A
WALK-ON
PART

ALSO BY MELANIE PFLAUM

Bolero
Windfall
The Insiders
The Gentle Tyrants
Ready by Wednesday
The Second Conquest
Costa Brava
The Maine Remembered
Lili
Safari
The Old Girls
Shadow of Doubt

French Editions
(Fleuve Noir, Paris)
Les Bonnes Familles
Bardon Larks a Disparu
Un Doux Tyran

German Edition
(Constanza, Hamburg)
Bolero

A
WALK-ON
PART

MELANIE PFLAUM

Pegasus

ISBN 0-908568-13-4

PRINTED IN NEW ZEALAND
AT THE PEGASUS PRESS
CHRISTCHURCH

DEDICATION

WE met in high school. He was Editor and I the Associate Editor of the *Hyde Park Weekly*, a high school newspaper on the South Side of Chicago. One day he came to my desk and asked me if I'd care to go with him to hear a debate on "Free Will versus Determinism" between a celebrated lawyer Clarence Darrow (who figured prominently in the famous Tennessee "Monkey Trial" on the question of Evolution) and a popular professor of Philosophy and Ethics at the University of Chicago, Thomas Vernon Smith. I was fifteen years old, he eighteen.

Our courtship was a stormy one. We broke up, and I went to Europe "to forget him", a romantic idea of the time, along with my best friend, Marjorie Gibson. On our return I became engaged to someone else.

I was to be married on a Saturday. The previous Thursday he invited me to have a "farewell lunch" with him at Henrici's restaurant in downtown Chicago. We both wept into our soup and he told me that the only reason he had not proposed to me before was his miniscule salary. We were both so overcome that we called our mothers to meet us at the City Hall where we were married by a judge. The rest is the story of my life.

That was fifty-five years ago. This week he died, and this book is dedicated to: my closest friend, the Man I Loved: Irving Peter Pflaum.

April 1985   M.P.

CONTENTS

Some of the material in this book has appeared in
*American Mercury, Independent Woman, Lookout, New
York Herald-Tribune, Progressive Magazine, Revista/
Review Interamericana, Vogue.*

SUCH AN INTERESTING LIFE

"You've had such an interesting life," people sometimes say to me. "Why don't you write your memoirs?"

Looking down at the Mediterranean, the orange groves, the scattered villas, I am tempted. Yes, my life has had its moments. But is the story worth telling? And if it is, how should it be told?

For once I have time. My twelfth novel, *Shadow of Doubt*, has been successfully published. A thirteenth? No. I am not superstitious, but. . . .

On my hilltop home there are no distractions that I do not choose to have. "What, no telephone?" American friends exclaim in horror. For so many years the telephone was like an umbilical cord. The *Sun-Times* had to be able to reach my husband on any foreign news-break — at a party, on the tennis court, anywhere, anytime. And I am one of those people who simply can't let it ring. Too curious.

Today there are no deadlines except the ultimate one, and judging by the longevity of my parents and grandparents, aunts and uncles, that should not be for a while yet.

"You've had such an interesting life. Why don't you write your memoirs?" I once asked a journalist-diplomat friend, Loren Carroll, during luncheon in his elegant apartment in Sicily, where he was U.S. Consul-General. He shook his head. "The kind of memoirs I would write aren't being read any more. The 'General de Gaulle said to me . . .' kind are obsolete. The only sort wanted now are the ones where you write, 'So I said to General de Gaulle . . .'."

And yet.

And yet. Is there not a place for the memories of someone to whom Charles de Gaulle never said anything, but who in the course of fifty years of journalism, travel and novel writing had occasion to meet many of the salient political, literary and revolutionary figures of the times? Someone, like me, who has brushed shoulders with History?

After all, I had seen (or believed I'd seen) the image of the Black Virgin of Lublin weeping for the sorrows of Poland. With my two-year-old son I had huddled in our Madrid *atico* when it was caught in crossfire during the first days of the Spanish Civil War. My second son Peter was born in the middle of a Barcelona air-raid. My husband and I had watched Hitler at the last *Partei* congress in Nuremburg and been appalled by the collective madness. We had interviewed King Carol and Madame Lupescu of Rumania, King Boris of Bulgaria, the dictator Metaxas of Greece, and attended the funeral of Kemal Ataturk of Turkey. Later there had been interviews with all the prime ministers of Western Europe, and extensive travels in Asia and Africa to provide background for current happenings. I think of Adenauer, Attlee, de Gaspari, Golda Meier, Madame Chiang, the Duke and Duchess of Windsor, Harry Truman, and wonder to what extent did their personalities shape the destinies of nations? More interesting, perhaps, are the natures of those whom we knew as friends, and never wrote about: Jean Monnet, father of Benelux and the E.E.C.; Richard Crossman, journalist and cabinet minister, who revealed the secrets of the British Government's inner strife in diaries published after his death; Claude Coxburn, whose great-grandfather burnt Washington in 1812, an upper-class Communist polemicist; Sefton Delmar, German-born *Daily Express* writer, who from a room in Woburn Abbey convinced millions of Germans that he was "Heinrich Eins", an officer broadcasting from within the Reich and telling how Hitler was losing the war.

Soon after the Second World War, during the series of interviews with European premiers that I have mentioned, I acted as interpreter for my husband. Long discussions with de Gaspari of Italy were followed by talks with his foreign minister on the problems of reconstruction, particularly in the south, the *mezzogiorno*. "Only God can save Italy," said the Minister piously. "But Signor de Gaspari and God are like this," and he held up his index and middle fingers tightly joined. Could this explain the almost forty years of Christian Democrat ascendancy that followed?

There are happy memories to cherish, and tragic scenes that are impossible to forget. One still haunts me — an enormous room in Majdanek, in Poland: a German concentration camp. On trestles reaching from one end of the room to the other are little children's shoes and the handmade toys — dolls, ships with cotton sails, carved wooden animals — that they carried with them on their last journey.

In theatrical terms one could say that I have had "a walk-on part" — been neither a star player nor yet a mere member of the chorus. Through many of the dramatic events of the last half-century I was at least in the wings.

Sometimes even that was too close, as when we were at the racecourse in Panama near the presidential box when President Remon, a man who had no enemies, was assassinated. The night before we had met him at a New Year's Eve party, and a few days earlier had seen him doing his Christmas shopping unaccompanied by bodyguards. In my novel, *The Insiders*, I explored possible motives but since the young gunman was killed on the spot and no one was ever indicted for conspiracy I will never know for certain how near I came to the truth.

If we were sometimes in danger when we least expected it, we were at other times not in as much danger as we feared. During the Czech crisis of 1938, living on the top floor of an apartment just across the street from the principal railway station on Woodrow Wilson Square, we heard the voice of Hans Kaltenborn, the dean of radio news commentators: "As the bomber flies, the German Air Force is only nineteen minutes from Prague." In imagination we could already hear Nazi planes revving up for take-off, coming to drop their loads on the strategic target right beside us. But of course they didn't. Because there was "Munich".

Later, back in Germany we found surprise and relief that Hitler had "got away with it" again. The Rhineland, Sudetenland, and earlier the *anschluss* with Austria, all won without a shot. In Mainz where we were staying, sallow youths with pick-axes tramped by singing the "Horst Wessel" song on their way

SUCH AN INTERESTING LIFE

to help build the West Wall (while their counterparts in France were working on the ill-fated Maginot Line). Air-raid shelters were being dug, though a knowledgeable engineer friend assured us, "They'd never stand up to bombing. They're just to keep people off the streets and out of the way."

In Paris, at the last prewar Foreign Correspondents' Dinner, we listened to Bill Bird of the *Baltimore Sun*, complete with Hitler moustache and heavy German accent, making a speech: "All I want is peace — a piece of Czechoslovakia, a piece of Poland, a piece of France. . . ." There was uneasy laughter. Before long most of those present would be War Correspondents.

What follows is as near as I am likely to come to writing my memoirs. It is not an autobiography, neatly arranged in chronological order, rather is it an untidy collection of impressions and descriptions, differing in length, varying in time and place, some written when the events occurred, others recollected if not in tranquility at least with the benefit of hindsight. I offer it as lines and scenes from the small walk-on part I have enjoyed playing.

MELANIE PFLAUM

El Tosalet
Javea (Alicante)
Spain

PART I

A RECURRING THEME

Chapter 1

"I'LL NEVER FORGET . . ."

MEMORY is a sly and deceptive thing. I have often said, "I'll never forget the eighteenth of July, nineteen thirty-six" — the day when what turned out to be the Spanish Civil War began. Now, almost half a century later, I try to remember what happened to me that day and the days that closely followed.

My husband, who was working for the United Press news agency on the Plaza de las Cortes in Madrid, our two-year-old son Juanito and I were living in an *atico* apartment on the Plaza de Atocha. It was a very small flat surrounded by enormous terraces — the roof of the building — where we had potted-plants, beach umbrellas, and a sandbox for Juanito, thus transforming the place into our "penthouse". The building was one of the tallest in Madrid. Miles away we could see the Cristo monument marking the geographic centre of Spain, and the tall Telefónica in the centre of the city, on the Gran Vía. We were eight stories up, counting the *entresuelo*. The lifts worked only sporadically because an engineers' strike meant they did not have a recent certificate of safety; often they were locked. Since I was six months pregnant, I stayed at home most of the time.

My husband worked from nine-thirty at night till five in the morning but seldom arrived home before eight o'clock as he usually stopped for coffee and *churros* on the way back. The morning of the eighteenth of July he did not arrive at all. Instead he sent a messenger to collect his razor and toothbrush and to tell me that he might not be home for several days. The messenger explained: On the night of the seventeenth, a *telegrafista* loyal to the Republic had informed the Government of the uprising in Morocco that was spreading to the mainland, where a *pronunciamento* by the generals proclaimed their inten-

15

tion to seize the country. The messenger, a lad of about eighteen who acted as a sort of copy-boy in the United Press office, added his own opinion that there was no need to worry; it was a mere nothing and would be over in a couple of days. We could hear gunfire and what sounded like the booming of cannons as he spoke.

The bureau manager, Jan de Gant, had left for Portugal several days earlier (on a tip-off, we learnt later), so the under-staffed agency was now working round the clock. As a rule, in terms of world news, Spain was fairly unimportant, but items from Madrid were always of great interest in Latin America, where the two Argentine newspapers, *La Prensa* and *La Critica*, were among the U.P.'s best clients.

Soon after this visit, what sounded like hailstones but proved to be bullets, began to hit the terraces, shattering the flowerpots, shredding the striped umbrellas, and burying themselves in Juanito's sandbox. Bullets ricocheted into the dining-room and the hall, and were embedded in the walls and ceilings. People were hanging white sheets from their windows, trying to indicate they were neutral. The sound of gunfire added to the various cracks, whistles and bangs nearby. Guardia de Asalto troops loyal to the Government had taken up position on the roof of the vast Obras Publicas building across the street and were firing at insurgents who had holed up in the Hotel Nacional on the other side of the square, a heavy barrage during which many of the bullets landed on our terrace. Juanito and I sought shelter in the kitchen which faced the inner court of the building.

In the great square below people were busy shooting at one another but since they were in doorways or windows they were invisible to us. Meanwhile, the Government radio assured us that "in Madrid absolute calm prevails". And from Seville, General Quiepo de Llano told us that the Military were now in control of the entire country.

A pounding at the front door. I opened it and six grim-faced militiamen pushed past me into the apartment.

"Where is he?"

It soon became clear they were under the impression that shots from a sniper were coming from the *atico*. Ignoring my protests, they proceeded to jab bayonets under the beds, fling open closets, even pull out drawers and toss their contents on the floor. At this point Juanito entered from the kitchen.

"Salud, Camaradas!" With a cheerful smile, he gave the clenched fist salute and the greeting which a friend of ours had taught him as a joke. Immediately the very young and trigger-happy militiamen burst into laughter, patted him on the head, apologised to me for "*la molestia*", and left.

The next three days are telescoped in my memory. The surrender of the Montana Barracks; the procession of trucks filled with guns and ammunition, from which *milicianos* handed down weapons to everyone who wanted them; singing brigades of coverall-clad men, boys and some girls, marching in irregular formations, carrying banners. Then, early in a clear starlit night, an aircraft with its navigation lights plainly visible dropped bombs on the War Ministry in the nearby Gran Via, most of them landing in the garden. It was my first experience of hearing an aerial bombardment. But not the last.

At noon the next day, during a sort of unofficial truce, the Plaza de Atocha was quiet although sounds of gunfire could still be heard in the distance. The lift was working again and I scuttled from doorway to doorway to a small shop nearby to buy food. There housewives were exchanging rumours, a mixture of fact and fantasy: the Moors had been stopped in the Guardarrama by Government clerks with old rifles, and shells in their jacket pockets. The Government was abdicating and the *militares* would march in tomorrow and restore order. The *militares* had surrendered, and the Government would allow the leaders to go into exile (as they had allowed General Sanjurjo to do in 1934 when he had led an unsuccessful *golpe de estado*).

Nomenclature had not yet hardened into "Nationalists" and "Reds". It was still "the Government" and "the Military". The terms "Loyalists", "Insurgents" and "Fascists" were also employed, depending on one's sympathies. (Of course, in July 1936, in Madrid, one did not openly support *les militares*.) The shopkeeper's elderly father explained to me that since the Government retained control of the principal cities — Madrid, Valencia, Bilbao, Santander — the *golpe de estado* had failed and the Military would surrender; this had happened many times in the past; these were the rules of the game. More confused than reassured, I hurried home with my straw basket of groceries.

Everyone wore coveralls, blue "*monos*", to indicate that he was a member of the working-class; it was the uniform. No-one wore a tie. No-one, that is, except for a few newspapermen. During the next lull in the fighting, my husband crossed the square wearing a (rumpled) white suit, shirt and tie, on the theory that only a foreigner would be seen in what had come to be thought of as "Rightist" clothing. No one shot him so he may have been correct. Or lucky. Soon he took up residence in the Palace Hotel close to the U.P. office on the Plaza de las Cortes.

The hospitals were filled with wounded; the noose was tightening round Madrid. Except for the road to Valencia and the railway line, Madrid was encircled, and both routes were under shellfire and sporadic bombing attacks. In September Juanito and I took what proved to be the last train to Barcelona. When my husband and I parted at the railway station, we were not sure that we'd ever see each other again. Madrid, it seemed, was doomed. The U.P. staffers sent a message to Earl Johnson, head of the agency in New York: "MORUTARI SALUTAMOS."

The train trip to Barcelona took thirty-four hours (normally it was about twelve). At every bridge the engine-driver climbed down and peered beneath the girders to see if charges of explosives had been placed there. Often the train just stopped for no apparent reason; sometimes we got off and picked grapes. We had brought no food, but Juanito would mix with the other passengers and return with a piece of chocolate, a handful of raisins or a chunk of sausage that we would share.

It was hot. The train was crowded. The journey seemed interminable. Juanito's comment on arrival was succinct. "*Mucho tren*," he declared.

Chapter 2

A LONG VIEW

FROM the terrace of our house on a high hill looking south you can see Ibiza. The island rises to three high points and an indistinct fourth one which may be Formentera. But it took us five years to see it, although our painter friend Mike Jordy kept pointing it out. "Look, right between those two low hills on the coast, can't you see?" We couldn't. Then one day, early in the morning, it was clearly there, and since then it has been there most of the time. Sometimes with binoculars you can make out buildings gleaming white against a tawny background.

We can't see Mallorca but it would be nice if we could. That was where our Spanish experience began over half a century ago. We lived in a peasant house on another high hill (we're partial to hills) looking down into a deep valley and the cove of Cala Mayor. The village was Genova, which some historians believe was the true birthplace of Christopher Columbus. Our house had no running water and an outside toilet but it did have electricity, and the previous tenant had put in French doors. There was no heating except the fireplace and charcoal *braseros*. A large terrace, a deep well, an enormous garden with almond, orange, tangerine, lemon and olive trees, and a profusion of flowers. For all this we paid twenty-seven pesetas a month to the peasant owner, who gave us half of the fruit he picked; at current exchange you could say about four dollars a month.

The house isn't there any more. A housing development has replaced it. Perhaps a fitting symbol of what the intervening years have wrought. Wolfe was right. You can't go home again. Because you are not the person who left, and it is no longer there.

A RECURRING THEME

Distances of sixty-five miles and fifty-five years separate the peasant house on the hill above the cove of Cala Mayor, Mallorca, and our present "chalet" on another high hill above Cap Marti, Javea, on the mainland. But more than time and distance divide us now from us then. A different world has emerged. Worse in some ways, better in others.

From the terrace of our house we look down on orange groves and the sea. As much sea as ever but fewer orange groves as the white villas with their orange-tiled roofs, with their circular, oblong or liver-shaped swimming pools, replace the citrus trees and pines. To the left the town of Javea, a peninsula called Cabo San Antonio with its lighthouse, and, towering above us, the town, the port, above everything: the Montgo. Like Kilimajaro or Everest, it dominates, affects the climate and the temperament of the natives, conceals archaeological secrets and presides over some three thousand years of history. Yet the Montgo is really not much of a mountain as mountains go. It is its location alone on the coastline, its mysterious transitions of colour and shape, the legends that have accrued, that fascinate its neighbours. A friend said to me, "When I am in Madrid I am active, energetic. But as soon as I return to live in the shadow of the Montgo I become listless, indifferent, lazy. I put things off until *mañana*, a never-reaching *mañana*. Nothing seems to matter much; no sustained effort is worthwhile."

The Montgo rises above the Mediterranean town and port of Javea which claims to be the most eastern point of mainland Spain ("El Amanecer de España" — The Dawn of Spain — it says on the car-stickers). It isn't, but the part of the Catalan coast that *is* doesn't mind. For about four hundred years this was the frontier between the Romans to the north and the Carthaginians to the south. And before that the Phoenicians, the Greeks, Celto-Iberians and the mysterious Tartesians. And later, the Goths, the Arabs; and later still, in very recent times, the tourists.

Division persists between the people of Javea and those of Denia on the other side of the Montgo. Denia was founded by the Greeks, Javea by (among others) the Arabs. "You can't trust Denia merchants," Javeans tell you. "Unreliable, those Greeks!" And the Denians say, "You won't find anything you want in Javea. No initiative, those Moors!" Yet the people of the two towns have been intermarrying for a thousand years.

Like a rough-cut diamond, the Montgo is many-faceted, catching every nuance of light and shadow. Sometimes a lion couchant, a sphinx, a volcano emitting a wisp of cloud from its summit, it can disappear completely in the mist, or leave its tip to hang ghostlike in the upper air struck by a shaft of sunlight. From dawn, beginning with pale pink, it changes colour to amber and tawny tones, then as the day progresses, to old gold, rose, mauve, lavender, deep blue, purple, and by moonlight to shining silver and ebony. Occasionally, from our house on the hill, we look down into impenetrable fog — the Mediterranean, the orange groves, the town of Javea, have all disappeared. But there above is the Montgo bathed in the warm sun. It is our Olympus, our Vesuvius, our Fujiyama.

The association with Olympus is not altogether fanciful. A large natural cave on the south-eastern slope was found to contain a Greek shrine, a statue of Aphrodite and votive urns by the Mayor of Javea, an archaeology buff who has also unearthed Roman coins and the foundations of watchtowers subsequently rebuilt by the Goths (from whom the mountain gets its name of Montgo — Mountain of the Goths) and used successively by Arabs and Christians to watch for each other's fleets. The fires lighted on the top of the Montgo could be seen as far as Gandia. Some of the towers are quite elaborate, with underground passages for storage of food and deep cisterns in which Roman artifacts have been discovered.

(It is an intriguing thought that the Greek, Roman and Carthaginian precursors of Pizarro and Cortez sought and found gold, silver, mercury and tin on the Iberian Peninsula — *their* Peru and Mexico — and worked the mines with Ibero-Celt slaves — *their* Incas and Aztecs — in an early rehearsal of the New World *Conquista*.)

As with all the fortresses, castles, walls and temples hereabouts, the Montgo watchtower reveals stratifications. The farther you go down the more expert the construction. The Romans built to last and in many places their work has lasted remarkably well. Subsequent builders were less skilled or perhaps they were in a greater hurry. Layer upon layer. Stratum upon stratum. Greeks, Tartesians, Celto-Iberians, Phoenicians, Romans, Carthaginians. When the Phoenicians pre-empted the sea lanes, the overland Greek route ran from Marseilles along the Mediterranean down past Gandia and Javea as far as Alicante, a Greek trading-post. Long afterwards came the people from the north, lumped together as *"Godos"*, and then the Arabs, who brought their architecture, their mathematics, their religion, and their comforts of life, (*almohada*, pillow; *alfombra*, rug), as well as many fruits and vegetables (*alcachofa*, artichoke), and systems of irrigation for terraces that remain on all the hillsides. They planted olive trees and almond trees, orange and lemon groves.

Descendants of these people still live here. Some Moslems and Jews who remained from the Arab occupation became Catholics and escaped expulsion by the *Reyes Catolicos*, Isabel and Ferdinand. And after hundreds of years of warfare, the completion of the *Reconquista* with the fall of Granada left a considerable number of unemployed soldiers and sailors available for other adventures and conquests with Columbus and his successors.

In recent times foreign settlers have continued to add new strata. In our immediate vicinity the earliest layer is British. Not from England, of course. Old Asia hands. Old Africa hands. A tea-planter from Malaya. An administrator from Brunei. A judge from Singapore. A game warden from what is now Kenya. The next stratum is American. NATO personnel retired. Men who had worked on the American bases, Torrejon and Las Rotas, either as Military or Navy, or civilians attached to these bases. They speak Spanish and often have Spanish wives, and they have been away from the U.S. too long (in Greece perhaps, or Turkey, or Korea) to "adapt". Many of them retain nebulous but profitable connections with the U.S. military establishment, enabling them to buy refrigerators, photographic and other supplies from the PX.

More or less overlapping this stratum are the old South American hands, British, Dutch, Canadian: mining engineers, oilmen from Venezuela, chiefly loners. Either widowers or bachelors or long since separated from wives who now live in Mexico City or Stockholm. They are easy prey for the still-attractive

English and American divorcees with cozy villas, standard poodles or large Alsatians, and regular incomes.

The most recent layer is German, the new-rich from Hamburg, Dusseldorf, Bremenhaven, but the Germans use their houses for only a month or so in the summertime, and they are still active in business or industry. However, now and then you meet elderly Germans who have lived in the region "for a long time". They are usually S.S. officers who managed to get out of Germany at the end of the war and married Spanish women, and who quickly change the subject when asked direct questions.

Until recently, life in Spain was cheaper than elsewhere in Europe. It is no longer, and many people have put their houses up for sale, intending to move to the Dordogne in France or "a cottage on the west coast" of England. When these houses are sold, the buyer is either a German or a Spaniard, sometimes a German with a Spanish wife. The Germans are the richest people in Europe, and well-to-do Spaniards prefer to invest in land and buildings rather than hold pesetas which buy less and less in Spain's inflationary economy.

Every summer a new invasion from the north sweeps down the Mediterranean coast — the tourists. They equal the population of Spain itself, so in theory every other person in summertime Spain is a tourist. What happens, of course, is that almost all of the foreign tourists are concentrated on the coast, so that it is not unusual to see a sign proclaiming *"Se Habla Español"* — Spanish Spoken Here — in the window of a seaside shop or restaurant.

Since the main highway runs about ten miles inland, most of the invaders from the north drive on south but each year more and more of them turn off and come to Javea or its port, called Aduanas del Mar. Mostly French-speaking, young and *très sportifs*, they throng the cafés, the shops, the narrow medieval streets. Wearing wetsuits, they spear fish underwater. In little round inflatable boats they bob around the bays and they water-ski behind speeding motor-boats. They pitch tents on the hillsides and crowd the two discotèques on Saturday nights until dawn. Then suddenly in the last days of August (when Continental schools begin) they disappear. And Javea resumes its tranquil existence.

But things change. When we bought our house on the hill, it stood all alone. We told visitors, "Just keep going on up and when you get to the house at the end of the road, that's ours." Now, a dozen or so years later, there are houses on both sides and below us and more being built. Nothing above, for that is a pinewood owned by the municipality and not for sale. Our view of the Montgo is unobstructed, as well as that of the sea, the port, and, on a clear day, Ibiza.

Not of Mallorca, although some people insist that the thin line on the horizon they can see with binoculars is Mallorca. In our private archaeology, the island of Mallorca corresponds to the Greek or Phoenician stratum of Javea, as our first home in Spain. In fact, our fifty-five years of marriage have contained three big layers of Spanish experience, with other places and thin wedges of travel sandwiched between them. The thick layers are Mallorca, Madrid and Javea.

Our eldest son, John (Juanito), was born on Mallorca at Genova, a village which claims Colon (Columbus), a claim dismissed as folklore until recently, when respected historians began to agree. (Letters from Columbus to the Pope were written not in bad Italian but in good Mallorquin.) My husband, Peter, worked on a newspaper, the *Palma Post*. We were late for the "movable feast"; Whit Burnett and Martha Foley had gone on to Vienna by then, and Robert MacAlmon had left, but Elliott Paul was there, and Robert Graves, and various poets, painters and novelists, some of whom became famous much later.

Shortly before we went to Mallorca we had met MacAlmon and listened to his tales from the magazine *Transition* and how he had been the first to publish Gertrude Stein, James Joyce and others; I remember how he spoke of taking Hemingway to Pamplona. Like us, he was staying at the Fonda in Torremolinos — at that time a vast sweep of beach with only a few fishermen's huts and at the southern tip the house of an Englishwoman who had a tennis court and took as many as three paying guests. Day after day heavy rain fell. So we played dominoes, drank red wine, and talked. MacAlmon did most of the talking. He knew *everyone*. We listened politely and did not believe him. It was not until some thirty years later that, on reading a series of articles called "Gertrude Stein and Her Circle", we found everything he had said was true.

Elliott Paul had a bridge club in El Terreno and played an arcane type of music called "boogie-woogie" on the tinny piano in the café, and Robert Graves, Laura Riding and their assorted brood of children lived in Deya not far from the Cartuja of Valdemosa where George Sand and Frederic Chopin spent their brief and unhealthy idyll.

In his job on the *Palma Post* my husband was at various times reporter, managing editor, circulation manager, social editor, copyreader, occasionally all of them simultaneously. One result was that we met and entertained the Duke of Windsor and Mrs Simpson, Bernard Shaw and his wife Charlotte, Douglas Fairbanks and Gertrude Lawrence, and, most important, Katherine Cornell who became our son Juanito's godmother. The social leader was Natasha Rambova, the widow of Rudolph Valentino, who gave lavish parties for distinguished visitors to the island.

When we "entertained" in the best restaurants and hotels, no bill was presented; the announcement of the event in the social columns of the *Palma Post* was considered sufficiently valuable promotion for the establishment.

Those were discreet times. A reader who followed society notes would be led to believe that during the stay of H.R.H. the Prince of Wales at the Hotel Mediterraneo, a Mrs Wallis Simpson just happened to be among the guests. A snapshot of them together on the beach in bathing-suits taken by an Englishman and bought by the *Daily Express* was never published.

We lived a double life. In our peasant house in Genova we ate sardines and rice, drank rough red wine (at a few cents a litre), but as a hostess I wore my millionaire aunt's cast-off original Chanel and Worth suits and dresses and we dined on squab and lobster and drank the finest champagne.

The village of Genova where our eldest son was born fortynine years ago consisted of the Can Moreno, an old-fashioned general store, dark and smelling of cheese, sausage, and spices — the bread was the size of a millstone, hard and coarse-grained — a barbershop, a café; that was it. The barber's father amused himself by playing flamenco music on his guitar and singing *canto hondo* for the benefit of anyone who wanted to listen.

Ordinary *coñac* and *sifon* was about two cents a glass. Every day the goatwoman led her goats up to our house, milked them into a can and provided us with fresh milk. The baker-boy brought us a flaky, fluffy, circular, breakfast-roll called an *ensaimada*, freshly baked. And the fishermen's wives carried flat baskets of sardines, squid, and anchovies up the hill on their heads. When the postman had accumulated enough letters for us to make it seem worth the climb, he would deliver them. We had a dog named Bozo, a cat named Feocha ("Little Ugly One").

Now, almost a half-century later, none of these services is available. This is what is known as progress. In Genova we kept butter cool on a ledge in the well. There was always water in the well. We had a charcoal stove and a big fireplace. We now have no well and if the electricity fails the electric stove and heaters are useless, the motor for the pump stops and we have neither light nor heat nor water. If the power failure lasts very long, everything in the fridge will go bad. Thus far such crises have been of short duration but we are not as independent as we were.

Our present furniture is an expensive copy of the olivewood chests, chairs and tables we once had, and we have nothing like the four-poster, canopied bed with inlaid headboard, bought for almost nothing. ("What do you want *that* for? It's so old!") We had it packed, crated, carried to the port of Palma in donkey-carts, shipped to Valencia, carried to Madrid by train, to our penthouse by truck, raised by pulleys to our eighth-floor terrace — where it was destroyed by incendiary bombs in October 1936.

Few foreigners lived in Genova. And few *"forasteros"* — people from other parts of Spain. One of these was an old gentleman who wore a Castilian cloak and greeted you in Castillano instead of Mallorquin. It was not until we attended a performance of the Capella Classica in the Cathedral of Palma and our neighbour arose to applause and cries of "Author!" that we realised he was Manuel de Falla. He lived in austere simplicity in a peasant house like ours, with his maiden sister, and his best friend was the village priest. Farther off in a crumbling fortress-palace above the sea lived the pianist George Copeland, who had introduced de Falla's works (as well as Debussy's) to the American public. But the composer and his most eminent interpreter never saw each other. De Falla disapproved of what he considered to be Copeland's sybaritic life and Copeland regarded the composer as a puritanical, priestridden ascetic.

Later, when we knew Copeland well, we would be invited for tea and would sit on the terrace jutting over the sea and listen to him playing Chopin, de Falla, and Debussy on the grand piano near the French doors of the living-room. The sun set, the stars came out. We remained motionless and spellbound, as the music continued. Finally, Francisco, Copeland's Italian companion and secretary, would begin to remove the cups and saucers. Alfred the cat would stretch and yawn. It was over.

Our closest friends were a Spanish couple, Fernando and Pazzis. Pazzis was a member of the Sureda family who had lived in the Cartuja while they were growing up, each child having a separate cell and private garden, a talented and tubercular family. Pazzis was a painter and sculptor. Another couple who were close friends were John and Laura Ferren, he an American painter who was later to become well known, and she, the daughter of a Basque art critic and a Polish mother, to make a career as an art director in motion pictures, and whom we were to meet again in Hollywood during World War II. But when we were in Mallorca, all this lay in the future. We were then very young, very poor and very hopeful.

We were offered positions on the staff of the École Internationale in Porte Pi. My husband could continue to work on the *Palma Post* but would also tutor a few of the older children in Latin. We were given the gardener's cottage, where we spent the week, returning to our house in the hills at weekends.

There never was and never will be another school like the École Internationale in Porto Pi, Mallorca. It was a marble palace on the sea, with vast marble terraces, a tennis court, its own jetty (for day-students who came by motor-boat), extensive gardens, a plantation of pines where on marble benches encircling marble tables a class of six or seven could study the ideas of Plato or discuss the theories of Archimedes. In a sense the school was favoured by the disasters of the era. Our music-teacher was the conductor of the Vienna Philharmonic, our science-teacher a world-famous biologist from Dresden, both refugees from Hitler's increasing hegemony. Teaching drama was Sybil Sutton Vane, playwright and sister of the author of *Journey's End*; art was the domain of Roy Jacobson, recently chief cartoonist for the *New York World*. But although each member of the staff "taught" some particular subject, the reality was quite different. L. Ray Ogden, the Director, eschewed such formal distinctions. As in life itself, history, philosophy, geography, language, architecture and the arts impinge on one another so none of us was limited to teaching any one thing. The year Peter and I entered the school was a Greek year; everyone studied Greek history, philosophy, geography and science. We produced and acted in *Antigone* and *The Clouds*.

We had thirty-five resident students and five day-students, ranging from five to sixteen years of age; they came from eighteen different countries, many of them children of diplomats in Madrid. No one age group or nationality was strong enough to dominate or exclude others, so everyone played together. Even our two-year-old toddler Juanito hid behind trees when the pupils were playing hide-and-seek, though no one knew he was playing!

Although the atmosphere seemed to arise spontaneously, it was really the product of Ogden's personality and beliefs. He created a peaceful community within the surrounding hatreds and prejudices of Europe. Sitting at the marble tables under the pines, where according to Robert Graves the ancient Greeks had worshipped the White Goddess, it seemed quite natural to talk about Socrates or Pericles. We all did everything: played recorders, acted in the plays, went swimming from the jetty, cared for the vegetable garden and the numerous pets. The food was simple but good. Ogden himself was an extraordinary man. Under the Near East Relief and the Red Cross he had set up schools for the "wild boys" in the Russian Caucasus and in Greece after the massacres of Armenians by the Turks; he spoke a dozen languages, played a very good game of tennis. The children adored him. He provided a father-figure for many of them who had been moved from place to place and school to school by their career-diplomat parents or, the victims of divorce, dragged from one European capital to another by their often attractive but frivolous mothers.

When the Spanish Civil War broke out (by then we were living in Madrid) the British cruiser *Ajax* went to Mallorca, picked up all the children and staff and took them to Nice; from there they moved into a big villa at Bordighera, in Italy. Parents were concerned by the threat of wider conflict in Europe, so once more the school was moved, this time to an estate in Virginia, where it dwindled and disappeared. Until his mid-eighties, Ogden directed a summer camp in Maine, lived in Florida, and kept in touch with his widely scattered "family", some in the diplomatic corps or the military services, others in theatre and the arts.

Peter and I have met them in Hong Kong, Copenhagen, Madrid, New Delhi, Paris, Vienna. One of them, Ernst, looked us up when we were living at Evanston in Illinois; he had seen my husband's photograph heading his daily column in the *Chicago Sun-Times*. We were delighted to see him and to learn he had survived the War — his father was an officer in the Wehrmacht, his mother half-Jewish.

"When the Germans occupied Paris, Mother and I managed to get away to Nice — in Vichy France."

"What did you live on?" I asked. "Didn't they send you back?"

"We had a ten thousand franc banknote."

"That wouldn't last long."

Ernst grinned. "All the refugees had to prove that they had private means and would not become public charges. They had to have at least ten thousand francs to show the official at the *mairie*. So we rented out our ten thousand franc banknote for a few francs an hour. That French official must have seen the same banknote hundreds of times and each time accepted it as proof. He was a good man."

At the age of sixteen Ernst joined the French Foreign Legion, and eventually was able to bring his mother to America.

French officials can be exasperating, but they can also be human. When towards the end of the Spanish Civil War my husband left Spain by car, the officials on the Spanish side of the frontier cut up the upholstery, took out everything movable and searched every inch of space (which included letting the air out of the spare tyre), looking for what — secret papers, weapons? At last, exhausted, and ill with a bad case of jaundice (we'd call it hepatitis now), he drove into France at Le Perthus where I was waiting for him. The French police agent demanded, among other things, his driver's licence. He'd never had one. When we had left Chicago such formalities were not required. Since then it had never occurred to him. We sat at a café table while he searched through his papers. Finally, he produced a Spanish document permitting him "to circulate at night" — a requirement by the Catalan government for all newsmen who went out after curfew. My husband showed it to the French official, who nodded gravely and waved us into France and, after Spain, freedom.

That was the last episode in our Civil War experience. When we next returned to Spain, Franco was in complete control and letters and documents were dated not according to the birth of Christ but as VII Year of Victory.

*　　　*　　　*

When the Spanish Civil War began my husband was working at the United Press bureau in Madrid and we were living on top of a tall apartment building. For a time we were caught in cross-fire but street-fighting lasted only a few days and then an uneasy calm descended. Trigger-happy young men and girls dressed in coverall-type uniforms drove round the city in commandeered cars enforcing "order". The Government had taken the unprecedented step of opening the arsenals and sending truck-loads of guns and ammunition into working-class districts and simply handing out weapons to everyone whose arm was raised to receive them. Since most trade unionists and civil servants, organized as militia, were soon away at the various fronts fighting, the "order" that prevailed was of a curious nature at best. At night men were taken from their homes to the outskirts of the city and shot. Sometimes they were factory managers or others against whom some worker had a grudge. The bodies were left there, often labelled with descriptive placards, and the newsmen went out at dawn to see them.

And yet total chaos did not reign. An elderly general, José

Miaja, one of the few ranking officers who did not join the uprising but remained loyal to the republic to which they had all pledged allegiance, organized the defence of Madrid. He went from one union headquarters to the next, one political club to another, asking quite simply for men who were prepared to die. And got them. They were the ones who went into the Guadarrama mountains with rifles and pistols and stopped the Moors and the Tercio — the Spanish Foreign Legion — dead in their tracks. He instituted a system of rationing for the dwindling supplies of a capital that was being slowly but inexorably surrounded. The buses, the streetcars, the subway functioned. The cafés flourished. There was electricity and water and garbage collection. And most of all there was a general air of excitement and hope.

As the circle closed round Madrid the children in the slums were collected, as in London during the Blitz, to be taken to convents and monasteries in the provinces controlled by the Government. Many children had been with their parents or grandparents at the seaside during their summer holidays, a holiday that was to last almost four years; some were shipped off to Russia, from which they returned to Spain after forty years.

Air-raids had become quite frequent events by the time Juanito and I left the city. I was expecting another child and knew all the Madrid hospitals and clinics had been taken over for war casualties.

The night in October 1936 that my second son was born in Barcelona, there was a heavy air-raid there too, and a report of insurgent landings on the coast north of the city. Every taxi and private car was commandeered to take militia to Roxas to repel the invasion, à la the Paris taxis at the Battle of the Marne. The *clinica* was high in the mountain above Barcelona and it seemed there was no way for me to get there. My physician, however, was equal to the emergency. He commandeered an ambulance and we sped through the blackened streets with the siren wailing. We were stopped at every crossroads; militia poked their heads into the back of the ambulance and we explained our haste, whereupon they waved us on — until the next intersection.

We just made it. My son Peter was born as the All-Clear sounded. As things turned out, there had been no attempt to land on the coast. It was, it seems, part of a "Fifth Column" plot to take Barcelona under cover of darkness while the local militia were lured away to repulse an imaginary invasion. My aunts and uncles and cousins in Chicago soon afterwards heard Walter Winchell, addressing "Mr and Mrs America" in his machine-gun staccato, tell of the "baby born under bombs" to an American newspaperman's wife in war-torn Barcelona.

Some twenty-two years later, Peter, by then a young man, was driving towards Barcelona. He had been at the wheel for almost twenty-four hours and was finding it hard to keep awake. When a traffic light turned red, his car nudged the truck in front of him. It would have been a minor collision except that it was something more than two vehicles; it was two concepts of citizenship that collided on the road to Barcelona. For the truck belonged to the Spanish Army. And when the officers saw Peter's passport, they wanted to know why he had failed to report when his class of recruits was called up. His passport showed he'd been born in Barcelona in 1936, hence according to Spanish law he had been an army deserter for four years. The penalty was four years in a military prison for each year of desertion, which would mean a total of sixteen years.

Peter was taken before a military court in a fortress. As Mark Twain said, the prospect of being hanged concentrates a man's mind wonderfully. In this case, the prospect of sixteen years in prison brought up from some depth of memory the name of a Spanish friend of ours who was working for the United States Information Service in Barcelona. Peter was granted permission to telephone him. Our friend — and a friend indeed — dropped everything and drove immediately to the fortress. He explained to the court that both Peter's parents were U.S. citizens, that Peter was registered in the U.S. Consulate of Barcelona and thus according to U.S. law he was an American citizen as well as (having been registered also in the Ayuntamiento of Barcelona) being Spanish.

Thanks to the advocacy of our friend Rafael, Peter was released after paying a small fine for damaging the army truck. Neither Peter nor Rafael told us of this incident until several years later. When we thanked Rafael for averting what could have been a very serious situation, he replied that we had saved his life in the past and this was the least he could do for us and our family.

What had happened was this: The Anarchist Utopia of Catalonia was shattered as Communist control moved first to Valencia with the Government, then to Barcelona. The Government itself was becoming a shadow; real power lay in the hands of the Communists who now ran the Ministry of the Interior and the Intelligence forces.

Rafael, who worked for the British Cable Company, was arrested. His mother, distraught, came to tell us that he was accused of communicating with the enemy. He was probably being held on one of the prison-ships in the harbour, which was by then under heavy and almost continuous bombardment. Could we do anything to help?

After fruitless visits to the Prime Minister, the Minister of the Interior and the Police Chief of Barcelona, we realized that no-one could assist us until we could tell them exactly where Rafael was. Communist security police were in control, and members of the Government were helpless. At this point, Rafael's colleagues in the Cable Company came to the rescue. They reported a break in the cable. Rafael, who had received specialised training in the United States in this type of engineering, was the only man who could pinpoint the break. In the face of this emergency, Rafael was "found" — in a house in Bonanova. We brought him fresh linen and a change of clothing. After long calculations he located the break in the cable and a ship went out to fix it — not much of a task, since it had never been broken! By this time we had alerted the British Foreign Office, the U.S. Government, and the United Press, all of whom were making official inquiries. Rafael was released.

On the night Peter was born, euphoric and still slightly "high" on the ether I had sniffed during the birth pains, I lay in bed and talked to the nurse, who belonged to a German nursing order and before becoming a nun had been a dancer and a friend of Mary Wigman. My son and I were fortunate. Four days after his birth, the German nuns were evacuated and the clinic was turned over to the army for wounded soldiers. And while my husband was flying to Barcelona to see us, our apartment in Madrid was hit by incendiary bombs.

A RECURRING THEME

To my husband, after grim and grubby Madrid-under-seige, Barcelona seemed a sunny, bountiful paradise. True there were bombings, and meat, olive oil, and eggs were rationed. But the flower stalls on the Rambla were overflowing with exuberant blossoms and the market with fruit and vegetables. The opera, concerts, movie-houses were well attended, and there was plenty of beer in the cafés. To his great surprise he found he could telephone his stories directly to London with no intervention. In Madrid everything was subjected to strict censorship; the censor sat by your elbow with a copy of your dispatch and if you departed from the text he clicked a key which cut the connection. This was early November 1936.

My husband returned to Madrid to the astonishment of government officials, who had believed that his departure on grounds of the birth of a son was simply an excuse to leave the beseiged city. He carried with him on toilet-paper an elaborate code invented by a colleague in Geneva and brought to us by a young woman, Winifred Scanlon, who was to become a close friend of ours. Every likely contingency had been covered: if for instance my husband asked for £50, that meant a truce was being arranged. Alas, none of the events anticipated ever occurred, so the code was never used. (Just as well, perhaps, remembering the newsman in Russia who had arranged that if the Government fell he would ask for £100. But the man on the cable desk the night the Kerensky Government fell had not been informed of the code, so cabled back £100!)

The raids on Barcelona became heavier. Goering's planes from Mallorca could glide over the city, cutting their motors so as to avoid alerting the anti-aircraft defences. Every day brought news of fresh Nationalist victories. The U.S. cruiser, *Raleigh*, came into the port of Barcelona to evacuate Americans. Juanito, baby Peter and I were given the first officer's cabin and enjoyed much attention en route to Marseilles. Oh, the joy of baked ham, candied sweet potatoes, apple pie with a slice of cheese!

*　　　　*　　　　*

In France, I rented a studio-house in Collioure, a fishing village near the Spanish border, found a capable housekeeper

34

and cook, then persuaded my mother to stay with the children while I, now armed with credentials (from N.E.A., a Scripps-Howard Syndicate), returned to Madrid. On the road it was a case of the faster you went the safer you were, especially in the mountain passes which were bad enough in normal times and now held the added danger of machine-gun nests and ambushes.

The Madrid to which I returned was a different place from the one I'd left. It was now the stage for a bloody, heroic tragedy, with elements of farce. Among the spectators were novelists, playwrights, congressmen and their wives, singers (like Paul Robeson), scientists (like Julian Huxley) and, of course newspaper-men and -women from practically every country on earth. Everyone, even the *New Yorker* types like Lilian Helman and Dorothy Parker, was there. Most stayed less than a week, took the official handouts and briefings, which they rewrote, and left. Others, like Ernest Hemingway, stayed. Besides, there were the permanent correspondents — Herbert Mathews of the *New York Times*; Sefton Delmar, *Daily Express*; Philip Jordan, *News Chronicle*; Richard Mowrer, *Chicago Daily News* (Jay Allen of the *Chicago Tribune* was back in the U.S.A.); and the agency men of the wire services — the United Press, the Associated Press, the International News Services, Reuters, Agence Havas — all of whom remained. Most fleeting were the brain-pickers, like John Gunther, who would come in, buy us an expensive meal and find out everything we knew but couldn't write about because of censorship — and leave.

We moved into the apartment of the head of the United Press bureau, Jan de Gant, who had departed just before the military uprising. On the door we put up an American flag and a notice saying this was the property of U.S. citizens, which saved us from being ousted by the militia. The neighbourhood was fairly free from damage because the people who were shelling Madrid came from homes in that area. The working-class districts, the centre of the city, and the newly built University City which became the front line, were the worst hit.

Compared with Rotterdam, London or Berlin later, or even Barcelona the following year, Madrid was not too badly off for a city under bombing. I remember a conversation with Henry

A RECURRING THEME

Gorrell, a U.P. newsman, who invited us to the Gran Vía Hotel where good beer was still available if you got there about noon, just when the insurgents started to shell the Telefónica across the street. When I demurred Gorrell said, "Don't worry, your chances of getting killed are less than that of a pedestrian in New York City. You wouldn't refuse to cross a street in New York, would you?" I still don't think it was a very sound argument, but he won it.

Our larder contained a curious mixture. Since one of the United Press staff was a Yorkshireman, we were permitted to buy such delicacies as herrings, tea, marmalade, and biscuits from the British Embassy. Our diet comprised whatever was available. Sometimes champagne and tinned peas. One night my husband arranged a party at the British-American Club, at which he produced a rare treat, roast lamb. He and our driver had bought a whole beast from a farmer near Escorial. They dragged the gory carcass over the marble floors under the haughty noses of the Royal Family whose portraits lined the *sala*. The staff, delighted at the meat that they would share, produced a memorable dinner, complete with vintage wines from the cellar.

The regular "beat" for the agency men was the front or fronts. The war could be reached by subway! Earlier, during the siege of Alcazar, it was to Toledo that they went daily. Every day the Republicans believed the fortress would surrender, but what was happening was that, as at Monte Cassino in World War II, they were hitting piles of rubble which acted as insulation to the elaborate network of underground rooms, corridors, and wells. Day after day, the Alcazar was shelled and day after day the rumours went round that Moscoso was going to surrender. Speculative stories of parleys, a possible truce, an exchange of prisoners (for, when holing up in the Alcazar, the military had gathered ordinary citizens of Toledo, some of them the wives and children of the men who were attacking the fortress, the "West Point" of Spain) filled the world press. On one occasion a group of *militianos*, accompanied by my husband, actually penetrated one of the underground entrances but were driven out again. Then the Republicans decided on a desperate final solution. Their engineers were ordered to construct tunnels, in which mines were laid, and the commander of the fortress was told that they would blow the Alcazar skyhigh if he didn't surrender. He refused. After hours of tense expectation and fear, a tremendous explosion shook Toledo — it sounded like the eruption of a volcano. When the dust settled, it was found that the force of the explosion had been directed *outwards* to the town instead of *inwards* to the Alcazar, which was more-or-less intact. The sappers were at once shot as Fifth Columnists and the atmosphere in Toledo, already hysterical, became that of a madhouse.

It was at this point that General Franco made a momentous decision: to relieve the siege of the Alcazar. The Nationalist army headed for Toledo. On the last day, as the insurgents were approaching, my husband found himself in Toledo without transport. He had sent a colleague back to Madrid to file his story and then return with the car. He stood at the gate of the city vainly seeking a lift. He explained his plight to an Anarchist soldier, whose sentry-box was the pulpit of a church, and the sentry promptly waved down a car filled with officials fleeing the doomed city and ordered them to make room for my husband. When they objected he poked his rifle inside and threatened to blow off the head of the driver. Not surprisingly, they agreed.

The remarkable aspect of this incident is that the soldier insisted on the officials taking my husband and not himself. He could see the Franco army approaching, and knew he would die when the Nationalists lifted the siege.

It is clear now that this diversion cost the insurgents Madrid, but at the time most military experts and newspaper editors believed that Madrid would fall very shortly. With this in mind, United Press asked Stewart Brown in the Rome bureau to write a story on the entrance of General Franco's forces into Madrid, to be used as soon as that event took place, which could not be long delayed. So a vivid description of excited crowds cheering the conquering troops was sent to every U.P. bureau, *including Madrid*, with a hold-for-release note attached. It was quite impossible for the United Press staffers in Madrid, Henry Gorrell, Harold Peters and my husband, to explain the arcane workings of the press agency system and it was only after protracted sessions with the censors that they avoided expulsion.

Three years later, when Madrid did fall, nothing described in Stewart Brown's article actually happened. The city was never taken, it was surrendered by the Government, then in Barcelona. Julian Besteiro, a Socialist Deputy, took the responsibility of effecting the peaceful and orderly transfer of power, for which he was promptly imprisoned and then died in agony from meningitis without medical help. Many of the troops came to the central city by subway, and according to a no doubt apocryphal story they were required to pay their fares.

But all this still lay ahead. Toledo fell. Every day other towns on the road to Madrid fell to the Nationalists and the fronts moved closer and closer. Dolores Iturrubi, "La Pasionaria", exhorted the militia to make a stand, saying that it was better to die on your feet than live on your knees, but she was no tactician and the places where she urged these last stands were impossible to defend. So the young men died, and La Pasionaria went to Moscow where she lived on in comfort.

*   *   *

Madrid's lifeline was the road to Valencia and the sea. Convoys of trucks arrived with supplies from time to time but there were severe shortages. One by one the animals disappeared from the zoo, and soon there were no *burros*, dogs or cats on the streets anymore. It was now a war of attrition. In University City men died defending a few feet of shattered classrooms or a portion of undemolished wall. Soldiers went to "work" — that is, to kill or be killed — in shifts, as to a factory, returning home afterwards. *If* they returned, for casualties were heavy on both sides.

Somehow the road to Valencia was kept open. To prove the falsity of a report by the *New York Times* correspondent, Carney, that it had been cut off, Mathews and my husband took a taxi along the part of the road supposedly closed. For some of the way the road was under machine-gun fire and occasional shelling but they managed to get back and write their stories, my husband for the United Press and Mathews for the *New York Times*. Among correspondents in Madrid it was said that the war had become a battle between Mathews and Carney.

38

Each section of the Madrid front was almost autonomous and different credentials were needed for, say, an F.A.I. (Federacion Anarchista Iberica) unit and a U.G.T. (Union General de Trabajadores, largely Socialist but increasingly Communist-controlled) one. In some sectors of Spain there were no Spaniards on either side: Italians, Moors, Germans faced Russians, Poles, anti-Nazi Germans, anti-Fascist Italians, Frenchmen, Englishmen, Americans. But neither Stalin's Russians nor Hitler's Germans fought as soldiers; they were there as experts and technicians.

When Franklin Delano Roosevelt opened the Michigan Avenue Bridge in Chicago, he made a speech about "quarantining the aggressors", and jubilant headlines in Madrid announced that help would soon be forthcoming from the U.S.A. The Spanish gold supply was still intact — the third largest in the world — enough to pay for everything needed. Of course, no U.S. aid of any kind ever came. It was only a speech. Except for an early shipment of rifles from Mexico, the Soviet Union was the only supplier of arms, grain — and ideology; and in return received the gold of Spain.

In the summer of 1937 I spent three months in the hot apartment on Goya Street, Madrid, translating a biography of General José Miaja, who more than anyone else was responsible for the stubborn defence of Madrid. When the following autumn I left Spain to go to France, I carried the manuscript with me. At the border it was seized, all five hundred pages of it. "But it's about your General," I protested. The officials assured me they would send it on and I realized that I would never see it again. General Miaja was not a Communist. He was not *their* General.

*   *   *

The grip on beseiged Madrid continued to tighten and the Republican Government moved to Valencia. Most of the news correspondents went too. We all stayed at the Grand Hotel Victoria, aptly named and apparently unchanged since that era of dark, cluttered furniture, faded damask and velvet, and tassels on lampshades, on curtains, on bedspreads. In the hotel bar we talked to English and French sea-captains who had managed to elude the blockade of German submarines, bringing in small quantities of supplies contributed by private citizens in their countries, an effort which was never publicized and therefore unappreciated by the Spanish beneficiaries.

Slowly but surely the Nationalists were winning and more and more Republican strongholds were being lost. The war of words became fiercer. In this sector, the Republic had all the heavy guns — Malraux, Hemingway, Orwell, as well as the best-known foreign correspondents. Still, the Nationalists attempted to discredit the testimony of reporters on the other side. When Noel Monks of the *Daily Express* described the savage bombing by the Germans of the Basque town of Guernica, Franco's propaganda ministry replied that no credence should be given to his account as he was known to be an alcoholic given to flights of imagination. They picked the wrong man. Of the entire press corps in Spain, Monks was probably the only one who was a total abstainer. He was also a vegetarian, and he was scrupulously accurate in his reports.

However, the pressure by news agencies to capture headlines, to scoop the competition, was unrelenting. When the German battleship *Scharnhorst* shelled Almeria, the Government offered to fly correspondents to the scene to see for themselves the destruction wrought on the ancient city. My husband, for the United Press, and Kennedy of Associated Press accepted the invitation. But when the plane took off, Kennedy was missing. My husband went to Almeria, wandered about, looked at the ruins, and interviewed people. Almost no one knew there had been any shelling. Bombing raids had been frequent, resulting in so much damage that the explosion of shells from naval guns had scarcely been noticed and the actual results had been minor. He wrote this story — and was scooped by Kennedy who had stayed behind and instead used the official press release describing the horror and destruction of the German shelling.

In some cases the Paris office of the United Press would simply double the numbers — planes, casualties, and so on — to make a better story. Similar treatment was applied to reports of atrocities. There were almost unbelievable (in those innocent days before Belsen and Buchenwald) atrocities on both sides.

However, after Franco's victory many people reported killed by the Reds reappeared, alive and well. And in recent years quite a few Republicans have come out of hiding. For just as we knew that Aurora, our cook in Madrid, was a nun in disguise, during the anti-clerical barbarities of the early days of the Civil War, so during the Franco years many were aware that their carpenters and gardeners, for instance, were schoolteachers and intellectuals living under assumed names in places where they were not known.

In addition to the Communists who went to Russia after Franco's victory, thousands of Republicans scattered to Mexico, Puerto Rico, France, Canada, and the United States. Picasso, Casals, Ramón Sender; the list is impressive. Now, at long last, some have realized the dream of returning. A few, like Salvador de Madariaga, too long established elsewhere, came for a brief visit to their families and to experience the joy of living for a while in the new climate of tolerance.

Returning exiles find themselves in an altogether different country. They are received as curiosities. Spaniards who have lived through the Franco years feel that these strangers have nothing to contribute now. Even the highly honoured Christian Democrat, Gil Robles, who had never dealt with the Franco régime, had to withdraw from the leadership of his party, not just because of his age (in his eighties) but mainly because of the widespread feeling that expatriates simply cannot understand the current political scene.

If the returning exiles are bewildered, who can blame them? We who have lived through the last years of Franco and the short post-Franco period are astounded. Is this Spain, we ask ourselves, the country where only yesterday censorship lay heavily upon the press, radio and television, where the Guardia Civil behaved with such arrogant ruthlessness, where a distinguished lawyer, defending a client accused of "insulting the Army", could be sentenced to seven years' imprisonment for questioning the veracity of an officer's statement? Yet Alice-in-Wonderland features of life still abound in Spain. Not long ago the editor of a respectable newspaper, *El Pais*, was fined heavily for running some articles by a British physician in which family planning was discussed in a general way. Yet "nudie" magazines and pornographic films are everywhere.

For years it was illegal to buy or sell contraceptives. How is it, then, that the Spanish birthrate is among the lowest in the world? One reason could be found in the fact that as many as three million young unmarried men were working abroad. Or consider the situation explained to me by a Spanish woman. Young married women use "the Pill", prescribed by their doctors for menstrual irregularities. On the bottle it warns that the tablets must be taken with care under the supervision of a physician, because of the danger that they may prevent conception!

Another example: a mass gathering of Communists in the largest bullring in Spain, and the meeting of Carillo, the head of the Spanish Communist Party, with Berlinger and Marais, the heads of the Italian and French parties respectively. Press releases about the occasion were published in all the papers and quoted widely on radio and television. Both the mass meeting and the Eurocommunist Summit were protected by the police and the Guardia Civil and the leaders provided with armed guards by the Government. Yet the Communist Party was illegal at the time and being a member of it was a crime. Wonderland, indeed.

Looking back over the years I can appreciate that Spain has been a recurring and major theme in the symphony of our lives. Today I am content to be on a hill overlooking the Mediterranean as we were when we began our Spanish adventure at a time of placid, bucolic contentment in Mallorca above the village of Genova while the United States was undergoing the trauma of the Depression. Now our hill is above the town of Javea. Over sixty miles of sea divide them. In February, when the almond blossoms are in bloom, the hills here are covered with pink and white flowers, just as they are there. Much has changed but much has remained the same.

We can't see Mallorca from our terrace. But on a clear day you can see Ibiza.

Chapter 3

HEMINGWAY AND MADRID

A BATTERED and grubby Tauchnitz edition of *The Sun Also Rises*. Throw it away? No, for on the grimy title-page is written: "To my future friend Juanito. Ernest Hemingway, Madrid, Autumn, 1937."

Juanito, our son John, born in Mallorca, was then three years old and, having been evacuated from Barcelona, was living with my parents in France.

That was the winter of the siege of Madrid. It was also The Autumn and Winter We Knew Hemingway. And for Hemingway himself it may have been His Finest Hour. Certainly all the elements were there. Danger, Grace under pressure. Heroism. Love (just then in the person of Martha Gelhorn). Beer (in our apartment). And Death — sudden, dramatic death.

Hemingway arrived in Madrid with a fine ambulance, fully equipped, as a gift to the Spanish Republic. All he wanted was correspondent's credentials and coupons for gasoline. What he got was the usual bureaucratic runaround. Frustrated and desperate, he turned to the United Press bureau — Hal Peters, Henry Gorrell, my husband, and a Yorkshireman, Jan Yndrich.

The beer had disappeared from the bars on the Gran Vía. And the shells kept falling and killing people because the Nationalists were trying to hit the Telefónica and missing. Peters, my husband, and a four-foot-tall Anarchist named Federico (our chauffeur, houseboy, informant, friend, and severest critic) decided to remedy the beer shortage. None of us had much technical knowledge but with the help of an associate of Federico's (who thought we were mad; Federico *knew* we were!) a spare closet in our apartment was rigged up with a pressure mechanism for dispensing draught beer. During an air-raid at

43

the censors' office, when everyone else was in the basement, my husband stole a sheaf of papers with the letterhead of the Ministry of Foreign Affairs. Next he had a rubber-stamp made that said: "U.S. Association of Correspondents of War." "WAR" was in big letters, and the whole thing looked not unlike the stamp of the War Ministry. He wrote a *vale*, "Good for One Barrel of Beer", stamped it with the rubber-stamp, signed an illegible scrawl of a signature, gave Federico one hundred pesetas and sent him to the brewery. Federico returned with a barrel of beer, a mission he successfully repeated at regular intervals all that winter and well into the spring.

Our apartment became one of the most popular spots in Madrid. Government officials, officers of the Republican Army (or armies, as there were different ones on the various fronts, with distinct political affiliations), artists and writers (such as André Malraux and Genevieve Tabouis), were delighted to drink our beer. Thus some of our stories came to us instead of our having to go out and get them. Among the visitors were mercenaries like Whitey Dahl, "The Harlem Eagle", who had flown for the Ethiopians during their war with Italy. But our favourite and most faithful guest was Ernest Hemingway. He would come late in the afternoon, sit on the floor, and listen. He talked very little.

I was caught up in a kind of Hemingway-type subtle sense of honour. We all were. It was a game, but a serious one, and perhaps the reason he kept coming. We treated him as just another correspondent and not as the Great Man and writer and novelist we knew him to be, and he knew we knew him to be. We didn't pick his brains or interview him or ask him to read our manuscripts or question him about Literature.

He was embarrassed by the fact that he was receiving a huge sum per word for his articles, whereas the agency men like my husband and Hank Gorrell were risking their necks daily for so little. And, like us, he resented the "trippers" who dropped in for a few days, got the VIP treatment, and then went out and wrote "definitive" pieces based entirely on Ministry of Information handouts.

Hemingway was a great listener. He listened with controlled excitement, hardly moving, just nodding his big head from time to time. He was not interested in theories or ideas, but he loved action. Yndrich returned from a four-day excursion into enemy territory, talking of travelling with Asturian *dinamiteros* (miners experienced in the use of TNT and what came to be known as Molotov cocktails) in an armoured car, blowing up bridges and roads over mountain passes. Hemingway listened, closing his eyes to picture it better.

My husband Peter talked of finding himself alone in the completely deserted town of Seseña, evacuated by the Republicans and rapidly approached by the Nationalists. Before leaving he took an unopened crate of X-ray machines and several large cartons of drugs for the hospital in Madrid which was in great need of them — AND the Royal typewriter that I am still using!

He was more fortunate than Gorrell, who was captured by a Moorish regiment reputed to kill anyone for the sake of a watch or a ring or even a gold tooth. He was rescued by an Italian whose one-man tank had overturned nearby. Gorrell spoke Italian and he and the tank commander retired to the nearest bar and were singing Fascist songs together when three British colleagues were marched by at bayonet point. Seeing Hank, they made signs of distress, but Gorrell in his ebullient mood took them as gestures of greeting and simply waved back. Finally, at headquarters, they were all released after promising to leave Spain. Which they did. But all returned.

While they were being held they were shown plans of Madrid defence positions — tank-traps, artillery, machine-gun nests — and asked if the information (supplied by spies and Fifth Columnists) appeared correct. Oh yes, they agreed; that was how it was. In actual fact, as far as they knew, none of it was there at all.

One afternoon when Hemingway arrived at our apartment he was greeted by a houseful of chickens. They were roosting on lamps and bookcases and coffee-tables, clucking, scratching the rugs, fluttering about the furniture. He shook his head, saying, "I don't believe it!" We explained that an American friend who had Madrid's best poultry and egg farm, had heard he was about to be *incautado* — taken over by the militia. So he called the United Press and Federico was dispatched to help himself to six dozen hens. Most of them were brought to the office, where they

45

were soon laying eggs in the typewriters and wastebaskets, but a dozen or so were left in the apartment. At least Aurora (the maid, really a nun in disguise) was delighted. She never liked the powdered eggs we were getting from the British Embassy.

Hemingway often accompanied my husband, Peters and Yndrich on their routine visits to the front. (One went to the front the way one goes to the office.) They had friends in each sector. One day I'd gone with them. (I was a correspondent for the Scripps Howard Syndicate, chiefly because life in Madrid was impossible for foreigners unless you had credentials.) A mortar shell landed very close and we were talking nonsensically, slightly punch-drunk from the scare. Someone had said that Hemingway was spending too much time with Communists and added, "You know, they say a man is judged by the company he keeps."

Idiotically, without thinking, I quipped, "And a woman by the men who keep her."

Hemingway turned on me, suddenly deeply serious, his eyes hurt and angry. "Martha makes more money than I do," he said. "*Collier's* pays her a thousand dollars a piece. I never give her anything."

Oh God! I hadn't thought of Martha. I found myself wishing another mortar shell would arrive.

I learnt something at that moment. Hemingway was very literal minded. Beware, I thought. He's a friend now, but he could change in a flash.

The Gran Vía Hotel, where Hank Gorrell had a room, was just across the street from the Telefónica. The Hotel Florida, where Hemingway and Martha Gelhorn were staying, was close by. For a couple of hours a day both hotels were being hit by shells intended for the Telefónica. Hemingway had been in the First World War and considered himself a military expert. He explained that the trajectory of the shells was such that they couldn't hit his and Martha's rooms facing the inner courtyard. He showed us his calculations on a notepad; we were impressed but unconvinced. It seemed to us that he was testing Martha's loyalty — to see how much she loved him and how much confidence she had in his judgement.

Indeed, their portion of the hotel did remain intact. Until the day after they left, when it received a direct hit and was completely demolished.

They had fixed up the sitting-room with cretonne covers for the couch and armchairs, some prints on the wall, and an electric heater (it was a cold winter and there was no central heating). They had a hot-plate to make tea, beef bouillon with Maggi cubes, or, when available, coffee.

One afternoon we were invited for drinks. Martha, whose blonde hair was shoulder length and who was a most attractive young woman, was standing in front of a long mirror in the bedroom, trying on a silver fox fur she'd just bought. "You like?" she asked Hemingway.

"You are a bitch," he replied deliberately, "taking advantage of starving people in a siege to buy yourself luxuries." He went on, just as the protagonist would do in his later play, *The Fifth Column*. When a phrase struck him as right, he remembered it, totally, with complete recall.

Two other incidents that would appear in the play involved us. One was at a party at Hank Gorrell's (neither Martha nor I was present). My husband saw a Moorish dancer steal money from Sefton Delman's jacket (he was the *Daily Express* correspondent) and stuff it in her blouse. He grabbed her, and in the scuffle that followed she bit him on the thigh.

The other happened later that week. A drunken militiaman in Chicote's bar — formerly Madrid's most fashionable café and an establishment with strong royalist leanings — wandered round the tables waving a flit gun and squirting customers. He sprayed a militia captain and his girl. The captain shot him dead on the spot.

The next day, at the same hour, Hal Peters went to Chicote's and walked round the tables with a flit gun, inquiring, "When is the next execution?" Federico followed him, pleading, "He's just a crazy American journalist. Don't pay any attention to him, *por favor!*"

All of this is in *The Fifth Column*. The protagonist is a composite of Hal Peter, Hank Gorrell, and my husband, plus a bit of Hemingway himself.

A RECURRING THEME

Federico's favourite saying was, *"Hay que complicar la vida* — One must complicate life."* He said it ironically, meaning, as though life wasn't difficult enough these days, these mad Americans have to complicate it further. Federico was loyal beyond belief. We used to drive up to the border and go into France to buy food, leaving him with all our pesetas and the car on the Spanish side. If he had wanted to take off with everything there was no law, no force, to stop him.

At another of Gorrell's parties a correspondent accused a militiaman of taking his wallet. Two officers pushed the man out into the corridor and were going to shoot him then and there. Everybody was drunk, and the correspondents were arguing with the officers and protesting at the proposed shooting. It was a matter of honour, the officers insisted, a stain on the Republic. People really talked that way then. Finally, tempers cooled; the wallet was returned, and everybody — culprit, executioners, and correspondents — returned to Gorrell's room for another drink.

Twenty years later, my husband and I were having dinner on the lovely island of Santa Marguerita off the coast of Venezuela with about fifteen correspondents, the Governor of the island, and his aide. During a pause in the conversation, the aide, who had been staring at my husband, leaned over the table and asked, "Weren't you in Madrid in the winter of '37?" My husband nodded. "I remember you. At a party at Señor Gorrell's room on the Gran Vía. We wanted to shoot someone, and you persuaded us not to. What I don't remember is why we thought we had to shoot him in the first place."

In exile in Venezuela, he was still nostalgic about Madrid and hoped to return "before I die".

In the days when we knew him, Hemingway was not the brawling "put-up-your-fists" sort of person his son Patrick describes in Bimini and Key West. Perhaps there was enough real danger and death about not to have to create excitement or, in Federico's words, *complicar la vida*. He did use similes and metaphors from the prizefighting, bullfighting, and hunting worlds. We believed that he was, or tried to be, overly simple and saw everything in terms of good guys versus bad guys. But that was before we read *For Whom the Bell Tolls*. Although we

48

hadn't realized it at the time, he had correctly appraised it all — the whole complicated bloody mess, the cruelty, the heroism, the treason, the increasingly tarnished ideals. It's all there, and the characters are right as rain.

I remember Hemingway as he was in our apartment that winter. A great big tough man (although Gertrude Stein said he was really fragile, always breaking legs or shoulders) whose face, despite the heavy moustache (this was before the Beard), suddenly looked like a small boy's. He sat on the floor amidst all the talk, his glass of beer next to him, listening creatively.

Chapter 4

THIS IS WHERE WE CAME IN

An air of euphoria. Bright hopes and ubiquitous dialogue. A
feeling of *déjà vu*. It has happened before; but where and when?
Certainly not in a previous incarnation. But, in a sense, yes. For,
in reality, are those two, young, recently-married, newspaper
correspondents whose friend Ramón raised the first flag of
Spain's Second Republic in the Plaza de Cibeles the same people
we are over half a century later?

Today under the aegis of the grandson of the king whose
departure ushered in a similar moment of happy expectation, a
heavy and cruel weight has been lifted from the spirit of
Spaniards. Once and for all the ancient jibe that the Bourbons
learnt nothing and forgot nothing has been confounded by King
Juan Carlos, determined on a reconciliation between the two
Spains.

When the young *telegrafista* raised the Republican flag over
the Palace of Communications — Madrid's central post office
— King Alfonso XIII was still in the Royal Palace, trying to
decide whether to stay or go. Hearing the shouts of *"Viva la
República!"* from the enormous gathering in front of the palace
he conferred with General Sanjurjo, Commander-in-Chief of the
Civil Guards. The General declared that he would not order his
troops to fire on the crowds, and the King decided to leave.

Amidst the wild celebrations that night of 14 April 1931 we
watched as youths climbed on top of tramcars and buses, shouting and singing. People surged through the streets, dancing,
cheering, all night long. In their republican enthusiasm, boys
beheaded the statues of medieval kings in the Plaza de Oriente
in front of the Royal Palace, although they had no idea who
they were. But there was no bloodshed. The atmosphere in the

early days of the Second Republic was joyous, hopeful; all men were brothers. At long last Spain was going to enter the Twentieth Century. Detained politicians left their well-furnished cells in prisons and fortresses to take over ministries and prepare a new constitution. Ideas of a secular state, of free, lay education, of agrarian reform, and prison reform, ideas of religious freedom, women's rights, civil marriage and — horror of horrors — divorce, ideas that had become commonplace elsewhere in Europe were for the first time being openly advanced in Spain.

It is easy now to regard this "Era of Good-Feeling" with the irony of hindsight. How naïve, how optimistic, how idealistic, how inexperienced they were, those founders of the Second Republic! All the dice were loaded against them. What *was* the Western world to which they looked so hopefully? A Germany of Brown Shirts and nascent Nazism. An Italy dominated by Mussolini's Fascists. A France torn apart by scandal and extremisms of Left and Right. An Appeasing England and an Isolationist U.S.A. Not to mention the worst Depression of the century. And in the east the monolithic Stalinist empire.

But for the young men like our friend Ramón, the poet Antonio Machado, educators like Fernando de los Ríos, even apolitical García Lorca, a new day had dawned. Unlimited possibilities lay ahead.

*   *   *

Some time ago our cook, Paquita, who like everyone else has been bombarded by radio, television, newspapers and billboards to vote in the referendum on constitutional reform, interrupted my typing. "Excuse the *molestia*, Señora." Pause. "May I ask you a question?"

"Of course."

"This referendum. Should I vote?"

"Certainly you should."

"Yes, but how? Should I vote '*Sí*' or '*No*'?"

"Well, if I were voting I'd vote '*Sí*'. But I'm a foreigner. You must decide for yourself."

"I want to vote '*Sí*', too." Another long pause. "But, Señora, is it safe?"

At first I thought she was asking if it was safe for Spain to embark on a new and untried political course, then I realized that that wasn't it at all. Despite continual assurances by all means of communications that this would be a free and secret ballot, Paquita was not sure there would not be repercussions if she voted the way *They* didn't want.

Who are *They*? No one who has not lived in Spain would understand. And even foreigners who have lived here in their foreign enclaves could not. *They* are the Guardia Civil, the police who dress as civilians, the millions of paid and unpaid informers — telephone operators, barbers, bartenders, anyone might be one.

The idea of a free election was simply too good to be true. Under Franco there had been Hitler-style *"Ya"* elections. But no one younger than sixty-five years of age had ever cast a free vote.

How remote Paquita and other working-class Spaniards are from politics was demonstrated for me the day after the Prime Minister of Spain, Carrero Blanco, was killed in a tremendous explosion that blew his car four stories on to a rooftop. I said to her, "What do you think about this assassination of Señor Carrero Blanco?"

She frowned, then asked, "Who is Señor Carrero Blanco?"

Her attitude reflected the reality of that time. Francisco Franco was the only person who mattered; the Council of Ministers, the members of the Cortes and other officials were only his creatures.

Public attitudes surfaced in popular sayings. One day we dropped Paquita off in front of the Guardia Civil Cuartel. "We'll let you off here at your friends'," my husband said jokingly as he opened the car door.

"Ni a sus madres!" she replied — meaning, "Not even to their mothers!" She added, "Having a Civil Guard as a friend is like having a bad *duro* [fifty cent piece] in your pocket."

*   *   *

And what of the thirty million foreigners who came to Spain every year and had nothing but praise for the tranquility and order created by the Franco régime? Since tourism is Spain's major industry, tourists are treated well and are not molested in any way. And resident foreigners led their *dolce vita* practically without restraint, in fact with fewer regulations than in France or Italy. Rarely do they come up against the facts of Spanish life, and when they do they are shocked. In the village where we live the English and Americans organized a theatre group and rehearsed *The Importance of Being Ernest*. On opening night cast and audience found themselves locked out of the town hall auditorium which the Mayor himself had provided. Why? Because it is necessary to obtain official permission for a meeting of more than six persons who are not members of the same family. The theatre group had no notion of the existence of such a regulation, and the Mayor had assumed that the usual steps had been taken. The Civil Governor of the Province was approached, bureaucratic wheels turned, and *The Importance of Being Ernest* was duly presented the following night.

To the average visitor the Civil Guards are extremely polite young men (and so good-looking!) who help stranded tourists, direct them to where they are trying to go, or telephone the nearest garage to come and fix a flat tyre. (Perhaps one should say there are not two Spains but three, the third Spain being that known to foreign tourists.)

Today, unlike the time of the Second Republic, the chasm between the two Spains — traditional and liberal — is only a gully. People and forces have changed sides. Most important, Church and Crown are now solidly in support of reform, the Church as represented by archbishops, bishops and priests, the Crown in the person of Juan Carlos and his Queen Sofia. And a new middle class has emerged. Our gardener first came to work on a bicycle, the next year on a motorbike, this year in a Volkswagen. The people who were said to have nothing to lose now have colour TV and paid holidays. The landless farm-workers are earning good money in German factories and sending home enough to buy a café or a garage in their village in a few years' time.

Against these forces stand the men known as "the Bunker", a last-ditch stand by those implacably opposed to democracy and a pluralistic society. Headed by an impressive orator, Blas

Piñar, they consider the present government a group of traitors who are betraying Francisco Franco's "Crusade". They are the well-dressed crowds who filled the Plaza de Oriente shouting "Franco! Franco!" a year after his death. They are the bully-boys who attacked bookstores, who wrecked movie-houses showing "liberal" films, who create chaos in the lecture-rooms of university professors with whose philosophy they disagree. They are also ordinary people for whom the Franco régime meant comfort and security. All they want is to keep things as they have been; they are afraid of reform because reform means change.

To see on prime time Spanish television a lengthy report of a Socialist Congress in Madrid (technically, the party was still illegal), with Willy Brandt, Olaf Palme, Michael Foot, François Mitterand and others embracing their Spanish colleagues, came as a shock after forty years of inflexible political censorship. This time the dice appear to be stacked in favour of reform instead of against it. The banks, foreign investments, economic and monetary interests, both national and international, support it. Perhaps the most important element is the King. Groomed by Franco as his successor and representing in his person the principles of legitimacy and continuity, this handsome young man has captured the popular imagination and is leading his people towards a freer and more just society. When he spoke to both houses of the U.S. Congress about his aims and ideals it was televised via satellite in Spain and we all knew then that this indeed was no puppet of Franco but the spokesman for a new era in Spain.

Prime Minister Adolfo Suárez, emerging from the Movimiente (formerly the Falange) as the King's man, manoeuvred the Reform Bill through the Cortes and the Council of the Realm, a seemingly impossible task since they were being asked to commit suicide and give way to a bicameral legislature elected by universal suffrage. Finally, after many hours, days and weeks of debate the Reform Bill was passed by an overwhelming majority and the clerk read out the official count: three hundred and fourteen for, thirteen against; and an exhausted but smiling Suárez responded to the applause of the Cortes by standing and applauding *them*.

*   *   *

The first Era of Good Feeling, in the 'thirties, lasted through the Presidency of Alcala Zamora, a deeply religious man and politically a moderate. Despite the grumbling of the clergy, whose salaries continued to be paid by the State, and much head-shaking by fat colonels, the surface of the political sea appeared calm. But with the accession of Manuel Azaña to the Presidency storm-clouds gathered rapidly. Amid strikes, bombings, assassinations and acts of violence by groups of *"incontrolables"*, the euphoria of the early days vanished and political lines hardened into class hatred. The privileged classes could accept in principle such things as prison reform, lay education and even women's suffrage (on obtaining the franchise the women voted into power the party that had opposed it!), but when the Government tried to implement agrarian reform — purchasing land at the value cited by the landowner for tax purposes — their opposition became deep and implacable enmity.

In the United Press office in Madrid where my husband worked, a daily box score was kept. So many churches burned, so many labour leaders shot. The assassination of a Guardia de Asalto was matched by the murder of a Falangist. A liberal judge's death was avenged by the killing of a Rightist lawyer. Almost every day saw a political funeral in which mourners were attacked by groups of spectators and the hearse was raked by machine-gun fire. After a union headquarters was bombed, a conservative casino would be destroyed. It was much like Northern Ireland today, except that since everyone was officially Catholic the division was between Right and Left (with the Church, as an institution and a vast landowner, on the Right).

In an attempt to solve the ever-growing number of industrial disputes, a byzantine system of *"jurados mixtos"* — arbitration boards — was established. Three members represented the union, three the employers, and one — the deciding vote — the government. My father, who had built the first milk-processing plant in Spain, found that when the government was Rightist the employer won, and when it was Leftist the union won, regardless of the merits of the argument. (Not that it mattered in his case, for during the Civil War his beautiful plant — designed by a Danish architect, and standing on the Paseo de la

Florida — was in the line of fire of the Nationalist artillery and was pounded to bits.)

Sabotage. Strikes and lockouts. Inflamatory editorials in the newspapers and vituperative speeches in the Cortes. In fact the day the Civil War started my grandmother in Chicago received a postcard from me, sent weeks before, which said: "I don't know what is going to happen here, but things can't continue like this. Such chaos!"

Yet despite everything, the danger and the inconvenience, life in Madrid was pleasant. (Or so it seems in later years, comparing Madrid with New York during a garbagemen's strike, or London when there was no light or heat during an electrical workers' strike, or Paris when the Metro and the buses were paralyzed.) I remember, in the long summer twilight, the walk down the Castellana or in the Retiro Park, the good beer and manzanilla wine, the *"tapas"* — tiny dishes of almonds, squid, clams, pickled fish, stuffed olives — served free with your drinks in the manzanilla bars along the Calle Sevilla.

My husband worked nights, from ten o'clock till about six in the morning. He walked the short distance from the United Press office in the Plaza de las Cortes to the Plaza de Atocha where we lived, sometimes stopping at the Casa Rosa for a drink just as they were putting their last customers out the door — guitar-players, men-about-town, ladies of the evening. To even things up we stayed out all night on his nights off. We had four Madrileño friends (including Ramón), all republicans with "advanced" ideas, who met for coffee every night at the Café Brasil. Every café was politically characterised; there was one for every shade of allegiance. We would join our friends after supper, almost midnight, and the night would pass in a twinkling, what with the talk, the pub crawl, beer and steak sandwiches on the Plaza Santa Ana, and, at dawn, coffee and *churros* in the Plaza del Sol. Often someone would accompany us home, still talking, determined to finish his peroration on politics, music, philosophy, or whatever we had been discussing. The dawns were unforgettable, the sky was so close, the air so clear. Men with hoses washed the streets. With our friends we went to the Fiesta of San Fermín in Pamplona (and were shocked to see our sophisticated Madrileño companions running in front of the bulls). Our friends were happily confident that the Republic would overcome its many problems and that an age of peace and social justice lay ahead.

Two of the four are still living, and their sons and daughters once again are breathing this strange new air of freedom.

*   *   *

As historians never tire of reminding us, Spain did not experience either the Enlightenment or the Revolution. In some respects, the Madrid of the early 'thirties resembled London of a previous century.

A family I will call Roca lived on the Calle Goya in Madrid: a widowed mother, her son and two daughters, living in genteel poverty. I often met "the girls" (who were then in their forties), Maria Carmen and Immaculada (known as Immy), for concerts in Retiro Park or coffee at the Café Kutz on the Castellana.

On one occasion we invited them to our apartment for drinks when some American diplomats were coming. Our other guests thought them charming, and the new U.S. Consul, an unmarried man, offered to give them a lift home in his car. The following week when I met them they were sad and woebegone. "Ay, *chica*, you can't imagine. . . ." Disgrace! Scandal! It seems that the young U.S. Consul had invited them to stop off at the Café Florida for a drink, and they accepted. None of the three — two innocent spinsters and a simple foreigner — were aware that this was the place where American executives of the I.T.T.- owned Telefónica across the street were in the habit of meeting their mistresses. Unfortunately for the sisters, a friend of their brother Manollo saw them and reported the fact. Scenes followed. Their widowed mother took to her bed and declared she would die of shame. Manollo said they had disgraced the good name of the Roca family, that he couldn't hold up his head among his colleagues at the office, and that he would never speak to "the girls" again. Señora Roca managed to survive the shock for some thirty more years but it was several months before Manollo would talk to his sisters; at mealtimes he communicated by gestures.

57

For many years, when Manollo was away from home working in another city, Señora Roca and her two daughters used to close the blinds and draw the curtains of their apartment on Goya Street and remain in their stifling quarters for the entire month of August, sending their little slavey maid scurrying out late at night for food supplies. Why? So that people would think they had gone to San Sebastian as they had in the days of their wealth.

We were at the Rocas' apartment when the parade celebrating the first anniversary of the Republic passed along Goya Street. Looking down from their balcony, Manollo sniffed disdainfully. "Scum!" he said. "They should be squashed [*aplastado*] like bugs!" I still remember his face; I had never seen that kind of hatred before.

Again Manollo. The date, 16 July 1936. Immaculada and Maria Carmen arrived late at the Café Kutz on the Castellana, both looking distraught. "Ay, *chica*," they said, as we exchanged kisses. "You can't imagine. . . ." The deputy from Galicia, Calvo Sotelo, had been assassinated and, according to Manollo, this was the last straw. The Republic was doomed.

Manollo was right.

*   *   *

Many years later, after the Second World War, I was back in Madrid, once again visiting the Rocas on Calle Goya. "We were for the Allies," Immy told me. "But Manollo favoured the Germans."

"The Germans should have won," Manollo said. "They had the plan, the organization, the military spirit. On the Allied side it was simply American industrial capacity." He implied it wasn't cricket to win as we had done.

Although Spain remained neutral in both World Wars, each time the conservatives favoured the Germans, the liberals the Allies.

At the end of World War II a journalist colleague — a Catholic and former philosophy professor — asked us to help in his research for some articles he was writing about Spanish attitudes to the wartime enemies as reflected in Spanish newspapers. We suggested our friend Ramón. Ramón went to the Biblioteca Nacional, the official archives, where among other things he unearthed the text of the telegram Franco sent to Emperor Hirohito congratulating him on the Japanese capture of Manila.

The journalist used the source material provided by Ramón in his articles published in the *New York Evening Post*. And shortly afterwards was called to the Foreign Office and told he was *persona non grata* and must leave Spain within ten hours. Ramón, who knew he himself was being followed, helped him to pack. "Don't worry," the journalist told him. "What can they do to me? I'm an American citizen."

And Ramón, in the tradition of don Quijote de la Mancha, forbore to reply that *he* was not an American citizen.

Nevertheless, nothing is simple in Spain. A friend of Ramón's in the police department warned him when his home would be raided. Ramón burnt everything that might be considered incriminating, including photographs of us and our children, and when the police searched they found nothing. Eventually Ramón was reinstated in his civil service job, though at near-starvation wages and minus the bonuses and perks that Falange members enjoyed. Gradually in the 'fifties and more rapidly in the mid-'sixties, life improved for men like Ramón whose only crime was sympathy with the Republic. In the early 'seventies, after years of not daring to meet old friends in public, he and these old friends (also by now in their early seventies) started gathering, in Café Gijon late on Saturday afternoons. "No politics," he explained; "mostly gossip. Who has died. Whose daughter has married whom. Not even bullfighting." (Ramón, an *aficionado* in the old days, believes that bullfights are now "staged" for the foreign visitors, who can be fooled by fancy footwork; "Juan Belmonte did not move his feet and let the bull charge to within millimetres, only turning his hips slightly to avoid the horns.")

Not all Ramón's friends were as fortunate as he was. One of them, Alfredo, who had become a fairly prosperous manufacturer, received a letter from a former comrade now in France, saying that a committee was being formed to help another colleague, in Paris, who was dying of tuberculosis. He sent some money, and within two days the police arrived and took him to gaol. Both letters had been seen by the Office of Censorship. At his trial he was accused of belonging to a subversive committee and was sentenced to two years' imprisonment.

Two other men whose letters had been intercepted received similar sentences. One of them, Adolfo, had a son who was studying law; he was so shocked by the travesty of justice that he dropped out of law school and went into his father's business. We saw Adolfo when he came out of prison a few months before his two-year-term was up. At first, he said, he was kept in a cell below the Interior Ministry on the Plaza del Sol. He was interrogated for hours and hours, kept awake by blinding lights, shaken from sleep for more interrogation. What the police wanted was the list of names of other people on the committee. But not one of the prisoners broke down and after a month they were sent to an ordinary prison for the remainder of their sentences. One of the people whose names were not revealed was Ramón.

Even during the harsh years of the 'fifties there was a curious form of double-think. Once while visiting friends in Mallorca my husband needed an extension of his visa. Our host, Fernando, who had been a leading republican though never joining any political organization, and who had spent over a year in a concentration camp doing road-work (where his fellow-prisoners mocked him for his white "*señorito's*" hands), took us to see the Civil Governor. He greeted us with great courtesy, offered us cigarettes, arranged the extension of the visa, and enquired most solicitously after the health of Doña Berta, Fernando's wife.

After we had been bowed out of the Governor's office with assurances that he was always at our disposal, I said, "I don't understand. I thought that man was your enemy."

"Yes, we were enemies," Fernando said. "But no more." He told us a strange story. After his trial, at which he was found not guilty — all that time in the concentration camp was *before* the trial! — he returned home, but he was still harrassed and kept under surveillance. One night he and his wife went to a nearby cinema where a double-bill was being shown. They decided one full-length feature was enough for them and left before the second one. A few minutes after they reached their house there was a knock on the door. The police. "Why did you leave the theatre like that?" they demanded.

Fernando explained. "No, no, that isn't the true reason," one of the police officers declared. "It was because the picture of the Caudillo is shown between the two features and you did not want to stand and salute him." They departed with warnings that his conduct had been noted.

Fernando had already taken his son away from school because the boy reported that he had been asked to spy on his parents and at great sacrifice Fernando had engaged a tutor. But that incident after the cinema was the "*colmo*", the limit, the last straw. The next morning he went to the Civil Governor. "I cannot live this way," he said. "If this harrassment is not stopped I will kill myself."

"How long will you give me?" the Governor asked.

"Two weeks at the utmost."

"Very well. Come back here in a fortnight and I will let you know what I can do."

When Fernando returned, the Civil Governor told him, "I assure you, on my word of honour, you will not be molested any more."

And he wasn't.

*   *   *

Not long ago my husband and I attended a luncheon at the Press Club in Madrid. The occasion was the publication of a book called *España Fue Noticia (Spain Was News)*, to which foreign correspondents on both sides of the Civil War had contributed episodes and reminiscences. We saw journalists we hadn't seen for forty years. There were Germans and Italians, Poles, Frenchmen, British and Americans. Men stared at one another, then embraced as they recognized the young correspondents they had known under the disguise of paunch and balding pate. The whole occasion was further evidence of a climate of tolerance.

Such books sell readily. A whole new generation is curious about the personalities, the battles, the ideologies of Spain's Civil War. But their interest is academic, much like that of a university student in the United States who has become an American Civil War buff. The young people have discounted their parents' and grandparents' accounts of atrocities and privations; they say they want to know *what really happened.*

One of the tragedies of the Spanish war is that each side became what its enemies called it. At the beginning both sides were composed of alliances of disparate elements. For the Nationalists these were the Army, the Guardia Civil, the Church (except in the Basque provinces), the Carlists, the Requetes, the Falange. On the Republic side the spectrum ranged from the Sindico-Anarchists, the Trotskyite P.O.U.M., the labour unions and Socialists as far to the Right as the Christian Democrats and the Radical Socialists (who were neither radical nor socialist). And, of course, both sides conscripted the young men who happened to be on that particular side when the shooting started. Early in the war the Republicans began calling the Nationalists "Fascists" and the Nationalists started to call the Republicans "Reds" and "Communists", although at that time there were only two Communists in the entire Cortes. And before the end of the war the Falange had absolute domination over what were by then the Franco forces, and the Republican territory was under the complete control of the Communists.

Whereas aid — in the form of money, planes, guns, Italian soldiers, German technicians, supplies of all kinds — poured in for the insurgents, the Democracies did nothing for the embattled republic. The so-called Non-Intervention policy prohibited a recognized government from buying arms to defend itself, though the Spanish Government had gold, tons of gold. So finally, reluctantly, the Republicans turned to Russia, who sold them wheat and arms, swallowed up their gold, and gradually but implacably took over. Only Communists units received arms, there were none for Anarchist or Republican forces. Communists quickly infiltrated censorship, communications, the ports, and the border controls It is my belief that the U.S.S.R.'s policy towards the Civil War in Spain was not to win it but to keep it going. It was the time of the Popular Front and Spain was a rallying cry that could unify liberal and radical forces throughout Europe.

As for the famous International Brigade, we in Spain knew little about them except what was told to us by their political commissars. You could visit any other sector of the front much more easily than theirs. For years I have met people who, on learning I was in Spain during the Civil War, say, "Oh, I wonder if you knew So-and-So; he was in the International Brigade." And, of course, I didn't. Because before he was guided across the Pyrenees he handed over his passport and was given another name. And if he became fed up with Communist propaganda and discipline and tried to get out (after all, he had volunteered), he was more than likely shot as a deserter or killed in an "accident". The irony was that what the Spanish republic did *not* need was men, even brave men, who were not trained soldiers. High-school teachers, librarians, even hillbillies from the Ozarks arrived. They had neither technical nor military experience required for fighting a war.

The amazing thing is not that the Nationalists won but that it took them so long. They had all the armed forces, aviation, tanks, artillery, all the trained officers and specialists, and they never lacked supplies. There were occasional rifts between commands (once we heard General Queipo del Llano making a speech on the radio during which he said that his troops would have to take Burgos, Franco's headquarters, before they took Madrid; he was drunk), but there was nothing on the Nationalist side like the war-within-a-war at Barcelona between the Trotskyites and the Stalinist Communists, when for almost ten days the centre of the city was divided by barricades from behind which there came constant gunfire. About midday there was a half-hour's truce so that people could carry on their lives and pass from one side to the other. And while the Communists were busily shooting at one another, the Ebro front was collapsing not many miles away.

*　　　　*　　　　*

For me the most memorable part of the war in Spain was the period when the Anarcho-Sindicalists controlled Cataluña. (That does not sound right, because anarchists are against control, against government of any kind; better to say perhaps that Barcelona and all of Cataluña were living on Sindico-Anarchist principles.) There were no "forces of Law and Order". No police. No censorship. Every factory, every shop, even the little *pension* where I lived was organized as a *"sindicato"*. In our *pension* the energetic but illiterate cook was elected president; the German owner became the accountant-treasurer. Every decision had to be presented to the entire group and voted upon. Even the great textile mills, the automotive plants, and department stores were run in this way.

Yet there was practically no crime. My father and I would go to the movies and walk through the Barrio Chino at one o'clock in the morning without fear. Despite occasional bombing raids, Barcelona at that time was the most peaceful city I have ever lived in.

How does one explain this? First, of course, every able-bodied young man was in the Army. Second, the owners and managers of factories, shops and hotels were quite sure the Nationalists would win and were able to keep an eye on things in the meantime, while playing what they regarded as a silly game. But as well, and this is the sinister part, there was an unseen but real terror. Since the Anarchists were trying to establish an ideal society, criminals were deemed unfit to live in it. A shoplifter might be shot dead on the spot because by his act he had shown himself unworthy of "El Communismo Libre". Too bad for him, but that was how it was. *Muerte sin odio* — death without hate.

When they burnt churches — or rather the interiors of churches since the buildings themselves were of stone — a committee (always committees!) was constituted; all the pictures and holy images were brought out for inspection and whatever was considered "art" was saved and whatever was "superstition" was consigned to the flames. How this fine distinction was made is a mystery

Some of their actions were charming. Since they opposed uniforms of any kind, they dyed the ugly grey pinafores of the orphans so that the children wore pink and baby-blue, cerise and lavender. The vast convents (the nuns who had escaped being murdered were in hiding) became communes for children evacuated from Madrid, where everyone did something under the confused direction of dedicated young women, resulting in cheerful chaos. I thought the youngsters, ranging in age from four to fourteen, looked fairly clean and certainly better fed than they were in the slums of Madrid.

*   *   *

The worst years for the Franco régime and for the people of Spain followed World War II. Ostracized by all of the postwar governments of Western Europe, who in any case needed aid themselves, Spain went through a severe economic crisis. Petroleum, bread, all the basic ingredients of life were in short supply. Marshall Plan aid was pouring into Europe. Only Juan Perón came to Franco's assistance with grain shipments and massive credits. (Later Franco was able to show his appreciation to Perón, who lived in splendour just outside Madrid after his fall from power and until his ill-judged return to Argentina three decades later.)

Things were in a bad way: the rolling-stock of the railways falling apart and without replacements, the bread almost inedible, the olive oil rancid; people were grumbling audibly. The situation was quite different from the prosperity that followed the First World War, for Spain's economy had not recovered from the devastation of its own Civil War when the Second World War prevented all development. It seemed that the régime of Francisco Franco might crumble when, lo and behold, enter the U.S. Navy, to negotiate the first contract for a naval base, followed by contracts for air bases. Millions, billions of dollars, to say nothing of grain, petroleum and other supplies, poured into Spain. Once again, Francisco Franco was saved.

This occurred during the administration of President Truman, whom my husband used to see regularly to obtain background material for his daily column in the *Chicago Times*. On one occasion Truman was sitting for his portrait in the full regalia of the Masonic Order. He was concerned about the rights of Protestants in Spain. At that time they had none; hotel clerks would give people addresses where Protestant religious services were held on Sunday mornings the way they would give you the address of a speakeasy during Prohibition. There could be no indication or sign of a church. Only marriages celebrated by

Catholic clergy were legal. Burial of a Protestant was an almost clandestine affair and the funeral cortège was limited to the back streets. Masons were lumped with Jews and Reds as the enemies of Franco's Crusade.

"So you're telling me Protestants in Spain are second-class citizens," Truman said.

My husband replied that since no Spaniard had any rights, *everyone* in Spain was a second-class citizen. Perhaps Protestants were third- or fourth-class.

Franco controlled even the Catholic Church through his privilege of selecting the candidates from whom the Pope chose the archbishops — a unique arrangement. However, early in the 'fifties a change took place in the thinking of priests, monks, and even bishops. They began saying that the Church's position in the Civil War as the bulwark of wealth and privilege had been wrong, that the Church should be concerned with social justice and should speak out on such matters. And over the years since then, both officially and unofficially, churchmen have become increasingly articulate. Pastoral letters have been banned by the state censor, priests jailed, and bishops and archbishops put under house arrest. When we first came to Spain churches were attended only on holidays, by well-dressed people, few men and mostly very old women. Nowadays they are well attended by people of all classes. And recently Spain relinquished its special privileges voluntarily in a new Concordat with the Vatican.

*   *   *

There are some interesting parallels between the two Eras of Good-Feeling. In the first case, a dictator chose to give up power; in the second, a dictator held on to power until the last moment before his death. In one the dictator dragged the king down with him; in the other the king, by a miraculous legerdemain, overnight became the symbol of the very forces that had been suppressed by the dictator for four decades.

The dictatorship of Primo de Rivera fell as the result of the disastrous Moroccan campaigns and the financial crash of 1929.

Perhaps the worst episode was an ambush in which a large contingent of Spanish troops was annihilated in a mountain pass at Anual, and there were rumours of mutiny in the army. Spain had done well economically in the First World War, selling to both sides, but the days of prosperity were over. In the face of all this, Primo de Rivera, Marques de Estella, resigned — a most undictatorial act.

In the municipal elections, republican candidates won overwhelming majorities, despites the *caciques* or local political bosses. Seing the crowds and hearing the shouts of *"Viva la República!"*, King Alphonso XIII left his palace and went into exile. The ascension of his grandson, King Juan Carlos, as head of state has been as enthusiastically cheered by the multitudes as was the proclamation of the Second Republic some forty-five years before. Day after day, he and his wife — a most photogenic young couple — have been received with wild ovations wherever they appeared, even by those who prophesied the King would be known as Juan Carlos El Breve (the Short-Lived) and who feared he would carry on "Franquismo" without Franco.

Western heads of state now make it clear that Spain is no longer a sort of pariah but a part of Europe. In the recent past Western Europe's attitude towards Spain has been ambivalent. U.S. bases are an integral part of the Western defence strategy. Spain welcomes yearly as many tourists as there are Spaniards. Expatriate Spanish workers have been doing many hard and unpleasant tasks that no German, Frenchman or Belgian wanted to do. But Europeans have long memories of the part Franco played in World War II. Quite obviously, Franco's sympathies were with the Axis. He admired Hitler and Mussolini, kept autographed photographs of them on his desk. Both of them had helped him to win the Civil War, and his political ideas were in sympathy with theirs. Yet, whenever I've talked to people about Spain's rôle during the Second World War, someone always says, "But you must admit, Franco kept Hitler from taking Spain."

But did he? It is true the Germans never invaded Spain. And also true that the Allies wanted to keep the Germans away from the Straits of Gibraltar before, during and after the landings in

North Africa. At this time I was the Acting Chief of the Iberian Section of the U.S. Board of Economic Warfare. We were buying Spanish supplies for Allied forces and buying preclusively to keep strategic materials out of the hands of the Germans. Our agents bought tin and tungsten, mercury, cork, wool, sardines, turpentine, sharkskins. We really needed the tin and the tungsten after our principal sources, Singapore and the Malay Peninsula, fell to the Japanese. For our part we supplied the Franco government with high octane aviation fuels (carefully calculated for their needs, with none left over to give the Germans), ordinary gasoline, lubricants and diesel oil, and other essential products without which the Spanish economy would have ground to a halt. Our policy was to keep Franco at least neutral enough to protect our supply lines to North Africa. And, as is now history, Rommel's Afrika Corps ran out of fuel and to the Allies went the final "Desert Victory".

However, at one point I was given a high-priority assignment: U.S. Intelligence wanted to know what the Germans would get if they moved into Spain — what railroad stock, hydro-electric power, fuel reserves, motor vehicles, manufacturing plants, harvested crops, fishing fleet, harbour and dock facilities. Working night and day I produced a comprehensive report. As everyone knows now, nothing happened. But Intelligence was correct. The date was correct; both Count Ciano's and Air Marshal Goering's memoirs confirmed it. But Hitler changed his mind and the Reichswehr moved against Russia instead. So it was Hitler and not Franco who kept the German Army out of Spain.

Franco's admirers sometimes point to the account of the meeting between Franco and Hitler; "Hitler came to meet Franco and Franco kept him waiting," they say. Which is true enough. But there were many advantages for the Germans in *not* occupying Spain. It was a major source of supplies in a bomb-free area whose economy was kept going by the U.S. In other words, the Germans could get agricultural and mineral products, fuels and spare parts, thanks to the United States. And as their own labour supply dwindled, they could depend on Spain for manufactured goods and minerals, whereas German factories had to be hidden underground and German mining plants and railway lines were subject to continual Allied bombing.

Franco did play his cards astutely. Why should he, the all-powerful Dictator of Spain, become another Gauleiter of the German Reich? He flattered Hitler, and managed to keep proper, albeit cold, relations with the Allies — relations which became less cold with each Allied victory. The Spanish Blue Division which fought with the Germans against the Russians became less and less prominent in press reports.

And, thanks to Spain's neutrality, thousands of people escaped from Occupied Europe. Many otherwise would have died in gas chambers or concentration camps. But it must be added that when the war ended thousands of Nazis, including war criminals, made their way to Spain and from there to South America. Not all; quite a few remain here in Spain.

In any case, how could Franco's army have stopped the Wehrmacht and the Luftwaffe? His forces were poorly equipped to fight a modern war. The Pyrenees was no longer an obstacle. Still the myth persists. Shades of Goya's famous cartoons showing courageous, bare-breasted, peasant women fighting Napoleon's soldiers with pitchforks! The matrons of Madrid pouring boiling water down upon the French invaders! Yet even at that time the heroic resistance of the Spanish populace would have been futile without Wellington's Peninsular Campaign, the Battle of Trafalgar and, finally, Waterloo. And there is another, embarrassing point: the workers, miners and city slum-dwellers of Spain were no partisans of Franco. They were precisely the ones who had been defeated in the Civil War. Most of them were bitter and in no mood to defend a régime which regarded them with suspicion and treated them with severity.

Until quite recently, reconciliation was a dirty word in Spain. Never forgive an enemy. Nor his son. Nor his daughter. I know of many cases in which well qualified young men and women were passed over for appointments because their parents — in some cases, grandparents — had been republicans. Students were unable to get passports and exit visas if they were "*fichado*". Listed; suspected of being unsympathetic to the government. It was done in a devious way. No student was ever told that he or she was "*fichado*". But when he applied to go abroad his application was lost, somehow the papers never went through. Of course, anyone could leave Spain during the tourist season, when there is no time to check all the thousands of foreign cars that daily cross the frontier; the problem for such students is not getting out, it is getting back in! So they stay.

In the last years of Franco the idea of reconciliation became respectable; exiles began to drift back, newspapers appeared to be more free. Occasional issues of *Time* magazine were still confiscated from news-stands but copies mailed to subscribers went through. Conditions today provide reason for the belief that the new Era of Good-Feeling may last longer than that of the 'thirties. From its birth the Second Republic was beset by enormous difficulties: an archaic economy, powerful banks, huge *latifundios* with absentee-owners, a wealthy church deeply involved in temporal affairs, an army which was becoming increasingly uncontrollable; add to these a surge towards independence on the part of the two most advanced regions, Catalonia and Euzkadi, and a small intellectual élite whose ideas were light-years distant from those of the general public. Around Toledo, for example, farm workers lived on *sopa de ajo* — garlic soup and chunks of bread; meat was for Christmas or Easter. Basically, their lives were little different from those of their ancestors in the fifteenth century. Child mortality was high, tuberculosis was commonplace. Illiteracy was estimated at between seventy and eighty per cent.

All that has changed. In the last fifteen years the standard of living has soared, and while there are some depressed areas there are no starving peasants. In part this is due to a need, albeit temporary, of Western industry for unskilled and semi-skilled workers. For a time as many as three million Spaniards were abroad in Germany, France, Switzerland, Belgium and Sweden, under government-to-government contracts, and the monthly payments to their families brought the Spanish Treasury an amount of foreign currency second only to that provided by tourism. So many left Spain to work abroad that it became not uncommon to see Moroccan workers on construction sites, brought to Spain to redress a shortage of labour.

The new Era of Good-Feeling may not last. The Socialist government of Felipe Gonsalez has to deal with grave challenges

— deficits, industrial disputes, annual inflation at around thirty per cent; Basque separatism. But it has a lot going for it as well. King Juan Carlos and Prime Minister Adolfo Suárez did not leave prison or return from exile. They came directly out of the Franco régime itself, the King as the approved successor of the Generalissimo, Suárez out of the *Movimiento*, the only legal political body in Spain. Despite the murmurs of "the Bunker", they represented Legitimacy and their proposed reform was finally accepted by Franco's hand-picked Council of the Realm and members of the Cortes. If peaceful transition from a dictatorship to a constitutional monarchy with a pluralistic parliamentary government is possible, then such a transition has occurred in Spain and continued under Prime Minister Gonsalez.

"*Ojala!*" the Spaniards say: a word derived from Arabic, meaning "May it be thus!"

*　　　*　　　*

L'ENVOI

"Alas," sighs my neighbour, the General's wife. "If only Franco were alive, none of this would be happening." She is thinking of the robberies, muggings and drug-related crimes in Madrid, Barcelona and other large cities in Spain. "Such peace and tranquility then, such a sense of security!" She shakes her head sadly.

I do not argue. She is a good neighbour and a good friend. We are the same age.

But it is like an Englishwoman saying, "If only Queen Victoria were on the throne today, everything would be fine!" If we could turn the calendar back a century or so, would we really be better off? People like me and like the General's wife might be, although I'm not so sure. If we'd survived childhood, smallpox and tuberculosis, we might both have died in childbirth (I have three children, she has seven!).

Of course, it *was* safer to live, to walk in the streets, to travel on a bus, to attend the theatre, to return home late at night in Madrid than it is now. In this, she is right. But anyone our age can say the same thing about London or Paris or New York. In Spain, one reason you *felt* safe was that crimes were not reported in the newspapers so that unless you knew someone whose purse had been taken, you believed that there were no pickpockets. Since El Caudillo and press and radio and television censorship disappeared at the same time, the sudden deluge of news about crime made us believe that it had suddenly developed.

The Twentieth Century arrived late in Spain; widespread urban crime, the drug culture, came late, too. Now that Spain has entered the Common Market and NATO, has a modern Constitution and a Constitutional Monarchy, both the blessings and the evils of the last decades of the century are upon us.

The high hopes of the old Spanish Republic were doomed. In a Europe where Hitler and Mussolini were the rising powers, with Russia ruled by a bloodthirsty Stalin, disunited France, isolationist England and America, Spain's young idealists were bound to be swept away by the Fascist "wave of the future".

Today Spain is entering a democratic Europe as an equal (even if, in George Orwell's words, some — like France — are more equal than others). The present government of Felipe Gonzalez and his successors face problems of unemployment, inflation, the need to restructure major industries like shipbuilding and textiles previously protected by heavy duties, the need to modernize the whole military edifice and thus avoid future "*golpes*" like the absurd Tejero melodrama when the Cortes was seized by insurgent officers. Some of these problems are universal ones. And the threat of nuclear extinction faces us all. But Spanish society today is more stable, more prosperous and more self-confident than it has been at any time during the half a century and more I have lived in and visited this fascinating country.

PART II

LOOKING BACK

Chapter 5

THE GREAT CHICAGO FIRE

In the history of nearly every place there is an event so crucial that its residents date everything as happening before or after it. The old families of the city of Panama divide their past into two parts: before and after the sacking of the town by the English pirate Morgan. (Since Spain and England were at war, instead of being hanged for his crimes he was made Governor of Jamaica.) In the South of the United States people date events as occurring before or after what they call "The War Between the States" (never the Civil War). In Chicago, where my family lived and still lives, the watershed of history was the Great Chicago Fire.

My grandmother Melanie, after whom I was named, remembered it vividly and after many tellings I find it seems almost as though it happened to me.

She was ten years old on 8 October 1871, a few days after the fire had started, and people in hansom cabs, in buggies, on horseback, on bicycles, and on foot, carrying whatever they could salvage from the destruction of their homes, surged past her home on North State Street. There were ladies in high-heeled slippers, burdened with weighty heirlooms, family portraits, or even birdcages; housewives struggling with baskets of linen and china; men with mattresses and cabinets on their shoulders. No one was helping anyone else. It was every man for himself. Screams and wails and drunken laughter floated by on the sea of people that swept past the house.

The cook and the chambermaid had fled with the rest, taking with them hampers of clothing. Melanie was alone with her mother, an invalid. She was told to lock the front and back doors

75

and to draw the blinds throughout the house. Heavy iron shutters protected the downstairs windows and, using all her strength, Melanie slowly managed to pull them together and lock them. The noise of the people outside grew louder and closer. What looked like a solid wall of fire was approaching the river. All the gas mains were broken, so Melanie lighted candles and sat with her mother, listening and waiting.

But the fire stopped at the river. The next morning people began to seep back, and there were knocks on the door. Friends who had passed the house the night before, not caring to remember that an invalid and a child were inside, now arrived asking for shelter. They had been "burned out", their homes levelled. Could they be put up temporarily? Melanie brought the messages to her mother, Madeleine. There were twenty-five families, almost a hundred persons. Some knew Melanie's family well, some were slight acquaintances, and others were total strangers.

"Tell them they may stay here," Madeleine said. Melanie was shocked. Her fastidious mother, allowing their home to become an encampment for these unsightly refugees! What would her father say when he returned from his trip to Wisconsin to buy lumber?

Melanie watched, fascinated, as Captain Steve Edwards, late of the Union Army, wounded at Antietam, organized the communal living. First he ordered the younger men to return to the fire- and bucket-brigades in the burning city. He conscripted a commissary department among the women. Even the children were assigned chores of cleaning and carrying water from a nearby pump. He found mattresses and blankets. He read the Bible and prayed for the victims and everyone knelt and said "Amen". And Captain Edwards promised "to shoot personally anyone caught stealing in the house".

That was Saturday. The blaze was still a towering cliff of flame that threatened to cross the Chicago River. All day Sunday the firemen and volunteer bucket-brigades fought a losing battle. The Courthouse with its records dating back to Fort Dearborn days, Crosby's Opera House, the New Union Station, Tremont House, the City Hall — all were reduced to ashes.

It was almost dawn on the morning of Monday, 9 October, when helped by a steady wind the fire jumped the river to the

North Side. Bridges and river-boats caught fire, and windborne planks and spars carried the flames along. The Historical Society, where the first draft of the Emancipation Proclamation was kept, and the mansions near the waterworks were engulfed, despite the efforts of General Sheridan to blast with dynamite a fire-break that the flames could not cross.

Once again screaming mobs stormed down North State Street, joined now by some of the refugees who had been sheltered by Madeleine. But Captain Edwards remained. Those who stayed watched from Madeleine's upstairs sitting-room as the crowds shoved their way through the streets, carrying their belongings and those of others. For despite the warnings of Pinkerton's police, posted in great placards, that anyone caught looting would be shot on the spot, looting had begun. Goods from the abandoned department-stores had been snatched by passers-by. Paintings, silver and precious porcelain were taken from the empty mansions. Stocks from liquor stores were being consumed en route. Amidst the throngs, horses maddened by falling sparks plunged and kicked over their traces, trampled children, and crashed against walls.

Captain Edwards stood his rifle against the window-ledge. Then he took out his small and battered Bible, cleared his throat and began to read aloud. To Melanie, the sound of the captain's voice gave a sense of assurance greater than the words themselves. As windows and doors were shuttered and bolted, the air inside became hot and stifling, like an oven. The stench of burning horseflesh, a sickening sweet odour, mingled with the other smells. The air became so thick with smoke that the Captain choked and coughed, but he continued to read.

When dawn came they opened the windows and shutters and blinds and looked out. A few of the other stone houses nearby were still standing but beyond was smoking desolation. On the west side of the river a bank of flames a hundred feet high and two miles long still advanced, burning the wooden shanties — the slums of De Koven and Clinton streets.

The Captain yawned, and stretched his arms. He patted Melanie's bright hair, smiled at Madeleine. "Guess the danger's past," he announced. "Always did prefer to hold a good well-entrenched position rather than make a strategic retreat."

Later he could be found sleeping soundly under the kitchen table, his head nestled on a wooden rolling-pin.

At dusk that day Melanie opened the door and sat on the top step of the front stairs. To the south and west, flames still rose against the sky. The air still smelt of smoke. The clanging of bells and the sharp roar of distant dynamite broke the quietness of evening. Melanie thought carefully about everything that had happened during the past days so that she could fix it in her memory. Captain Edwards had said, "This is something you will tell your grandchildren."

She did. To another Melanie. Me.

Chapter 6

WORDS AND MUSIC

THE fires had hardly died out when a curious sight could be seen on the blustery windswept streets of Chicago. An old horse drew a rickety wagon driven by a small, red-cheeked boy who called out, "R-r-r-rags and old i-r-r-ron!" Whenever he stopped people brought him scorched, fused and tangled remnants of household possessions, kitchen utensils, pots and pans, even melted coins. The lad weighed the metal objects carefully on his scales, paid the owners, then continued on his way.

He was older than he appeared: almost nineteen, though he looked about fourteen. He called the horse Rosinante. He had come to Chicago just after the Fire, used his savings (from a year's work as a bellhop in New York) to buy the horse and wagon and to rent a stall in a stable. An immigrant, he had come to America from France. Alone.

This was Maurice. My maternal grandfather.

He spoke good English (with a French accent that people were later to say sounded like Maurice Chevalier's). That and an interest in metals and mineralogy had been acquired from the Benedictine friars in France, where he had received whatever formal education he had. Whereas Leon, the father of his future wife, was ruined by the Fire (his great lumber yards on the river were destroyed and the insurance companies were unable to meet all the claims from such a huge disaster), Maurice built his fortune on the scrap metal that remained after the Great Chicago Fire. Leon and Maurice had one thing in common: they were both French, unusual in Chicago except for a few descendants of the intrepid *coureurs de bois* who had traded with the Indians and then sold beaver, muskrat and fox furs at Fort Dearborn, a trading post and fort set up where the river joined

Lake Michigan. Still, the difference between Leon's daughter, Melanie, who lived in a fine stone house on North State Street and the immigrant boy shivering on his rickety wagon was enormous.

Even when I knew them as my grandmother and grandfather, after they had raised three daughters and a son (the eldest daughter being my mother), they seemed to live in different worlds. In fact, Maurice was seldom seen in his own home. He rose at dawn, returned from work late at night, seven days a week, never took a vacation. Part of the week he spent in Sandoval in southern Illinois, where his Illinois Smelting & Refining Company employed most of the local population.

Aside from his work, he had one passion — opera. During Chicago's opera seasons patrons had become used to the little Frenchman who sat upstairs in the gallery and his reaction to the singing was awaited with amusement. His shouts of "Bravo!" could be heard everywhere, as could his equally loud disapproval (in French) — he once called Mary Garden an "assassin" during a performance of *Lachmé*: she had "assassinated" the aria!

On Sunday evenings after supper, when he was home, he would take me into his study and play records on the wind-up gramophone. He particularly admired Caruso and would sing with him in his own clear tenor voice. He told me the plots of the operas, then played selections on the Victrola for me. Except for Wagner, he loved them all — Gounod, Verdi, the lot.

My musical education was continued by my Uncle George. A doctor with a private practice, he was also the official house physician for the Opera House. The Auditorium on Michigan Avenue, built by Henri Luis Sullivan, possessed the finest acoustics in America (no amplifiers or electronic devices needed there).

Uncle George, Russian-born, who later married my Aunt Erma, graduated from Rush Medical College and had his licence to practise medicine when he was so young his professors advised him to study in Paris for a year or two. It was the best possible time to be in Paris — he met Axel Munthe, Pavlova, Isadora Duncan, Daghiliev, Seurat, Derain — painters, writers, dancers, singers, pianists. Later, when some of them came to Chicago, they greeted him as an old friend. My aunt didn't "care much" for opera, so Uncle George took me instead, somewhat against my parents' wishes ("so late at night"). Dressed in my best white dress with a blue satin sash, high white socks and white shoes, I sat in the box with my uncle, who was often called away when a dancer turned an ankle or a singer demanded a throat spray. Thus I met Pavlova in her dressing-room. She kissed me and gave me a long-stemmed rose. I remember Isadore Duncan explaining to a bewildered audience: "I do not dance, I just listen to the music."

Chaliapin, who came to Uncle George's for dinner, picked me up and kissed me on both cheeks, and said something in Russian. Uncle George translated: "What a solemn child!" An only child, I was accustomed to the company of adults. I was fascinated by their talk, even when I didn't understand it. Still, something is perceived. I was "much too young" to read Shakespeare, Dickens, Thackeray, George Elliott, Mark Twain (except for *Tom Sawyer*), but I did. I missed a great deal, yet I absorbed more than I realized: words, sentence rhythms, the poetry of language.

In the same way, I wasn't "taught" French by Maurice, when he read aloud to me, for his own delight, plays like *Cyrano de Bergerac* (after a brief translation of the story), but the French I picked up sounded French as that of my schoolfriends with their American teachers would never do. It gave me a feeling of confidence that made it possible many years later for me to appear on a nationwide TV show in Paris — "Author Meets Critic" — when the French edition of my novel *The Gentle Tyrants (Un Doux Tyran)* was published by Fleuve Noir, answering the critics' questions in correct French.

The time that adults spend with children is never wasted. How much I learned from them — my parents, my grandparents (Melanie, Maurice, Berthold — my paternal grandmother, Sophia, died when I was an infant), my Uncle George! Not only facts but ideas about life, honour, responsibility, human destiny. They and my Sunday School teacher, Dr Stone (at All Souls' Unitarian Church) had far greater influence on me than most of my teachers and professors later in life.

LOOKING BACK

Maurice used to quote a poem (by Baudelaire, I think):

> La vie est vaine;
> Un peu d'amour,
> Un peu de haine,
> Et puis, bonjour!
>
> La vie est brève;
> Un peu de joie,
> Un peu de rêve,
> Et puis, bon soir!

That just about sums it up, doesn't it?

Chapter 7

MOTHER WAS A SUFFRAGIST

UNLIKE the British suffragettes, the American suffragists were nonviolent and ladylike. Whereas Mrs Pankhurst and her followers were jailed and force-fed, and chained themselves to the gates of Buckingham Palace, the Americans relied on the feminine art of persuasion.

As a child, I was taken by my mother to the capitals of all of the states that had "Friendly Governors", a phrase that conjured up pictures of something like Tweedle-Dum and Tweedle-Dee from my *Alice in Wonderland* book, but which in fact meant governors who were friendly towards the idea of women's suffrage. We were sometimes put up in the gubernatorial mansions and Mother made speeches to civic organizations whose members might influence the state legislature to pass the **Amendment** which would give women the right to vote.

At banquets, sitting on a pile of telephone books so that I could reach my plate, I listened to The Speech. Mother's speech was always the same one. It was reassuring. In the days of the pioneers, she said, women controlled the health and education of their children. They knew where the food came from — their own gardens; they could oversee the activities of their young, teach them to read and write and do sums, instill good habits. But now (accompanied by a wide sweep of the right hand), all this has been taken away from her. She is no longer able to insure that her children's food is pure, that their health is protected, that what they learn is sound. All the suffragists want, Mother explained, is to regain the rights and duties in an increasingly urban and industrial society that they had in the days of log cabins.

It was a successful appeal. Men did not feel threatened by it,
and Mother's well-modulated voice and the fact that she greatly
resembled a small version of Lily Langtry, the Beauty of their
youthful memories, did not detract from its effectiveness.

But it was not always easy. Especially in the South, where
Southern gentlemen felt bound to protect their gentlewomen
from the tobacco-scented, rowdy atmosphere of the polling
booths. A friend of mine remembers listening to a Florida poli-
tician earnestly explaining to a large auditorium that "Women
don't really *want* the vote" — while some ten thousand women
from all over the country marched past the windows in teeming
rain, their storm-soaked banners demanding "VOTES FOR
WOMEN".

At home, rolled up in the closet for use at meetings of the
"Political Equality League", were large posters. Three figures
were depicted: an Indian warrior with tomahawk, scalps on
his belt; a dangerous criminal gazing balefully from behind the
bars of a prison cell; and Whistler's Mother, the Perfect Lady,
in her rocking-chair. These, the legend explained, were the three
classes of people who couldn't vote. (Long afterwards someone
suggested that women should have been included in the Four-
teenth Amendment, which provided that no one should be
deprived of rights because of race, colour, or *previous condition
of servitude.*)

Finally, the women of the U.S.A. did get the vote. And I was
to be the mascot for our victory march — dressed in a bright
yellow bloomer dress. I was even interviewed by the *Chicago
Tribune* and my picture was published along with my ideas on
Women's Suffrage, Socialism and Immortality. But the day of
the Parade I came down with the measles.

As a protégée of Jane Addams, Mother taught English to
classes of immigrant women living in the slums surrounding Hull
House and became concerned about their conditions. On one
occasion she returned to her home on Prairie Avenue with her
percale blouse torn and her skirt mud-streaked. She tried to
creep upstairs unnoticed but was stopped by my grandmother.
She explained that she had joined a march by striking gar-

84

ment-workers which had been dispersed by mounted policemen
— "like Cossacks! I was carrying a placard and I fell into a
puddle."

"What did the placard say?" my grandmother asked, shocked
that her daughter should be mixed up in such activities.

Mother, scratched and muddy as she was, broke into laughter.
"I don't know," she admitted. "It was in Yiddish."

When she married, my father encouraged her "radical" interests. Thus, the "Womens Lib." movement in the 'sixties sounded
to me like a strident parody of what I'd heard as a child. My
friend Sandy Bennett, a doctor of medicine — whose mother
Anna Blount was the first woman to graduate from Rush Medical School and who was a colleague of Margaret Sanger's —
had much the same reaction. As her daughter Ann said, "In our
family, the women have been liberated for three generations."
Sandy's father, an eminent physiology professor, shared the
household responsibilities (few as they were, since both they
and we had servants) and took as much interest in his wife's
career as in his own.

Nevertheless, until recently it was taken for granted that when
the chips were down the decision would go on the side of the
husband. When Sandy's anaesthetist husband was offered a
position in Texas, she gave up her practice and went with him.
Without a qualm I relinquished a career in government to return
to Chicago when my husband went back to the *Chicago Times*
after the Second World War. On the other hand, my son Peter
and his wife Susanna went their separate ways when their
careers divided them geographically, which led finally to divorce.
Until their generation, the husband came first. Always. Auto-
matically. Except perhaps for opera singers and movie stars!

One of Mother's most endearing qualities was her enthusiastic faith in me and my friends. Her encouragement took practical forms. After her death my father and I received many
letters from people whom she had helped — an introduction
here, an available scholarship there, an invitation to show paintings or to speak at the Chicago club of which she was president.
From the actress Beulah Bondi came a letter saying that when,
after a small part in *Street Scene* in New York, Stanley Walker
had suggested that she go to Hollywood, her family was horrified.

85

Broadway was bad enough, but Hollywood was a Den of Iniquity. Mother sent her five hundred dollars (a lot of money in those days) and told her it was a gift not a loan. "If you succeed, Beulah, I will feel more than repaid." Beulah became one of the leading character actresses of the films, but we had never known of Mother's part in her career.

Beulah's mother, Eve Bondi, was a suffragist but she was also a follower of the Coué dictum, "Every Day in Every Way I am Getting Better and Better". A wearer of silk scarves — as much a symbol then as the beads and long hair were to be for the Flower Children many decades later — Eve Bondi inspired my parents to buy a cabin in the sand dunes of Indiana.

Nothing could possibly be the way I remember "The Dunes" because in my memory they were, quite simply, Paradise. An enormous stretch of shifting sand along the Indiana and Michigan shores of Lake Michigan. In the hollows behind the dunes were woods, swamps, and fields of wildflowers that, starting with arbutus, "Indian paintbrush", dogtoothed violets in the spring, ran rampant into daisies, "bachelor buttons" and wild roses, and a mixture of plants and birds almost never found together elsewhere in the same latitude, because of the unique ecological system of the dunes.

It was my kingdom, my fief, my empire, to be shared later with a friend who was a boy, but not a boyfriend. With horses hired for the season, we galloped along the hard sand near the lake, played at Lawrence of Arabia as we flew along the crest of the dunes. We explored the little river as Father Marquette and Joliet in a birchbark canoe, went swimming in the lake, and covered enormous distances through the woods, following what we believed to be and might even have been old Indian trails. Late in the spring our cabin had to be dug out of the sand that covered it up to the window-sills during the winter. It was really just a big screen-enclosed porch. No glass windows, only heavy wooden shutters that could be let down, and which banged deliciously in storms. No electricity. A handpump for water. An outhouse. A primus stove for cooking. Complete freedom, independence, privacy. And several hundred books from the Chicago

Public Library — with a small deposit you could take them out for the whole summer. At night, campfires and roasted weenies and marshmallows under the stars.

Mother and I stayed there from early June until Labour Day in September. Father came over at weekends on the Illinois Central railway. A summer was a blissful eternity with plenty of time for everything: no pressures, no appointments, just sky, water, sand-dunes — and books.

Chapter 8

HURRAH FOR GRANDPARENTS!

GRANDPARENTS are a wonderful invention. The relationship between a grandparent and a grandchild is so much easier, more relaxed, less complicated than that between parents and offspring. We have established firm friendship with four of our seven grandchildren (the seventh was but lately born), have travelled with them, and they have spent long periods of their childhood living with us. We took the two eldest, Michael and Lara, with us round the world (when they were four and six), and Lara later came with us to New Zealand for six months. We took them to Hawaii when we taught there one summer, and to Holland, Austria, Spain and Morocco another summer. They remember riding camels in Marrakesh, dancers wielding spears in Fiji, a pet turtle they found in New Caledonia (and which they kept with them, unknown to us, all the way back to Hawaii).

Grandparents played important parts in both my husband's youth and in mine. When he was seven years old he was seriously ill with what was later called rheumatic fever and had to spend a whole year in bed. His principal nurse and companion was his grandmother, Molly. She used to tell him stories of pre-Civil-War Texas (she was born in Marshall, Texas), of the war in which her four elder brothers fought for the Confederacy, and of the arrival of the Yankee troops, who, she said, much to her own and everyone else's surprise, behaved "almost like gentlemen". Molly's stories were vivid. She described the slaves shouting for joy when they heard Lincoln's "Emancipation Proclamation", many setting off then and there for destinations unknown.

She told of a shootout in the main drygoods store on the town square and how she and her mother, Caroline, rushed with the crowd to the door of the shop. People surrounded a dead man and Caroline could see only his boots, recognized them as her husband's and promptly fainted. When she was revived, she discovered that while they were indeed her husband's boots, the dead man had stolen them from her house, had then tried to hold up the drygoods store but had been shot dead by the owner.

Other tales recounted by Molly concerned "the Plague" — Yellow Fever, a worse enemy than the Yankees. The whole family drove in the carriage, with two horses, to Shreveport, in Louisiana, to stay with relatives and avoid the disease. When the Yellow Fever reached Louisiana, they went north to Memphis, and more relatives, and finally when the epidemic spread to Memphis, they fled "way North" to St Louis, where they stayed in rooming-houses. It was on one of these trips that Molly, now married, gave birth to her daughter Claudia in a room above a salon in Fort Worth, Texas, owned by one of her brothers. Many years later Caroline and Claudia were attending the St Louis Exposition and met a young Chicagoan named Herbert Pflaum, also visiting the Exposition. It was love at first sight. Herbert and Claudia eloped, were married, and nine months later my husband-to-be was born.

Once in a cinema with Claudia (by then my mother-in-law), I saw and listened to Judy Garland singing "Meet Me in St Louis, Louis [both pronounced Looey], Meet Me at the Fair". I, too, began to weep. Why? I couldn't have said — the transitory nature of life, the passing of youth and young love, perhaps.

Whereas Molly's brothers bore arms for the Confederacy, Herbert's father, Isaac, was an officer in the Grand Army of the Republic and was wounded at the Battle of Gettysburg. We knew this because his commissions (the first as a major in the Illinois Volunteers, the second as a captain in the Union Army) hung in our house. What we did not know was that he was a drinking companion of Ulysses S. Grant when, cashiered from the Army for intemperance, Grant was a storekeeper in Galena, Illinois. A graduate student doing research on the General found scores of notes from Grant to Isaac Pflaum and replies from Isaac, often making arrangements to meet at the Palmer House, one of the best hotels in the Chicago Loop. Since most of the army officers were Southerners, Grant was recalled to service when war broke out, and, according to a story of the period, when President Lincoln was criticized for his selection of a general who drank, he countered with the remark that the critic should find out what brand of liquor Grant drank and he'd give some to the other Northern generals.

Later, after the war, Isaac ran for Assessor of the township of Hyde Park on the Republican ticket, with "Grant and Colfax: Peace and Prosperity" as presidential and vice-presidential candidates. (A reader of the *Sun-Times* sent my husband a model ballot.) They won.

Isaac died when Herbert was fifteen, so neither my husband nor I knew him. But as interest grew in U.S. Grant memorabilia his name emerged frequently in doctoral theses. A well-to-do realtor in Chicago, Isaac owned land in the Loop (so-named because the elevated railway makes a loop in the city centre), including the block on which the Morrison Hotel was located. He exchanged this property for a farm on the outskirts of the city, which later was purchased by the city (for a trifling sum) to make a playground.

The original owner of our house in Evanston, Illinois, was named U. S. Grant also — he was a nephew of the General, and his was one of the two first houses built for professors of Northwestern University on what was then a large meadow near Lake Michigan. Our house was always known as "the Grant house". In the deed it was specified that "no alcoholic liquors shall be purveyed, stored or consumed on these premises" — Evanston was until quite recently a "dry" community and the headquarters of the W.C.T.U., the Women's Christian Temperance Union. I remember the peonies, phlox, and the Japanese lilac trees planted by the General's nephew-professor that still bloomed in the garden, and his widow, aged over ninety, came every year on the anniversary of his death and sat on a bench, remembering. It was there that his ashes had been scattered in accordance with his testament.

The house that really represented elegance to me as a child was that of my Grandfather Berthold, my father's father, on Kimbank Avenue in the Woodlawn district of Chicago. I loved the library, where you could spend hours curled in the leather-cushioned window-seats, built into deep recesses and overlooking the garden. And the greatest marvel of all: the ballroom on the third floor had a *real stage*!

Claiming seniority (by six months), I wrote, produced and directed plays in which my twin cousins, Louis and Louise, and I acted. There were other cousins who could be brought in for small parts such as footmen, soldiers, courtiers, or slaves. Louise was always the heroine. Louis was the hero. Sometimes I cast myself as the villain.

The greatest marvel of all was a huge box of costumes — pierrots, kings and queens and princesses, devils, Roman togas, medieval chateleines, ropes of pearls, diadems and crowns, sceptres, pilgrims's capes and staffs, an incredible collection. Musty and battered they might be, but they were *there*. Nothing would fit us but by the artful use of safety-pins, string, and even rubber-bands, we made do. No-one could remember where the box came from, but Lizzie — who had been my father's nurse and was still living in the house, mending, and complaining constantly about the way the other servants wasted my grand-father's money — thought that it went back to the time when my grandparents as a young married couple (in a different house) used to give masquerade parties.

I cannot remember any of the plays I wrote, directed and produced, but I do know they were written for the costumes instead of the other way round. Then we dragooned aunts and uncles, friends and neighbours, anyone we could get, to attend the performance. Grandfather rewarded their fortitude by serving coffee and chocolate cake after the show.

Chapter 9

A THIRST FOR WORDS

My father was an inventor, a Socialist, an agnostic; a tall, strong, good-looking man. Yet none of these labels reaches the core. Above all, he was a Reader of Books. A chain-reader (like a chain-smoker), he finished one only to reach for another. He read in the bath, even walked down the street reading, read at mealtimes, in bed; on the streetcar or bus, waiting in line, he always had a book at hand or pulling his overcoat pocket out of shape.

He sold his farm in Indiana chiefly because he had literally read all the books in the nearby public library of Michigan City. He drew the line at poetry, mystery stories, and "cheap [meaning sexy or violent] novels"; his preferred fare was history, biography, archaeology. Our set of Gibbon's works was bent and frayed from repeated readings. Among his favourite authors were Bernard Shaw and H. G. Wells, whom he had met (as well as Sydney and Beatrice Webb) when a very young man; all Fabian Socialists, too.

His death was almost dramatically appropriate. My mother had died a year before and he had come to live with us in Puerto Rico. It was a year in which my father and I became re-acquainted after several decades of physical separation. Since my husband and I were both teaching at university (and writing books), an excellent library was available to us — and to him. One spring evening he was sitting in an armchair in the living-room reading a recently-published *History of the Roman Empire: from Nero to Marcus Aurelius*. He must have known something was wrong and he had time to place his leather bookmark at the page he had reached before losing consciousness. He never recovered.

Geneticists have not yet found a reading-related gene, but I seem to have inherited my father's tropism for the printed word. While papering a shelf, I have caught myself reading the death notices in a two-year-old Madrid newspaper, enjoying the mellifluous-sounding names. Through this thirst for words I have picked up from unremembered sources unrelated bits and pieces of information on an astonishing number of subjects, from the life-cycle of a jellyfish to the construction intricacies of an observatory telescope.

Practically every one of the many jobs I have held has had to do with words and their use. My first job was at the offices of the American Medical Association where the weekly *A.M.A. Journal*, the seven monthly *Archives [of Surgery, of Diseases of Children,* etc.], and a popular magazine called *Hygeia* were edited. At the then (in the early 'thirties) magnificent salary of twenty-seven dollars and fifty cents a week, I became a manuscript editor, learning the chemical equivalents of popular or proprietary names (not aspirin but acetylsalicilic acid), the right medical terms (not leprosy but Hansen's Disease), and the correct printed style. The stylebook was our Bible, the medical dictionary our Tree of Knowledge.

The editorial offices were run on the principles of a convent or a Reform School for Wayward Girls. This created a bond of friendship between the six of us that lasted all our lives (only two are still living). If we wanted to communicate with one another, we had to wait until the office-boy came round to deliver new manuscripts or take away a finished one, then hand him a note ("Are you free for lunch?") to deliver to a colleague, who might reply with a nod or a thumb and index finger circle: OK. Or even by a *sotto voce* exchange when two of us "happened" to coincide at the Greek or Latin dictionaries or at the Ladies' "washroom".

Just before the three-day Christmas break, we would be invited upstairs to the lunchroom, which was decorated with holly, red crêpe paper and a large Christmas tree. We stood in line, like serfs at the castle, and each of us received from the flabby hand of Maurice Fishbein, the Editor, an envelope containing a ten-dollar gold coin, for which we expressed thanks and wished him a Merry Christmas. We did not have to curtsy but the mood was distinctly feudal. After that we drank lemonade from a cardboard cup, munched two cookies, wiped our fingers on paper napkins, and went back to work. The revels were over.

If you received a telephone call, you had to take it at the desk of Miss Jewel Whelan, the editorial slave-driver and *de facto* office manager, who glared at you while you were speaking and never failed to remind you that it was not permitted to receive personal calls in the office. A poorly educated woman who had risen from being a filing clerk to a position of power in the organization, she was a toady to her superiors and a petty tyrant to her subordinates. Looking back over the years, I realize now that her evident animosity was partly justified; we were young, clever, articulate, and we had beaus. She was fat, middle-aged, and lonely. How could she *not* hate us?

Still, we learned a great deal at the A.M.A. — medical nomenclature, diseases and their symptoms, more Italian and Greek, some physiology, pathology, chemistry and biology. Since we were constantly shifted from one of the *Archives* to another, we knew something about otolaryngology, opthamology, dermatology and surgery. We learnt also to read proofs and to write legends for illustrations, and, above all, to put badly written, often confused prose into comprehensible and grammatical English.

These skills, it turned out, were not without value. We knew we could always fall back on ghost-writing for doctors (many of whom seem to be illiterate), or on editorial work for publishers of medical and scientific books, and the numerous state and regional medical journals. In later years I worked for the Medical Yearbooks and even returned to the A.M.A. itself when we had two sons at university and needed the money. By that time even the A.M.A. had become humane. Jewel Whelan was dead; a scholarly gentleman named Murdock had replaced her. We had weekly editorial conferences where changes in the once sacred Stylebook were suggested and discussed, and we were told about the latest advances in medical science. In short, the American Medical Association had entered the Twentieth Century.

I finally left the A.M.A. under dramatic circumstances. A novel of mine, called *Bolero,* that I had been writing (and rewriting) for more than five years, was accepted by one of the most prestigious publishers of fiction in England: William Heinemann. The day after I received the contract and a large (for those days) advance royalty payment, I gave notice.

Although I had written as a foreign correspondent, and had been published in such magazines as *Vogue, American Mercury* and *The Reporter,* the acceptance of my first novel was one of the greatest thrills of my life. Like the birth of my first son, it remains in my mind as a once-in-a-lifetime experience that nothing else can rival. I knew I could write, but now I was a Novelist.

After my initial stint of "work" at the A.M.A. — that is, doing something for which I was paid — nothing I did thereafter seemed like work to me. Writing scripts for educational films (some fifty in all, free-lancing for Coronet and Encyclopedia Britannica Films); doing a science show on radio (called "This Wonderful World"), to which a million Chicago schoolchildren listened every Friday and for which I received an award from the U.S. Army when it was later done in Japanese and Korean; teaching as a professor of English Literature at three universities — all this was so interesting that I often had a slight sense of guilt at being paid for doing something that was so much fun! (The last was somewhat mitigated by the minor frustrations of the job — rewriting scripts, grading term papers, interminable faculty meetings.) Even my wartime service as a bureaucrat — head of the Iberian Division of the Board of Economic Warfare — was too exciting to be considered work; besides, we were helping to Win the War.

All this time I was raising a family, running a large household (with the indispensable help of Martine Richards, our cook-housekeeper, who was with us for almost thirty years), writing short stories and travel sketches, and, in the small hours of the morning, pecking away on my ancient Royal typewrtier, working on the novels which were eventually published, though not in the order in which they were written.

Chapter 10

MY LIFE IN THE HOTEL BUSINESS

An advertisement in the *Mallorca Sun* caught my eye. The manager of the Camp de Mar Hotel needed a bilingual secretary. I needed a job. The United States had gone off the gold standard, and my savings were evaporating quickly. So I applied and was accepted immediately. That should have told me something.

In the early 'thirties Camp de Mar was the *crème de la crème*, its secluded beach the haunt of dukes and duchesses, knights and ladies, millionaires and fortune-hunters. I was picked up by a large Hispano-Suiza and seated in front with the chauffeur. The back-seat passengers, just off the S.S. *Exeter,* conformed to my expectations: British, elegant and, during the long drive through Palma and on to Camp de Mar, silent. I was dying to ask the chauffeur all about my employer but didn't dare. So the silence was total.

Mr Corelli (I will give him that name) was tall, cadaverous and bald. And an Argentine. As he escorted me to my quarters, he expressed profuse apologies, explaining that because the hotel was overcrowded my temporary accommodation was less adequate than he would have wished. Near the garage at the back of the hotel was a dreary little cell that adjoined the laundry, from which nauseous fumes and steam were emitted. A tiny airless bathroom. One frayed towel. My dreams of a luxurious paid vacation were fading. Paid? No one had yet mentioned salary.

Back in the office, Mr Corelli sketched in my duties. He was, he said, delighted to find that I could handle French as well as Spanish and English conversation, and also correspondence. I did not reveal my typing limitations or that I knew no shorthand. I needn't have worried. It soon became clear there would be little time for secretarial work. For I was the receptionist, desk-clerk, telephone-operator, mail-sorter, message-taker, accountant (recording charges for trays sent up to the rooms), information-centre ("When does the next boat leave for Barcelona?", "Where can I get a copy of the *Daily Express*?"), crisis-controller ("I'm locked out of my room; send someone at once to let me in."); in fact, I *was* the office staff.

My first and most pressing task was to type thirty-six menus, eighteen for luncheon and eighteen for dinner. No copies were possible as the menus were on thick crested cards. I made a start, being careful with the spacing and restraining myself from correcting the bad French. It was hot work, interrupted constantly by telephone calls and guests asking difficult questions. I cheered myself by thinking that at least the menus promised I would enjoy some fine meals.

At one o'clock Mr Corelli appeared, beaming, and with a regal gesture told me that he would take my place at the desk while I had lunch. I repaired my make-up in the "LADIES" off the hotel lounge and sailed into the dining-room, anticipating a gourmet treat.

The headwaiter led me to a small table near the doors into the kitchen. I was not offered a menu. My meal was served on fine china covered with silver tureens but when the waiter removed the covers I saw that instead of the cold salmon, pheasant, avocado salad and lemon mousse with French pastry that I'd been typing all morning, I had a sort of greasy stew, a few slices of tomato, and an orange! I looked round and could see that all the guests were receiving the menu fare.

Before long I hurried back to the office, boiling to express my indignation at this treatment, but when Mr Corelli saw me approach he smiled and rushed away. I was at once besieged by guests and the never-ending telephone.

Mr Corelli materialised again about six o'clock and said that if I would like a swim before dinner he would be glad to take over the office. This was my chance to speak but guests were all around and I lacked the courage to stage a scene in public.

I changed and went down to the beach. What ecstasy it was to strike out in the cool turquoise water, nerves relaxing, the frustrations of the day left behind on the shore. I'll think about it later, I told myself. But when I returned to my cell the fumes from the laundry were still seeping through the transit window. As I showered and put on a dinner dress I wondered how on earth I would be able to spend the night there.

Dinner was a repeat performance. Beautifully served food that would have disgraced a third-rate restaurant. This was it, I told myself. I rehearsed in my mind the devastating speech I would make to Mr Corelli. Simmering with indigation, I marched to the desk.

Mr Corelli was not there. A pale youth looked at me and mumbled, "Can I help you?", apparently under the impression that I was a guest.

"Who are you?"

"I am the night-clerk."

"Where's the manager?"

"I don't know. He didn't say."

Frustrated, I roamed about the lounge seeking the elusive Mr Corelli. Finally I gave up and went to the little writing-room off the hall and sat at one of the beautifully designed writing-tables furnished with crested paper and envelopes.

I had scarcely begun when Mr Corelli appeared at my elbow. "The writing-room is for *guests*," he hissed. We were alone, not a guest in sight. This was my chance. But words failed me. In another moment he was gone. Furious with myself as well as with Mr Corelli I rushed out of the hotel, down to the beach. My heart was still pounding, I walked along the sands till eventually I came to a fishermen's bar. It was crowded with locals, talking loudly in Mallorquin which I did not understand. But I quickly became conscious of their inquisitive looks in my direction. I had forgotten my black sheath dress, cut low at the back, the single strand of pearls, the silver slippers. Unescorted women did not frequent fishermen's bars. And I had no money in my flat brocaded purse. I retreated, followed by stares and raucous laughter.

Removing my shoes, I walked back along the beach. It was a clear starlit night. The air was cool and the sand felt cold under my feet. The fatigue of the day's happenings was beginning to overcome my repugnance for the waiting cell, so I returned to it and tried to sleep despite the all-pervasive smell.

I did sleep for a while but I awoke before dawn, determined to escape what I had come to think of as Corelli's Evil Kingdom. I saw lights on in the garage, so I dressed and went outside. The chauffeur who had driven me to the hotel — could it possibly be less than twenty-four hours earlier? — was tinkering with the engine of the Hispano-Suiza. I asked him if he was going to Palma that morning. Yes, he replied, he had to pick up some guests who were arriving on the cruise ship *Stella Polaris*. As though reading my mind, he added that if I could be ready in ten minutes, while he changed into his uniform, I was welcome to go with him.

I know how a galley-slave who has been ransomed must have felt. Glorious freedom! Soon I was sitting next to the chauffeur, smartly uniformed in dove-grey, as we glided through the dark. Dawn broke as we passed the headland of Porto Pi and the sun was shining brightly on the *Stella Polaris* by the time we reached the port of Palma de Mallorca.

It was a day or two before a question arose in my mind. Why did the chauffeur show no surprise at my early morning appearance and my evident desire to leave so soon after I'd arrived? Perhaps it was not the first time this had happened.

By the end of the week the advertisement announcing that the manager of the Camp de Mar Hotel required a bilingual secretary was back in the *Mallorca Sun*. And during the course of several months I met four young women, two British, a German and a Swede, all of whom had had much the same experience. The Swede had stuck it out for three days, a record. None of us had received payment.

But then the advertisement had not said anything about a salary.

Chapter 11

CHICAGO, CHICAGO

KNOWLEDGE is a wonderful thing. But ignorance has its uses. When I was hired by David Smart, owner of *Coronet* magazine and Coronet Educational Films, to write scripts I confessed that I knew nothing at all about film-making and that my knowledge of photography had been restricted to the manipulation of a box Brownie camera.

He laughed. "You write the scenario of the film you want to see; it's our business to produce it." And because I thought of my films in terms of the audience for which they were intended, in this case schoolchildren, I was a great innovator. Realizing that they looked up not down into shop-windows, saw thighs, legs and shoes in crowds, I gave directions to the cameramen that they were not to raise the camera above three feet in films they were making for kindergartens. Thus, although these films might look strange to us as adults, they portrayed the world to which a young audience was accustomed. It seems no-one had thought of doing that before.

In another series of films, on the background to the American Revolution (which won the Valley Forge Award), I decided against the use of second-rate actors dressed up to look like George Washington, Thomas Jefferson or Patrick Henry. Instead I showed a group of people in colonial dress watching delegates arriving at the Continental Congress in Philadelphia. "Look! There's General Washington!" "Sam Adams has a new suit!" You could see the silhouette of Jefferson writing against the wall of the terrace at Monticello, a back view of Lafayette as his hands offered his leather pouch of credentials into the hands of (presumably) General Washington.

CHICAGO, CHICAGO

When I was given the assignment of doing a film on clothes
for showing to high-school girls, I protested: "But I don't really
know anything about the latest styles and fashions." I was told
that since to be financially successful the film had to last for
about ten years the styles of the moment were of no importance.
What the film was concerned with was colour and design —
which colours favoured which type of complexion and hair,
which basic designs suited which kind of figure.

I even wrote scripts on, for me, most arcane matters, such as
"Safety in the Machine-Shop". If the completed film (based on
careful reading of the material I was given) told me what I
should know in a way I could understand, it would tell anyone.

In these films, as in the radio science shows I did, you must
capture your audience within the first thirty seconds. You must
tell them what you are going to tell them, then tell them, and
than tell them what you have told them, all in a way that will
hold their attention. Otherwise, a captive classroom audience
may be physically present but imaginatively elsewhere.

When I was teaching in various universities, I tried to make
use of the technique I had acquired in script-writing. Since I was
dealing with books and authors (Eng. Lit.), which to me are the
most interesting subjects in the world, I tried to pass on my
enthusiasm to my students, with a fair degree of success. My
classes were "popular", a pejorative adjective to some faculties,
where being dull was held to be scholarly. Yet, when I look
back on my own university student years, I realize the best professors were also the best showmen.

Where, I now wonder, did my husband and I get the energy
to do all the things we did simultaneously? For four years, while
being the Foreign Editor of the *Sun-Times* in charge of all
foreign news, writing a daily column ("Behind World Headlines"), serving as a full professor at Northwestern University
with a normal class-load, broadcasting a five-times-a-week radio
news-commentary on the CBS station WBBM, writing "Front-
of-the-Book" background for the *Atlantic Monthly* and articles
for *Harper's*, he was also a public speaker at groups like the
Council of Foreign Relations and the League of Women Voters.
I helped — I did much of the research, and by the time he
reached the studio in the Wrigley Building (rushing from his

class in Northwestern University in Evanston, Illinois, twenty miles away — the traffic cops knew his licence-plate and let him stretch the speed limit), I had prepared his commentary so that he could glance through it quickly and go on the air. Before he arrived I had read all the wire stories, decided on the principal item and written the commentary in his style of speaking, vocabulary and sentence structure.

As well as all this, we led an active social and family life, entertaining visiting foreign celebrities at big dinners and cocktail parties. We played tennis, swam in Lake Michigan, took our sons walking in Harms Woods. We made what seemed a lot of money, paid enormous income-taxes, and enjoyed our crowded lifestyle while it lasted.

So much of the Twentieth Century began in Chicago — and then moved away. Architecture: Louis Sullivan and Frank Lloyd Wright; the Monadnock Building where I worked for Medical Yearbooks was the world's first, true, steel skyscraper. Literature: as a baby I was carried by my parents in a basket to the studio-shops of 57th Street (ramshackle buildings that remained from the Chicago World's Fair), where Floyd Dell and Sherwood Anderson and Theodore Dreiser gave parties (beer and pretzels) and talked about writing. Economics: the Chicago Stockyards were the locale of Upton Sinclair's first and most powerful documentary novel, *The Jungle*. Intended to reveal the appalling conditions of the immigrant workers, it succeeded in alarming the Chicago public about the complete lack of hygiene in the slaughter-houses where the city's meat was prepared. "I aimed at the public heart and hit it in the stomach." Poetry: Harriet Monroe started *Poetry* magazine, publishing Edgar Lee Masters, Vachel Lindsay and just about everyone else who later became popular. Journalism: *The Front Page*, a play written by Charles MacArthur and Ben Hecht who had worked as reporters symbolized the rough-and-tumble, no-holds-barred excitement of American journalism. James Farrell, Studs Terkel, Nelson Algren were to continue the tradition of realism as contemporaries of mine. Radio: Station KYW in the Tribune Tower hired friends of ours to write what became known as "soap operas". Katherine Chase's "The Story of Helen Trent" continued for several decades.

Yet, despite the superb Symphony Orchestra, the Art Institute with its great collection of French Impressionists, the new Mies van der Rohe apartment buildings, the excellence of its newspapers (in particular, the *Chicago Daily News*), and the University of Chicago (where nuclear physicists Fermi, Urey and their colleagues conducted the first chain-reaction experiments under the stands of the football stadium), despite such triumphs Chicago had remained somehow provincial, and isolationist — "America First", as championed by the *Chicago Tribune*.

In the days before the Second World War none of my husband's colleagues had been out of the U.S., except perhaps for some fishing trips to Canada. Thus we were encouraged to entertain foreign dignitaries in our home, as it often led to interviews for the newspaper. This meant we could entertain freely on an expense account. Martine, our housekeeper, marshalled her "troops" — her friend Louella, her daughter Johnie Mae, plus Chester Chambers, an ex-prizefighter, whom we called in to act as barman. Martine gave the orders and everyone else obeyed. None of the four was white, yet to call them black is absurd. Martine's brother lived in an all-white neighbourhood and had married a Swedish woman. He was a barber, and said he sometimes stood with his straight razor while a soap-covered face proclaimed, "I can allus tella nigra — their fingernails is purple," thinking how easy it would be to let the "cut-throat" blade live up to its name!

Early in the war we moved to Virginia and Martine came with us. She had to travel at the back of the bus while our small boys had to sit in front; she couldn't go forward with them and they couldn't go back with her. Martine, who spoke Creole French, hailed from Louisiana and had learnt cooking as assistant to the French chef in the household of the Nashes on their estate near Chicago (they were one of the two families in the "Kelly-Nash Machine" which ran Chicago politics). Long before Middle Westerners were "into" gourmet cooking, our guests were enjoying her mousses, her crêpe suzettes, her soufflés, as well as shrimp gumbos and Creole dishes she had brought from Louisiana. In fact, she was too good. A local publisher, the French Ambassador, a steel tycoon, the president of a university, all tried to entice her to their kitchens, attempts which she duly reported to us. She remained loyal. For our part, my husband provided her with front seats for concerts by such artists as Marion Anderson and for the final game of the World Series, when they were virtually unobtainable. Furthermore, when our boys went to summer camp she took the whole summer off. And she told me later, "You never asked me where I would be on my day off, 'In case I want to reach you'; when I was off, I was off!"

When we moved from Virginia back to Evanston, Martine was jubilant. The difference between discrimination as practised in the North and the kind of aparteid that prevailed in the South was enormous. Indeed, when my husband and I were in South Africa a few years ago, and were shocked by the "WHITES ONLY" signs on buses, park benches, and beaches, we suddenly remembered where we'd seen those signs before — in Georgia and Mississippi.

PART III

WAR AND PEACE

Chapter 12

COLLIOURE REVISITED

In the early 'fifties I returned to a French town where I had lived for a time during the Spanish Civil War. In the taxi from Perpigan I talked to the driver about the World War that followed.

"How did Collioure get on?" I asked. "What happened when the Germans came?

"They made the townspeople leave. And the fishermen. They didn't allow anyone to go fishing. Afraid they might escape to North Africa, I suppose."

"I wonder if I'll find anyone I used to know.". There was no reply, so I asked, "Were you here during that time?"

The taxi-driver shook his head. "No. I was in a prison camp in Germany. We were liberated by the Russians at the very end."

During the war I had often wondered about Collioure. I wanted to go back there and find out how the people whom I knew so well had met the challenges of defeat, occupation and liberation. As individuals and as a community, how had they weathered the spiritual and material storms which had been unleashed upon France? A nation is too big; even a city like Paris is too big — it had to be a little town where I knew everyone and everyone knew me. They would talk to me, and perhaps then I would understand.

In Collioure, I was known. I was "*L'Américaine*". We had a house known as "*Les Terrasses*" that jutted out on rocks overhanging the Mediterranean. I had two small boys, a maid, Jeanette, from the village, and, occasionally, a husband who came out of Spain to visit us.

Everyone's politics was known. The majority of the three thousand people were fishermen and their families. The fishermen were "Red", anti-clerical, and violent in their sympathy for the Spanish Loyalists. They helped load supply-boats without pay, for their Catalan cousins across the border. They smuggled members of the International Brigade into Spain in their fishing-boats or over the little-used passes of the Pyrenees.

All the people of the middle class — that is, the people who wore shoes instead of the rope-soled espadrilles and business suits instead of the faded blue wash trousers and jackets of the fishermen — were pro-Franco during the Spanish Civil War. They feared an invasion of the "Red" hordes from Spain, whom they believed would run amok and kill them all. Their Rightist press played up the atrocities committed by the Republicans, failed to mention those of the Insurgents. On this side were the owner of the anchovy canning factory and its manager, the shopkeepers, the druggist, the doctor, the banker, town officials, the village priest and the nuns who ran the kindergarten, and the Bonapartist, who was a wine salesman.

The schoolmaster, however, whose best friend was a Catalan Nationalist poet, was for the Spanish Republic and said so. The middle class people talked of sending their children to Perpigan to school to get them away from his influence. The fishermen said he was an intellectual but a good man.

So Franco victories were toasted by the shopkeepers, Republican successes were celebrated by the fishermen. René, the owner of the Café du Sport, served both groups of customers with equal affability.

The French Catalans and the Spanish Catalans managed to ignore the frontier, despite all controls and regulations. Throughout the Spanish Civil War, the Second World War, and any other time the border between France and Spain was officially closed, families on both sides continued to visit one another and keep one another supplied with food and other scarce commodities. During the Spanish Civil War, the French Catalans fed their Spanish cousins. During World War II and the Occupation of France, when German patrols with fierce dogs guarded the border, the Spanish Catalans brought bread and olive oil to their hungry French relatives. And they hid French Maquis, just as

Spanish Republicans were sheltered by fishermen and mountain people on the other side of the frontier. The wartime border could be closed on both sides, with neither mail nor goods nor train nor car able to pass from one country to the other, but the unofficial traffic continued. Spain has no secrets from the people of Collioure.

In the winter, when there was little fishing, the fishermen would spend the long evenings playing dominoes in the café. Then, a fisherman would drink only a small glass of *Banyuls*, the local wine, all evening. But in summer, when the sardine and anchovy fishing was good, the men bought beer, *Pernods*, or an apéritif before dinner and coffee and cognac afterwards. They never saved money, so each winter was a fresh and unexpected disaster.

They fished by night. From our great studio windows we used to watch the fishing fleet go out at sunset. Pink, blue and lavender sails against a flaming sky. Before dawn they returned, their lanterns twinkling in the dark.

Sometimes, when the catch was heavy, they made two trips a night and returned with holds gleaming with scales. A fish auction was held by lantern-light on the beach. The manager of the anchovy canning plant and the fish-buyers from the inland villages bid for the fish which the fishermen brought out in great baskets. The auctioneer started at a high figure and counted downwards rapidly until someone called "Sold!" — the catch would go at the last figure spoken.

The patron, or owner of the boat, received two-fifths of the proceeds; the other three fishermen each received a fifth. It was never very much.

Old women, always dressed in black, mended torn nets and gossiped on the beach in the early morning. The fishermen sat on the promenade, smoked, and watched people pass by. They did not sleep until after dinner at noon; then they napped until late afternoon, when they went to the café for their apéritif. In the summer evenings they were off to sea before twilight.

José, his brothers and his father were fishermen, but they were different. Their boat was newer, trimmer, whiter, and it had a motor. Instead of fishing for sardines or anchovy, they went farther out in the sea to catch salmonet and larger fish, which were sold in Collioure instead of to the canners. They studied the currents, the winds and the tides, the seasonal variations in the habits of the fish with scientific absorption. You never saw them in the café. But in winter they ate regularly.

René, the café owner; Monsieur le Curé; Jacques, the schoolmaster; Jeanette, my maid; José, who by now was her husband; his brothers; Madame Quintana, the hotel-keeper; Monsieur Duclos, the Bonapartist; André, the young pilot whose family spent the summer in Collioure; and the fishermen and the shopkeepers — how many of them would I find?

My thoughts were interrupted by a sudden swerving of the taxi as we descended the hill to Collioure. There was the beach, the old fort on the hill. Now we were in front of the Café du Sport and René was standing in the midst of the tables. I waved to him, and an incredulous look came into his face. The taxi squeaked to a stop and we shook hands, both trying to find words. "You are back. Welcome. Welcome. You are just the same. I am . . . we are so happy," he blurted out.

Later that evening, René plied me with extremely bad beer (at first I thought there was soap in the glass) and questions about my sons and myself. Finally, I had an opportunity to ask him, "How was it here during the War?"

"Quiet. So they say. I was called up, of course, and my wife ran the café. There was almost nothing to serve the clientele, no beer, no liqueurs, just watered wine and syrups."

"Who were the clientele?" I asked.

René's large ears turned dark red. "Germans, for the most part." His eyes looked steadily at me. His wife, who had sat down beside him, shook her head.

"It is a public café," she said. "We must serve the customers or close." She laughed bitterly. "The Reds don't come here anymore; they call us the 'White' café — the Café de la Poste on the corner gets their trade now, and welcome to it!"

"Didn't the Poste stay open during the Occupation?"

"Yes, it was open, but they said I smiled at the Germans, while Madame Pons frowned at them. It's true enough; I have always been one to smile, and she has always scowled, still does." René's wife shrugged her shoulders. But it was clear that she cared.

Looking about, I noted that the café was well filled with fishermen. "I don't see much difference," I said.

"It's the younger ones. They were boys when you were here."

So the townspeople didn't have to leave when the Germans moved in. The version from the taxi-driver was beginning to falter.

The next morning I went looking for Jeanette. I found her easily, in the same, dank, cold, stone house. She wept and embraced me. "I have prayed for this moment, but I thought God would not grant it to me," she said. "Look at this jersey and skirt — you gave them to me over ten years ago and they still serve." She had three children, two boys and a girl — fair like José her husband. He came in and greeted me, and the children acknowledged their introduction with grave courtesy.

"That night in November when the Germans came," José recalled later, "we thought it was the whole Reichswehr. So much noise. Tanks clattering through the streets, gun-carriers and armoured-cars — they kept on coming. Later we found there really weren't so many. The same ones went round and round again and again. I suppose it was to impress us." He laughed. "Do you know what we were living on? Turnips and bread that tasted like sawdust."

"I never ate those turnips," Jeanette interrupted.

"Was there less food after the Germans arrived?"

"No, it was about the same. But *they* ate very well. Especially the officers, and the women who were their friends."

"From Collioure?"

"Plenty of them."

There was silence.

"I wouldn't have anything to do with the Germans," said Jeanette with pride. "They would come and ask me to wash their clothes; they paid well — they had butter and bacon and everything. But I would say, 'Nichts. Pas de savon.' They would say, 'We can get you soap', but I would point to the children and say, 'Nichts. Viel arbeit — kinder'."

Jeanette beamed as she recounted her resistance record and José patted her hand. "There weren't many like Jeanette."

So the townspeople didn't leave, and some of them had been on friendly terms with the Germans.

"What happened to these women — after the Liberation?"

"Nothing. Their husbands, back from prison-camps, they didn't ask questions. They knew better."

"But didn't they get their heads shaved, or anything?"

"No. It was not like in Ariege, where we were at the end of the war." Jeanette explained, "There in Ariege we saw two young girls executed. They were very pretty. It made me feel sick. It was right for them to die, but it was an awful thing to see."

"In Ariege the Maquis were strong," José said. "These girls had betrayed Résistance leaders to the Germans. Reprisals were taken against many harmless villagers. Here in Collioure we sheltered the Maquis, but only two men of the town *were* Maquis. Ouradour-sur-Glace, where the Germans burnt alive all the women and children in the church and the men in a stable, it was a centre of the Résistance. Here the Germans didn't get so mad at us.

"Still, it was not easy. At first they forbade fishing. But then they had no fish for themselves, so they permitted daytime fishing. Sometimes the commander of the fort would be bored and he would order target practice — the gunners would aim all round the fishing-boats to see how close they could get; I can tell you, we were frightened — with shells hitting the water a few metres from the bow of our boat. We headed for port.

"Later on they allowed fishing at night, occasionally. They would put two German soldiers with loaded machine-guns on each boat. It's an all-night trip and sometimes we offered them a sandwich. They didn't dare accept — for fear of being poisoned! They wouldn't even drink any water." José laughed heartily at the recollection.

"As you see, they made fortifications all along the coast. Paid high wages, too. But I wouldn't work for them — I'd rather have starved."

I inquired about José's father and his brothers.

"My father is well. But my two brothers are dead. They were captured, along with many other French soldiers. But they were taken to Dachau and died slowly. The Germans knew they were Anarchists. Someday I want to find the Frenchman who betrayed them."

"Do you think there were many Frenchmen in the pay of the Germans — before the War, I mean?"

"I don't know. What I do know is that some joined the Vichy Militia, which looked for Résistance leaders to turn them over to the Gestapo. Your friend the Bonapartist was one of those. We hated them worse than the Germans."

I asked how the Militia operated.

"They would join the Maquis, and when they knew the plan for some raid they would tip off the Germans. Or sometimes they were 'Black Maquis'."

"What was that?"

"Those were the ones who acted to make a bad impression. They would go into a village and take food — hams, eggs, poultry, everything — without paying; they would even rape young girls; and they would say, 'We are Maquis'. The villages would think, these Maquis are bad people."

He told me about one brush he had with the Militia. "It was in Ariege. I was working there in the vineyards; it is inland, you see, and there are no fish. Some men came up to me and said, 'You there, can you drive a truck?' I said I could and they offered me a hundred francs a day to drive for them. I was earning only eight francs a day in the vineyard. But I said, 'Why do you want me to drive a truck — what are you up to?' They said, 'Oh, we're going hunting that's all. We want to catch some Reds.' They were Vichy Militia. So I told them no, I wouldn't drive a truck for them, even for the hundred francs a day.'

"What sort of people were these Militia?"

"Some of them were rich young men, like the heir to the anchovy canning plant here; some were just louts. And some, well, they were like your friend the Bonapartist: they believed France should be part of the New Order. At the end, most of them fought for the Germans after they knew the Germans had lost. In Perpignan there was house-to-house fighting. They ran over the rooftops, the way you see in the cinema, and they jumped over walls and fought in cellars and attics. Your friend the Bonapartist was shot. He was lucky; he died fighting instead of being tried and executed like the ones taken alive."

"I see some are still being tried in Perpignan."

"Yes, the trials will go on for years. The last ones to be tried are the most fortunate; the people hated the first ones so much, they got the death sentence. Now it's usually seven to nine years at hard labour. In a few more months they will probably be let off with no sentence at all."

I asked if that meant they were forgiven.

"No. But people get tired of hating. And now they begin to be divided all over again — the Left and the Right — and they are so busy quarrelling with each other they forget to hate the *collaborateurs*. In the last month, for example, there have been no death sentences."

I inquired what had happened to André, the young pilot who used to spend his summers here.

José looked at me with an expression of feigned disbelief. "Didn't you hear what happened to the French air force? He was killed, of course. Shot to pieces by the Germans. In the first week, when they broke through at Sedan. He knew he would be killed. He always said, 'What chance do we have against the Luftwaffe in these obsolete old crates of ours?' He used to say he had to live quickly, because he didn't have much time."

For a while there was no more talk. Jeanette fed her children and sent the two older boys out to play. She put the youngest child to bed for her nap. "We almost lost her, you know," she said to me. "Because of American milk."

"What do you mean?"

"The American Red Cross sent us canned milk. Everyone was grateful. But then a shipment came that must have been bad. Twenty children in the village died; my niece was one. Our baby almost died; she would have if I had not told the doctors, 'The milk she is eating is poison; I will give her water and onion soup.' They pumped out her stomach, and she was so weak she could not even cry. But she lived. Still, she has been delicate since then."

I could not discover what sort of milk the Red Cross had sent the village. Or if it had come from America or been purchased in Switzerland. But the story was quite true. Twenty children in Collioure had died from the milk. It is also true that many more would have died if no milk had been sent, but people do not think of that.

In the days that followed I saw Jeanette and her husband frequently. One day they invited me for dinner. There had been a good catch that night. I brought the ration stamps I had been given at the frontier and Jeanette appeared very pleased to have them. "Usually all our stamps are used up in the first few days of the month. The rest of the time we buy in the black market. We have not seen meat for three months."

Later I inquired about the Curé

José answered, "You know I never liked him. I don't believe, nor does my father. But the Curé is a man; he was not afraid of the Germans; he stood up to them and said what he thought was right. He hid the Maquis in the church and fed them — and they, too, were not believers. I do not go to church; I have not the habit. But Jeanette may go and so may the children, and I will no longer make fun of it."

Madame Quintana was the innkeeper. We had stayed with her while we waited for our house to be made ready, and after we moved in we had returned once a week for dinner. The *bouillabaise* at Madame Quintana's was second to none. She is a plump, white-skinned woman, with a high nervous voice, a sharp temper, and an insatiable curiosity about the lives of everyone about her.

During the Occupation, the inn of Madame Quintana had been Gestapo headquarters. A German colonel and his staff had stayed there. It seemed strange that she was still doing business as usual.

First I had dinner at the inn a few times, to re-establish my acquaintance with her. Then one afternoon I paid a formal call. I wore hat and gloves; she wore her best black *moiré*, and we sat in the garden and sipped tea.

"Ah, the things that have passed in this town since you left. *Incroyable*! They have made me an old woman."

"No," I protested. "Really, you've hardly changed." This was not true, and we both knew it.

"If the inn could talk, you would hear some strange tales. The scenes that went on under this roof!" She nodded her head, remembering. "You know, I suppose, that this was headquarters for the Gestapo?"

I nodded.

"My son was captured; he was in a German prison camp all the time they were here. You may suppose my sentiments towards them. But I was very nice to the Colonel, very nice. He liked the cooking, and we fed him well. He knew a little French and he liked to practise it with me. A little at a time, he began to tell me things. I believe he trusted me.

"Then, when people would be denounced as Reds, he would ask, 'Madame, tell me, is So-and-So a Red?' Once, for instance, he said, 'Your friend José has been denounced, and, of course, it is common knowledge that he is an Anarchist.' I said, 'That is nonsense. I have known José, his father and his family all my life. They are fishermen, with no politics. They work hard, and I wager the man who denounced José is envious of his fine white boat and wants it for himself.' The first time José was denounced I warned Jeanette, and José went to the mountains and hid till I told him to come back. The second time the denunciation was anonymous. The Colonel showed it to me and said, 'The man who wrote this is a coward because he does not sign his name,' and he threw the paper into the fire.

"Not a single person in the village of Collioure was tortured or killed. No matter how Red they were, I would tell the Colonel they had no politics. The Colonel was not a bad man, though a German. But the officers would have parties that lasted for days and some of the women in the village would come and drink with them and go to bed with them. It was a disgrace. Then I would keep out of the way; not that they ever molested me — but at those times I was ashamed of being a Frenchwoman."

I asked about Madame Quintana in the village, and her story was true. People had always disliked her, because she was such a gossip, but now they had a great respect for her, almost amounting to a liking. Most families had received warnings from time to time, that it would be healthier for some member to go to the mountains. There was a widespread conviction that she used her position to help the villagers, to defend them and to inform them of danger.

The Rightist Mayor, too, had helped the villagers. There were three hundred or so Leftist votes in every election and about a hundred and fifty men had declared themselves to be Communists. However, when the Germans came to the *mairie* and asked for the list of Communists, the Mayor replied, "There has never been a Communist in Collioure. This has always been a strong village of the Right." It was just as well the Germans didn't investigate the returns for past elections.

Now, as far the fishermen are concerned, the Mayor can go being in the *mairie* as long as he wishes. His election last time was unopposed.

The entire coast was fortified, as José had told me, and the Germans paid relatively good wages for work on the fortifications. (They were paying with French francs.) And the beaches were heavily mined.

"After the Liberation," Jeanette explained, "the authorities sent back German prisoners to pick up the mines. Some of them were the same engineers who had directed the mining. But what a difference! They were like skeletons. Much as I hated them, I felt sorry when they returned. Some could hardly walk. I and other women would give them a little bread now and then. They are human beings, after all."

My former landlady was no longer to be found. She had sold the house and moved away to another province.

"She was happy when the Germans came. She believed, like old Pétain, that our troubles were God's punishment for our sins. She had prophesied that France was going to the dogs, and she was pleased that at long last her predictions had come true. There was nothing too good for the Germans who lived in your house; she was obsequious and servile," René explained.

"'What happened to her after the Liberation?"

"She is an old woman, perhaps a little crazy. But there was feeling against her in the village, so when she went to the baker he would say there was no bread, and the *épicerie* was always out of everything she wanted, and the butcher shop had nothing for her. You remember, she was a miser, and when her precious money would not buy anything she became even crazier. So she sold her house and moved away."

Collioure revisited, I wrote afterwards, looks much the way it did when I was there ten years ago: the coral and salmon roofs lie snugly against the green hills; the dark rocks and white sands sweep round the old tower, and the little church and the crucifix stand out against the sea. The people, too, are the same people; some were lost in the War, but most of them continue their lives as they were before. The fishing-boats all have motors now; the coloured sails are gone. And René has a little nightclub with an American bar and dance recordings, as well as the Café du Sport.

But almost all of the three thousand individuals in the town have undergone a profound moral crisis, brought into their lives by the War, the Occupation, and the Liberation. And in a small but to its inhabitants unforgettable way, the experience of Collioure has become part of the history of France.

Chapter 13

THE ORIENT EXPRESS

It is good to know that the famous Orient Express has been revived, even if it is only in truncated form, for there is little enough romance in the world these days. I travelled on the Express in its heyday, just before the Second World War swept so much into oblivion. We were on assignment to Bucharest from Budapest, and were ushered into a first class compartment with its elegant if somewhat rickety fixtures, polished mahogany, silver-framed mirrors, and deferential stewards. Outside the fields were blanketed by snow. We passed through desolate little villages at dusk, then, later, fairytale moonlit forests. It was a few minutes after midnight when we reached the border. The train stopped and the Rumanian police came into our carriage.

"Passports!"

We handed them over. Two men looked at the documents, then one shook his head and left, returning with a higher-ranking officer who examined them and announced sternly: "No good!"

In response to our obvious consternation, the smartly-clad official pointed to our documents and then to his watch. Our Rumanian passports had expired at midnight, our elaborate press visas obtained in the Rumanian Embassy in Paris a few weeks earlier were now worthless. With a great show of severity he ordered porters to open the window; they were then told to pitch our suitcases out into the snow. As people watched and nudged one another ("International spies!"), we were escorted off the train and led to a wooden hut. Surely they weren't going to shoot us?

I was told to sit in the cold outer office while my husband was bustled inside and the door closed behind him. I caught a glimpse of someone in uniform sitting at a wooden table. The officer who had removed us from the carriage came out and sat next to me on the bench. He did not say anything or look at me but kept inching closer and closer. Outside two soldiers with rifles stood guard, and the great Orient Express — puffing and steaming — waited.

A few but very long minutes later my husband emerged. Everyone shook our hands warmly; we were conducted back to the train, I being helped gallantly up the high step. Policemen and soldiers saluted, porters dusted the snow off our suitcases and replaced them carefully in the baggage-racks above our heads, bowing and touching their caps. The other passengers looked disappointed.

What had happened? When we were moving again, my husband explained. "He didn't seem to understand what I was saying so I simply kept handing him *lei* banknotes until he smiled. Then he said in excellent English that it was all an unfortunate mistake and we should never have been inconvenienced. He stamped our papers, shook me by the hand, and wished us both a pleasant stay in his beautiful country."

Bucharest was supposed to be the Paris of Eastern Europe. Most business was carried out in cafés; theatres and concert-halls and nightclubs flourished; the brutal repression of the Fascist Iron Guards was condoned or ignored. Rumania was supplying petroleum and grain to Nazi Germany and receiving in return such valuable items as Tyroleon hats and mouth-organs.

I interviewed Magda Lupescu, King Carol's mistress, who was believed to wield a powerful influence on the government. Red-haired, white-skinned, and with amazing green eyes, Madame Lupesco talked in French and spoke only about art, particularly painting, music and Rumanian composers, about which she was clearly interested and well-informed. No mention was made of politics, national or international.

The Father of modern Turkey, Kemel Ataturk, died about this time and my husband was sent to cover the funeral. In Ankara we watched a million Turks openly mourn the man who had transformed the crumbling remnants of the Ottoman Empire into a strong, twentieth century nation. He had taken the women out of purdah, eliminated their veils, banned the fez, and opened up the mosques to outsiders. He was quite ruthless, hanging his opponents on lamp-posts, but comparing him today with Iran's Khomenei, who is engaged on the opposite task of dragging his country back to the Middle Ages, he seems almost moderate.

Istambul fascinated me, with its great mosques, especially the Blue Mosque and St Sofia, its markets in the labyrinth of narrow streets just wide enough for a donkey with a panier of vegetables and a child on its back to pass while you flattened yourself against the wall, the cries of the vendors who hammered brass and silver. The rugs and leatherwork were a combination of ancient Byzantine and Moslem and (ugly) "modern" elements.

Bulgaria, however, was where we saw the most magnificent Byzantine churches, mosaics and icons, much of which had been covered by white paint during the long Ottoman rule when the churches were used as mosques and human representations were forbidden. King Boris of Bulgaria was far more interested in railways than in antiquities. With enormous pride he exhibited his model steam-engine. Wearing the classic engineer's cap and coveralls, he drove his little locomotive, puffing and tooting, on a single railway track that encircled the palace park.

In Greece, we travelled by bus, stopping in primitive village inns, and everywhere, even in the most remote places, meeting Greeks who spoke fluent American-English. They had owned ice-cream parlors, fruit and vegetable stalls, or barber shops in places like Chicago, Detroit, St Louis, Los Angeles. In the face of the Depression, they had taken their savings and returned to Greece and their home towns where they could live more cheaply and help their families. But now, they told us, they could not go back to America. By returning to their country of origin they had lost their U.S. citizenship and would have to enter under the quota. No one had advised them and they felt betrayed. Many years later, the law which distinguished between naturalized citizens and those who were born in the United States was abrogated. The Supreme Court declared that a U.S. citizen remained a U.S. citizen wherever he went.

At this period Greece was governed by a strongman, a dictator called Metaxas, and republicans and liberals were in prison or exiled to remote islands. The U.S. Justice Department was trying to secure the extradition of a financier called Samuel Insull, whose empire of holdings had collapsed, and the press was taking a great interest in the matter. There was no extradition treaty between Greece and the United States.

A Greek journalist working for the United Press obtained a world-wide scoop when he broke the news that Insull would be returned to the U.S. for trial. As the Greek court's decision was not made public until some time later, we asked him how he had managed this. During a dinner of roast lamb, eggplant and salad, we had all consumed several bottles of the typical resinated wine, so perhaps he had become indiscreet. "The truth of the matter is," he said, "I sent the cable before the court's decision was made." He added, "You see, besides being a journalist, I am a lawyer. After reading all the legal arguments from both sides, I knew they would have to decide as they did."

Neither my husband nor I said anything, but we both had the same thought. He could have been mistaken; then what would have happened to his career?

Nothing, probably. Many famous journalists' careers began with just such a gamble: Roy Howard's false news of an armistice in the First World War, preceding the real one by several days, was the start of a career that led to the top of the United Press organization, not to mention his marriage into the Scripps family, owners of a powerful newspaper chain. But it's not the sort of thing to teach journalism students.

Chapter 14

HOLLYWOOD HO!

EVERY newspaper has one indispensable character: the practical joker. Ed Groshelle held that post on the *Chicago Sun-Times*. Short and stocky, with powerful arms and shoulders, and inexhaustible energy, a highly competent newspaperman, he never missed an opportunity to create chaos and confusion in the lives of his colleagues. It was he who dreamed up the headline, "LONG LOVE THE KING", on the occasion of Edward VIII's abdication. And when the rival *Tribune*, urging its readers to elect Dewey, ran a daily banner, "TEN [or whatever] DAYS TO SAVE YOUR COUNTRY", Ed's *Sun-Times*, after Truman had won, printed simply, "SIXTY-TWO DAYS TILL CHRISTMAS"; the point was not wasted on Chicagoans.

Shortly after we had returned to Chicago, after living and working in Europe since the early 1930s, and my husband had become Foreign Editor of the *Sun-Times*, I called him at his office. "Mr Pflaum, please."

A man's voice replied. "Sorry, he's just gone out to lunch with his wife." This was typical of Groshelle's sense of humour. There was no end to the kinds of mischief he could make.

One Saturday night we were giving a dinner party when the telephone rang for my husband. Later, he said to me, "You'd never guess what that was all about. The copyboy read out what he said was a telegram from someone called Colonel Jason Joy, asking me to collaborate on a film about foreign correspondents and offering five hundred dollars a week for two weeks and expenses."

"How marvellous!" I said. "When do we leave?"

"I said I couldn't accept. Too busy." My surprise must have

showed, because he laughed. "Don't you see? It's a typical Groshelle gambit. Especially that fake name — Colonel Jason Joy. If Ed thought I'd fall for that he can think again!"

On Monday morning when he went to the office another telegram was on his desk. This time Colonel Jason Joy was offering a thousand dollars a week for three weeks, plus all expenses. It could have been faked, because there was a Western Union desk in the building and there was no limit to the amount of trouble Groshelle would go to in pursuit of a good "joke", so my husband walked several blocks to another Western Union office and, to put an end to the nonsense, sent a reply accepting the proposition and asking for a thousand dollars advance expenses.

Later in the day when he came in there was a note to call the Chicago office of Twentieth Century Fox. A sultry voice told him, "Mr Pflaum, I have a wire here telling me to pay you one thousand dollars. How do you want your money?"

So there *was* a real Colonel Jason Joy, and it was a real offer, not an elaborate Ed Groshelle hoax. Somewhat dazed, my husband went to see the editor, Richard Finnegan, and obtained three weeks' leave. Then he called me with the news that we were leaving that evening on the Superchief train for California and the Never-Never, Make-Believe Land of Hollywood.

A suite at the Beverly-Wiltshire Hotel had been reserved for us, and we could sign for drinks, meals, or whatever we wanted. No limit. Thus began one of the most amazing interludes of our lives.

My husband was assigned to work with Lamar Trotti, one of the best directors in Hollywood, and remembered for award-winning films like *The Oxbow Incident*. His *Woodrow Wilson* and *The Purple Heart* were critical as well as box-office successes. A well-educated, soft-spoken Southerner, Trotti was the complete opposite of the stereotype director-producer. Through the Trottis and their friends we were introduced to a part of the Hollywood scene that we'd never heard of before. No wild parties with beautiful women in evening gowns being thrown into swimming-pools, no orgies with shapely starlets rising to stardom by way of the casting couch, no Babylonian extravagance and display. That side of Hollywood still existed but the directors and producers, actors and writers that we met were literate, hard-working people, not unlike their counterparts in New York or London.

The first morning my husband was assigned an office close to that of Lamar Trotti (after meeting Colonel Jason Joy in the flesh. Far from being an imaginary figure, he was a solid man with gold watch-chain across his ample middle and a deep voice). Trotti explained the situation frankly. My husband was to help write a script for a film about foreign correspondents, since he had been one himself and presumably knew all about their lives. The film was meant to be based on a 1942 wartime bestseller, *Only the Stars are Neutral* by Quentin Reynolds. One of the top executives, Daryl Zanuck, had met Reynolds, liked him, and had bought the movie rights then and there for $30,000. No one at Twentieth Century Fox knew if he had even read the book, and no one dared to ask. But when Trotti was told to produce it he found there was no story, only a series of incidents and personal experiences: no narrative, no drama; in the popular movie sense — no film.

My husband was given a typewriter and offered the use of a secretary if he needed one, which he didn't. Somehow, between him and Trotti, a script was created — a derring-do, adventure-type story about two foreign correspondents, a man and a woman of course, for whom Trotti cast Humprey Bogart and Ida Lupino. The final typing of this great opus was encased in leather binding on which "TWENTIETH CENTURY FOX" stood out in gold-embossed letters.

"This is a face-saving operation," Trotti explained. "The film will probably never see the light of day, but we do the work we're being paid for."

"Whose face is being saved?"

"Zanuck's, of course. He can't let be known that he bought a book without reading it. Now, when people ask why it hasn't been produced, he can say, high production costs — lots of reasons. This sort of thing happens all the time."

Trotti took us one day to the set on which *The Song of Bernadette* was being filmed. The stand-ins for the principal actors were being placed for a scene while lights were shifted and furniture arranged. In the scene the mayor shows the lawyer a newspaper referring to the Miracle and says, "We shall be the laughing-stock of France." The set was brilliantly lit. We were sitting in the dark far at the back of the studio. A voice that sounded somehow familiar called out, "Take the handkerchief out of your pocket and put it in your left sleeve." The stand-in mayor obeyed. Then, "And move a little to your right so I can see the shadow of the tree on the wall." The stand-in obeyed. The mayor picked up the newspaper as the script required, but the voice interrupted again: "That paper. It's the wrong one!"

"It can't be," someone objected. "We've researched it."

"But not enough,' said the voice. "There certainly was such a newspaper but its not the sort the mayor would read."

Finally, at long last, when the stand-ins' positions had been clearly marked for the actors, and the furniture placed to the satisfaction of the strangely familiar voice, the lights in the studio went up and we recognized the assistant art director as a close friend, Laura Ferren, whom we had known in Spain.

Once away from the set, she said, "Those ridiculous comments of mine, all those changes. They make me laugh. But if you don't say anything they think you're not doing your job." She smote her forehead dramatically. "What really kills me is something I can't mention. Lourdes is in the Midi — flat roofs. These are high-pitched Parisian roofs — I think they must have taken the sets from *The Hunchback of Notre Dame*. But it would be too expensive to change, so I suffer in silence."

We had lost contact with Laura when the German entered Paris. Before the war we often used to meet in the Café Flore. At that time she was working with the French director Jean Renoir on the films *The Baker's Wife* and *La Bête Humain* (with Jean Gabin), both of which were to become classics. During the Occupation she had managed to get out of France to Spain, then to South America, and finally to Hollywood. She and John Ferren were now divorced.

The Ferrens had been our closest neighbours and best friends when we lived in Mallorca. John was a painter. In the winter we usually had supper together, the four of us. John and Peter made spaghetti, partly over the open fireplace and partly on the little primus stove. Laura or I made salad; we all drank red wine, then later, coñac. The Ferrens' three cats and dog and our two cats and dog Bozo made a noisy and indignant picket-line outside the door of whichever house the meal was being served.

Laura's father was a Basque painter and critic who had known most of the Impressionists — Derain, Matisse, Renoir, van Gogh — and much of the talk was about painting and painters, often lasting till the fire was dying out near dawn. Somehow Peter always managed to get to the *Palma Post* office on time to dispatch his copy, a heroic feat. He sped down the mountain road on his bicycle, and sometimes came home holding on to the back of the tram as it circled up from El Terreno.

Now here we were, with Laura, in Hollywood.

At several dinner-parties we attended, Olivia de Haviland and John Huston were present. "I've always wanted to meet a real Melanie," she said to me. The sister of a Southern newspaper-man friend of our, James Young, had coached her in the right Atlanta accent for her part in *Gone with the Wind*. And we had met her mother and younger sister (as beautiful as Olivia) at Beulah Bondi's tower-like house (one room to a floor) over-looking the Hollywood Bowl. Once, after dinner, when Olivia and I were powdering our noses, she said, "I have to get up at five o'clock tomorrow to be on the set by six. I don't want to break up the party, so I'll just sneak quietly out. Please tell John later. In about an hour from now he will look around and say, 'Where's Olivia?'." Sure enough, an hour later, John Huston, who had been holding the floor as the centre of conversation, looked round the living-room. "Where's Olivia?" he demanded.

We met actors, directors, designers, musicians, dancers; we enjoyed an exciting whirl of activity — luncheons, cocktail-parties, dinners — travelling what I considered enormous distances from one to the other: Los Angeles covers most of Southern California and people seem to think nothing of driving fifty miles to someone's house just for a drink. We were visiting firemen; we were not out for anyone's job, we threatened no one. We were just passing through, not staying.

And when the three weeks were up, we left.

Chapter 15

COME TO MARTINIQUE

OSTENSIBLY as a newspaperman, actually on a private mission for President Roosevelt, my husband was sent to Martinique during World War II when control of the island was held by the Vichy French under Admiral Robert.

Gold from the Bank of France had been sent to Canada for safekeeping and was still on board ship in the St Lawrence River when France surrendered. The *Emil Bertin* which carried the gold was one of the fastest cruisers afloat; under orders, she managed to get through the nets and mines protecting the St Lawrence against enemy submarines and to strike out for the island of Martinique. Then followed a crazy chase down the Atlantic coast and into the Caribbean, with the British Navy trying to intercept the cruiser and her treasure, and the American Navy running interference. (The United States was not in the war then and did not want any naval engagements so close to home.) The French ship was too fast for her pursuers and reached Martinique safely, as also did the great aircraft-carrier *Berne*, with fifty brand-new fighter planes and their pilots, en route to France at the time of the surrender.

Roosevelt persuaded Churchill not to attack Martinique but in return Churchill demanded assurance from Vichy that German submarines would not be refuelled there to prey on allied shipping, as they had been doing since the surrender. My husband's task was to discover if he could how well the French were keeping to their side of the bargain.

The pilot of the Pan Am flying-boat that took my husband from Trinidad to Martinique warned him that the plane would have to take off again immediately after alighting and there was no way of knowing when (or if) it would return for him.

To his amazement Peter was welcomed with a salute from a very correct detachment of French marines. Customs and immigration formalities were waïved before he had a chance to produce his passport, and he was driven in a limousine to the Hotel de Paris where the manager, all bows and smiles, conducted him to a suite of rooms where fruit, champagne on ice, tempting pastries, and a huge basket of flowers awaited him. Since no-one in Martinique had been told of his visit, let alone its true nature, the reception was all the more surprising.

Deciding not to look a gift horse in the mouth, my husband took a shower and changed into fresh clothes, and was about to open the champagne when there was a knock on the door. A short man in a badly fitting, blue serge suit, flanked by two large and muscular young men, stood before him. Behind them he could see the anxious-looking manager.

"Who are you?" the man asked tersely in American-English. The tone implied, "Who the devil are you?"

"Who are you?" my husband replied.

Looking thoroughly uncomfortable, the man said in a low voice, "I think there's been a mistake. May I come in for a moment?"

Leaving the others in the corridor he entered the room and closed the door behind him. When he saw the champagne and the flowers he seemed amused. "Ah, the French!" he said. "So polite. So logical."

Eventually, after some cautious exchanges, explanations emerged. It appeared that he was Admiral Greenslade, in charge of the U.S. Atlantic Fleet, who had arrived to hold "hush-hush" talks with Admiral Robert. (Which accounts for the ill-fitting civilian clothes, my husband thought to himself.) He had already guessed Peter was a newspaperman.

"Since I was expected and you turned up, the French reasoned that you were me," said the Admiral. "It won't do any harm, and may save embarrassment, to let them think you are one of our party. You can be helpful to me and I to you." He added, "Of course, everything I've told you here is off the record."

Thus it was that my husband and Admiral Greenslade dined together, walked together (followed by the aides at ten paces), and compared notes. When my husband's stories appeared in the *Chicago Times* there was no mention of the Admiral's visit.

Together they inspected the aircraft-carrier with its new U.S.-built planes, the fast cruiser, and the coins and bullion now held ashore in a fortress dungeon — a considerable portion of the gold supply of France. Attempting to uphold U.S. prestige, my husband played tennis with some young French officers in the heat of noon, won the game, and suffered sunstroke!

In private conversations, he found that most of the pilots and lower-ranking naval officers were opposed to the Pétain régime and wanted to get away to join LeClerc and the Free French troops then fighting in Chad. He was informed also that German submarines were refuelling in various sheltered coves round the island, and that the German agent in Fort de France was the American Ford dealer (after the Liberation he was shot as a collaborator). For the French servicemen stationed there, Martinique offered a life of safety with all possible comforts, including good food, excellent wines, and lovely *café-au-lait* girls. Yet a sense of frustration was evident. With the world in flames, even the most apolitical young man was nagged by a sense of guilt.

From Martinique my husband set out on a tremendous journey by air round the entire continent of South America. He travelled by hydroplanes that could fly only in daylight, which meant staying overnight in obscure, flea-bitten hotels. The plane would splash down on a river at dusk; boys would swim out and, diving down, attach wheels so that the plane could be pulled up a ramp by means of ropes. At dawn the next day the boys would swim out again and take off the wheels. On the Amazon, as the plane taxied out for take-off, the front windows were covered with muddy water and my husband had to stand beside the pilot, pulling the cord of the siren in the hope that any craft that happened to be in the way would move before a smash occurred.

At this stage of the war the so-called "Fifth Column" was very real in many parts of South America, with Nazi sympathizers among the German colonies in Brazil, Argentina, Chile and Paraguay, as well as El Salvador and Guatemala in Central America.

Chapter 16

MOSTLY ABOUT PRESIDENTS

BEFORE the Marshall Plan was formed, postwar Western Europe was a scene of devastation quite impossible for most people in America to envisage. Money was worthless; Paris went hungry, while in Normandy there was cheese and butter, duck, goose, lamb, eggs, and even pastry! In Holland and in Great Britain, on the whole, the hardships were shared fairly under systems of rationing, whereas in France and Belgium the black markets flourished.

A committee of United States congressmen was sent to Europe at this time, headed by Christian Herder, Undersecretary of State, and a close friend of ours, Bronson MacChesney, professor of law at Northwestern University, went along as legal advisor and a sort of courier. One day Bronson called us in Chicago and asked us to come over for "brunch". "A young congressman is here on his way back to California. He was on our committee and can give you his impressions. His name's Nixon."

In Bronson's apartment there were five of us: Richard Nixon, Bronson, a friend and colleague named Bill Cary, my husband and myself. The meal that started about noon prolonged itself with drinks until late in the afternoon.

Nixon, unlike some of the other congressmen who used the European trip as an excuse for a binge, had taken the assignment seriously. He went to coal-mines, visited steel-works, talked to workers (with Bronson translating), and he spoke to us volubly, giving facts and figures, assessments and analyses. More than any other member of the Herder committee, Bronson told us, Nixon "did his homework" and made a real contribution to the report which ultimately provided the basis of the Marshall Plan. It sems that when the ship returning to America approached New York harbour at dawn, the earnest Nixon raced up and down the corridors, awakening the dead-to-the-world congressmen by shouting, "Get up! Get up! You can see the Statue of Liberty!"

Another side of Nixon's character was described years later by a friend of ours, Senator Paul H. Douglas (formerly economics professor at the University of Chicago, whose course on Utopias neither my husband nor I would ever forget). Over-age though he was in World War II, he joined the Marines as a private and was wounded serving in the Pacific. "There are no laws to deal with a person like Richard M. Nixon," he said. "I'd like to challenge him to a duel, either kill him or get killed. He destroyed two of my best friends: Helen Gahagan Douglas, a liberal Democratic candidate for Congress, by a smear campaign implying that she was a whore and a Communist; and Jerry Vorhees, the President of the Farmers' Co-operative Movement, again by innuendoes, suggesting he was in the pay of Russia. Both fine, honourable Americans, whose lives he ruined politically and personally."

When the Watergate Scandal broke, many years later, Bronson MacChesney and his wife called on us. "I thought I should come and apologise," Bronson said. "Because, after all, I was the man who introduced you to Richard Nixon. And also to Alger Hiss."

My first impression of Alger Hiss (and the only one, since it was the one time I met him) was that of a cold, formal, "Establishment", Ivy League type. He was a member of the U.S. delegation at the first meeting of the United Nations, and a crowd of us were drinking in the bar of the Palace Hotel. His air of cautious conservatism contrasted sharply with the outspoken manner of the rather raucous journalists.

Some time later Hiss was invited to speak at a luncheon in Chicago given under the auspices of the Northwestern University Law School. My husband was seated between Hiss and an empty place intended for Adlai Stevenson. As it happened, Stevenson was unable to attend but this fact was not known to members of the press who had received advance notice of the programme — and this was the era of Joe McCarthy. Our phone was busy with calls from colleagues on the *Chicago Tribune* and other papers; McCarthy was suggesting the "guilt by association" of Adlai Stevenson, who was a candidate for President, and Alger Hiss on the basis of their supposed seating at the table of the luncheon!

Early in World War II, and before the U.S. was involved, the managing editor of the *Chicago Times*, Russ Stewart, came to my husband's desk looking unshaven and tired. "I've been playing poker on the Superchief all night and I'm bushed. The man I've been playing with is a senator from Missouri — he's head of some committee dealing with defence contracts — and he won't be leaving Chicago until late this afternoon. Be a great guy and look after him for me, will you?"

Outside the glass partition stood Harry Truman, neatly dressed, cleanly shaved, and looking as though he had had a full night's sleep. My husband took over, introduced him to Richard Finnegan, the editor, showed him through the plant, and brought him to the Tab Room, the Executives' dining-room on the top floor of the *Chicago Times* building, for lunch. (By the way, the only women till then ever invited to eat in the Tab Room were Eleanor Roosevelt, wife of the President, and the great actress Helen Hayes, whose brother-in-law Arthur MacArthur owned the building; her husband Charles MacArthur and Ben Hecht had written the classic play about Chicago journalism, *The Front Page*.) By the time my husband had put Harry Truman on the Capitol Limited late that afternoon they were friends. And one of the best-known news-photographs of the century is that published in the *Chicago Times*, showing a smiling Truman holding up a copy of the *Chicago Tribune* with the headline, "DEWEY WINS LANDSLIDE VICTORY" — an early edition well and truly upset by the surprising election of Truman.

During the Administration of Harry Truman my husband, who was then the foreign editor of the *Chicago Sun-Times*, saw the President at least once a month. He often shared sandwiches and glasses of milk at the President's desk when Truman was too busy to have a proper lunch. It was not an interview; it was a conversation understood to be off the record, and the talks were never published. However, they provided background for my husband's daily column in the newspaper; he knew what the President of the United States was thinking about. As soon as he left the White House, he would hurry back to the Carlton Hotel and type the entire conversation. He kept these notes and today they would be of historic interest but somewhere in our moves to New Zealand and then to Spain they have been lost.

Soon after Pearl Harbour he was invited to head a new agency called the Co-ordinator of Information, which was later divided into the Office of War Information and the Office of Strategic Services which in turn was to become the C.I.A. A vivid memory of those days is of the Roosevelt press conference when Winston Churchill came for a visit. When asked if he was pleased that the United States was now in the war alongside Great Britain, Churchill grinned and said, "If I may be permitted to borrow an American expression: 'And How!' " In his one-piece jumpsuit and with his ebullient manner, he completely stole the show from the President, who did not look at all pleased at being upstaged.

One of our friends tells this story about Lyndon B. Johnson when he was a senator. The friend is a Spaniard, Antonio Martinez, a professor of linguistics. When the Spanish Civil War started he was in Lisbon as a cultural attaché for the Republican Government. He could not return to Spain after the victory of Franco so he took a teaching post at the University of Texas. Isabel, his young wife, was with her family in Santiago de Compostela; she tried to obtain an exit visa to join her husband, but although she and her family had never taken any part in politics, permission was refused. Year after year she filled out all the forms required for the visa and year after year her application was rejected.

More than ten years passed. Antonio was by now an American citizen. Somebody suggested that he should go to Washington and see the Senator from Texas. Somewhat to his surprise, the Senator, Lyndon Johnson, received him in his office and listened to the whole story.

He picked up the telephone and called the U.S. Embassy in Madrid. "A good friend of mine is here," he said, (he had never seen him before in his life), "and he's been trying to get his wife out to join him in Austin, Texas. What's the matter with you sons of bitches? Besides, [looking at Antonio, a very handsome man,] if his wife doesn't get here soon the co-eds at the U. of Texas won't be safe." Johnson laughed at his own joke. "Now see here, I'll give you all the details, but I want Mrs Martinez to get her exit visa and be in Austin within a week."

She was.

Chapter 17

MIRACLE IN POLAND

WARSAW in 1949 was one of the most devastated cities on the devastated continent of Europe. After its heroic and futile uprising the Germans had declared that no Pole would ever live there again, so in addition to shelling and bombing, the German Army systematically dynamited house after house, street after street. From our hotel window we looked out upon a desolate landscape of rubble and the air was heavy with the stench of decay.

The only buildings that remained were ones, like our hotel, that had housed the German commanders and the Gestapo. Now the Communists were in control, a Russian general was at the head of the Polish Army, and Russian-occupied Poland was cut off from the rest of the country. In fact, said a Polish-American priest we knew who was visiting his homeland, "I can go anywhere else — to Moscow, to Leningrad — but I can't visit my mother in the Russian-occupied part of Poland." As some measure of compensation the Poles now had East Prussia, including Danzig (renamed Gdynia). The large Prussian estates were being divided and offered to Poles for settlement, but few took advantage of this offer. Most peasants preferred a small farm in Poland — the Germans will take back East Prussia or the Russians will give it back to them, the peasants said. After all, the history of Poland is the history of partitions.

In our hotel were journalists from various countries, the British-American press corps being represented by Dennis Weaver of the *News Chronicle*, Paul Kennedy of Associated Press, and my husband for the *Chicago Times*.

Kennedy lived alone in his room, seldom leaving the hotel. He listened to the Polish radio and he had had scores of informants who came and reported to him. But eventually there was only one left, an old aristocrat whom he called Francis Joseph (since he resembled the Hapsburg Emperor). All the others had been intimidated from visiting an American journalist, but Francis Joseph said, "At my age, what does it matter?" and continued to come.

Kennedy lived on tins of pork-and-beans and beer which he obtained from the U.S. Embassy. He usually went out only once a week, to the races. All this time his American salary was accumulating in a bank in the U.S. On the Sunday before he was to leave Poland he returned to the hotel carrying a suitcase, which was chockfull of zlotys. He had bet on a most improbable combination of horses which had paid eighty-five to one. Now what to do with the zlotys? The journalists all relieved him of what they needed to pay cable costs, hotel bills and living expenses, at an extremely favourable exchange rate, since Kennedy could not take Polish currency out of the country or change it for dollars officially. He still had many zlotys left. I don't know what became of them. I hope he gave them to Francis Joseph.

Dennis Weaver and his wife Kay lived in one room with a bathroom adjoining. They cooked most of their meals on a small electric hotplate and washed the dishes in the bathroom basin. But they had an ancient Mercedes-Benz car (liberated from the Wehrmacht) and welcomed the opportunity to leave Warsaw occasionally and get out into the country. From one of these trips a searing memory for me is of Majdanek, a Nazi death camp which has been preserved as a museum and Lest-We-Forget monument. There were the ovens where desperate victims had scratched the cement walls in their final agonies, and the ashes of their bodies lay below. Gold rings, gold teeth, spectacles and watches had been removed, carefully labelled and placed on shelves. The most terrible sight was the rows and rows of small children's shoes and pathetic handmade toys.

In the Weavers' battered Mercedes-Benz, which used as much oil as gasoline and threatened to break down continually but never did, we all drove to Lublin where according to rumour a miracle was taking place in the cathedral. The Black Virgin, a sixteenth century icon, was weeping for the people of Poland. The Vatican had not recognized the phenomenon as an authentic miracle, but in a sense the Communist Government of Poland had. No one was permitted to go to Lublin by train or bus, and there were virtually no private cars. Yet almost a million people had come to Lublin for the Miracle: on bicycles, by horse-drawn carts, on hayricks, on donkeys, but most of all on foot, from all over Poland. The town was crowded with peasants, the women in bright blouses and wide skirts, mountain-villagers wearing sleeveless, sheepskin vests despite the warm August weather.

The courtyard of the cathedral was packed solid with the faithful, who were singing religious songs, and in the street outside the cathedral another crowd marched past carrying red flags and singing revolutionary songs. It looked as though it would be quite impossible to get inside and we were about to turn away when a young woman who had spotted the press card in the window of the car motioned us to follow her. She squeezed her way through the crush, telling everyone that we were foreign journalists and should be let through to verify the Miracle. Holding my hand tightly, she led us into the vestry, explained our presence to the acolytes and still holding my hand (while I held Kay Weaver's) squeezed into a spot just in front of the altar, where mass was being celebrated. People were packed in so tightly that it was hard to breathe. And I was several months pregnant.

Light came from a skylight, from the stained-glass windows, and from many candles and tapers, the shafts of sun and the flickering flames making an ever-changing pattern. As the Bishop raised the Host, murmurs and loud whispers ran through the vast congregation: "*Teras. Teras.*" In the vibrant illumination both Kay and I felt sure that we saw tears coursing down the cheeks of the Black Virgin of Lublin. Our husbands who were farther back said they did not see anything. "*Teras*", which I thought meant "tears", apparently means "now".

After World War II a new shadow had fallen over Europe from Communism and Soviet Russia. The Premier of France, M. de Queille, told us in an interview about the strikes of coal-miners which were then paralyzing industry in the north: "The press calls for me to send troops up there. I wouldn't dare to — half of the soldiers in the French Army are carrying Communist membership cards, and a large percentage of the miners too. Not that they believe in Communism, but it's a form of insurance — just in case!"

Later the same day we interviewed Marcel Cachin, the editor of *Humanité*, the Communist paper. His wife and my father had been sweethearts some fifty years earlier when she was a young French teacher in New York. (This was before the Russian revolution and the subsequent deep split between Socialists and Communists.) My father married my mother; she returned to France and married Marcel Cachin. Both the Cachins were deputies in the French parliament. Marcel Cachin was a fair-skinned, blue-eyed Norman, with a theatrical flair. His wife was quiet and austerely dressed. She seemed to regard me with interest during the interview and I wondered if she was thinking of what-might-have-beens.

At that time the Communist victory in China was completed and Chiang Kai Chek had retreated to Taiwan. Cachin stood in front of a large map of the world on which Russia, all of Eastern Europe and all of China were coloured bright red. Waving his hands across that large portion of the globe he prophesied, "Soon the whole map will be the same colour — red!" It sounded just like the Nazi boast: "Tomorrow the World."

The break between Russian and China was still in the future. Cachin's prophesy and Queille's fears were equally unfounded. But had it not been for the Marshall Plan, perhaps they might not have been.

Chapter 18

WELCOME TO YUGOSLAVIA

You've been reading too many spy stories, I told myself. But I did catch a significant glance between the clerk and the manager of Thomas Cook & Company's office in Trieste. We had been getting road-maps for the Dalmatian coast of Jugoslavia and asking about motoring conditions. It was in 1949 and we were well prepared, with six jerrycans of petrol on top of our minute Renault, one of the first to come off the line after the war and possessing the then extraordinary feature of a motor at the back and the trunk compartment, or "boot", in front. We never had to lock the car when we went to a restaurant because it was always surrounded by a crowd of fascinated onlookers who studied it, climbed underneath to inspect it more thoroughly, and waited to see it and us go.

We carried the necessary *triptico*, the international driving permit, as well as Jugoslav visas (obtained from the friendly consul in Chicago) and essential press documents. We had everything we needed for the trip.

Not quite everything. We were stopped at the border by a large Jugoslav soldier carrying a machine-gun. We showed him all our papers. He was not impressed. He shook his head, and waved his hand in a way that made clear we should go back to Italy. We pointed to an official in the little guardhouse. The soldier shrugged and eventually returned with his superior to whom we again proffered our documentation.

He pondered. Then he said, in English, "The car may enter Jugoslavia. You both may enter Jugoslavia. But you may not enter *in* the car." After exhaustive discussion we gave up and returned to the hotel in Trieste which we had left a few hours earlier.

There we tried to work out what had gone wrong. In the end we decided it was the jerrycans of gasoline that had done it. Without them we would be controlled in our movements by having to keep within range of the far-from-plentiful gasoline pumps; with our ample tins and our tiny car we would be free to travel anywhere we liked, something the government did not encourage.

In any case, as we discovered much later, our travel plans contained another flaw. Because of the ubiquity of horse-drawn vehicles, Jugoslav roads were scattered with nails, and punctured tyres occurred every few miles — this from a French journalist who spoke from painful experience.

Back at square one, we went swimming at the beach and ate at the famous Hapsburg castle of Miramar, then occupied by the American forces (my husband's "simulated" rank was that of a full colonel), where pretty young wives from Kansas were tasting lobster for the first time in their lives, had nursemaids for their children, and were complaining to one another about the hardships of military life.

Still in Trieste, we interviewed two ideological opponents — a well-known Communist labour leader and a Catholic archbishop. The labour leader told us in American-English that he'd been many times to the U.S. — had jumped ship and used false passports. "Easy," he said. He knew every port and had pals everywhere.

The Archbishop was Italian, but we spoke French. He told us that he and the Communists had agreed to allow each other to answer accusations each had made, and to print them, respectively, in the communist newspaper and the diocesan magazine. "I got the best of the bargain," he laughed; "everyone reads the communist paper, no one reads my diocesan journal!"

Since we could not drive into Jugoslavia, we decided to go by train, and late one afternoon we boarded the express en route to Belgrade. The train was packed. Our second-class compartment was jammed. Our immediate companions, we had plenty of time to discover during the course of the next eighteen hours, comprised a neatly-attired, grey-haired lady, a stout man in a dark business-suit, an oafish young man in the blue uniform of the security police, and a huge, unshaven, badly-dressed man whose breath reeked of liquor.

The train started and for a time we jolted along in silence. I was thirsty and my husband handed me the thermos bottle filled with tea we had brought from the hotel. I drank from the screw-off cup. This broke the silence. The uniformed man asked the grey-haired lady a question, looking at us and the vacuum flask.

"Pardon me," she said. "May I inquire what you are drinking?"

"Tea," I replied.

When this was relayed to the man in uniform he muttered something that sounded like "Russians!", after which the grey-haired lady gave him a long harangue. Tito had but recently broken with Stalin and there was general fear among Yugoslavs of Russian sanctions and even of war.

The woman turned to me. "I have been telling him that many people besides Russians drink tea — Chinese, Japanese, Indians, Englishmen. These people, I told him, are Americans, not Russians." She smiled, and introduced herself. She was, she said, a physician, trained in Vienna, and was on her way to Belgrade to head a maternity clinic.

Looking out the windows I could see that logs lay everywhere along the sidings and that the forests seemed to have been decimated. The stout man nodded in agreement when I commented on this. "It is the Five Year Plan," he explained in German. "We will carry it out, even if it takes us a hundred years!"

The huge Serb had a bottle of beer which he offered from time to time to the other occupants of the compartment. We all declined politely, so he continued to take swigs from it himself. Our passports had been examined at the frontier but a second review was made after a short stop in what used to be Slovenia. Before the Serb replaced his papers he handed round to us photographs of his wife, his two young sons, and of himself as a Partisan during the war, leaning against a tree, his submachine-gun cradled in his arms. He was a steelworker, he told us, on his way home from his summer holiday, and he displayed his peeling, sunburnt arms with pride.

It was getting dark. The man in blue uniform (the letters on his cap announced "SECRET SERVICE", the doctor told us with amusement) dozed; he had removed his shoes and placed his rather smelly, stockinged feet on the space next to me and with the movement of the train they kept sliding into me. The Serb was now drinking slivovitz, which was much stronger than beer. The toilet was at the end of the car and his frequent visits there meant climbing over people who, not having seats, were standing, or sitting on their luggage, some holding children on their laps. All the windows were sealed shut and the air was foul with tobacco smoke and the smell of humanity.

The night seemed endless. At each station a new group of police would board the train and demand documents. Each time I managed to fall asleep I was jolted awake by another request for our passports. Everyone in the compartment showed great patience with these formalities, except the Serb, who mumbled what sounded like curses.

The night wore on. The "Secret" Service man snored and kept moving his feet onto my lap, from which I kept removing them. The Serb was on his second bottle of slivovitz. There was one small light in the ceiling, otherwise no illumination. Just when at last it seemed everyone was dozing, the train stopped with a jerk and the police entered with long flashlights, demanding once more to see our papers. The Serb's cursing was audible and unmistakeable now but seemed to be directed at life in general rather than the current situation. We were all tired, thirsty, hungry and dusty. This trip would never end; we were destined to go on jolting through an eternal night, seeing nothing but dimly-lit and deserted station platforms, endlessly producing official documenation. . . .

In the early dawn, on what proved to be the last stop before Belgrade, came more police and the familiar demands. The Serb, who had fallen into a drunken sleep, was shaken rudely by a police officer. "Documents! Documents!" he shouted. The Serb awoke with a start, he fumbled in his inside pocket for his wallet, and threw the contents on the floor — the photographs of his family, of himself as a Partisan, all his cards of registration and identity that everyone in an Eastern Europe country must carry. He shouted back at the policeman. There was little doubt now where his curses were directed.

The doctor quickly retrieved the papers from the floor and handed them to the officer, explaining that the man had had a little too much to drink. The policeman took them and retired. But at Belgrade the last we saw of the Serb was his tall figure being led from the station by a police escort, his tousled head a good eighteen inches or more above their uniform caps.

Unlike Vienna, Prague or Warsaw, Belgrade is a capital without charm. Wars between the Turks, the Slovenes, the Croats, the Dalmatians and the Serbs made Belgrade into a sort of frontier town, the provincial centre of a Hapsburg empire run by foreigners far away.

Because of the rupture between Tito and Stalin, security was (or was supposed to be) very tight. Whereas the other heads of government in Eastern Europe had been hand-picked from obscurity by the Russians, Tito had come to power with the backing of most of the population and the blessing of the Allies. Losses among his Partisans and supporting civilians had been heavy. Many had died at the hands of the Chetniks, the Right-wing faction, or in death camps in Germany.

We met several American businessmen who had come to buy minerals or to set up industries and factories, and they all had the same story to tell. "I was referred to government officials — our company wants to build a rolling-mill near Belgrade — and they set up a meeting at the Foreign Ministry. Everything goes well and we are to confer with the head of State Industries. Fine. We explain our project again. He seems enthusiastic. Come back tomorrow, he says. When we return next day a new man is there and we have to start all over again. Fine, he says; come back on Monday. On Monday he's gone and another man is in his place. It's a madhouse."

We had a taste of this sort of thing ourselves. The Foreign Minister (a school-friend of the Jugoslav consul in Chicago) was most helpful. "We have a large co-operative farm project at Skopieje on the Macedonian border," he told us. "It is most interesting. You simply must see it." My husband didn't think the *Sun-Times* readers would take much interest in a Jugoslav co-operative farm project, however large, but the Minister was pressing, we were polite, and it was all arranged. We arrived at the airport and presented our passports together with the tickets that had been furnished by the Ministry of Foreign Affairs. The man at the window examined them all and shook his head. "You cannot go," he said sadly.

"Why not?"

"You have no police permit to leave Belgrade."

"But we are going as guests of the Foreign Minister. Please call the Ministry and they will confirm this."

The man dialled a number, waited a moment and then hung up.

"Not there."

"But there must be someone there."

He looked at the big clock behind us. "It is our summer time," he explained. "They go to work at seven-thirty in the morning. It is now two-thirty in the afternoon. They have all left."

The plane was sitting on the tarmac. We watched as the doors were closed and the steps removed. The man handed us back our passports and the useless tickets. "Perhaps some other day," he said impassively.

I caught my husband's eye and we began to laugh. We hadn't wanted to go on this trip in the first place, but now that it was prevented by blind bureaucracy, visiting a large co-operative farm project on the Macedonian border was what wanted to do more than anything else in the world!

Postscript: Years later we did go to the beautiful Dalmatian coast and stayed at Dubrovnik and at Split. Dubrovnik was once a city state that dealt on equal terms with the kings of France and England, a wonderful walled city where we heard concerts every evening in the sixteenth century courtyard; and at Split's centre is Dioclecian's palace, a city in itself. It was worth waiting for.

Chapter 19

GUARDIAN ANGELS

WE had decided to spend the night in Pireus as the boat to Crete left early in the morning. It was almost dark when we checked into a second class "commercial hotel" near the docks. Our room on the fourth floor was clean, with two narrow beds, a washstand, and one window looking down to a small courtyard. There was no elevator. "Neat but not gaudy" was our standard phrase for places like this.

We left our small suitcases, locked the door, carefully descended the four flights of stairs, deposited the key at the desk, and went out into the badly lit streets of Pireus. It was clearly not a safe neighbourhood — with few lights in the windows and none of the friendly aromatic smells of cooking. Shabbily dressed men, with scarves over the lower part of their faces, shuffled by. As we rounded a corner we saw a brightly illuminated café, and we entered. Inside it was warm and smoky. We chose a small table and ordered coffee. On a stage at the far corner a plump bellydancer was gyrating to the oriental strains of a flute but she was scarcely visible through the cloud of smoke. Afterwards, we remembered being served the thick, black, sweet "Turkish" coffee. And drinking or starting to drink it.

And that is all.

The next thing I knew was finding myself, fully dressed, still wearing my hat, my handbag firmly clutched under my arm, laid out like a dummy (or a corpse) on one of the narrow beds in the hotel room. From the other bed, my husband Peter also fully dressed, his hat on the pillow (men wore hats in those days), was staring at me.

Dazed and squeamish, we checked our possessions — passports, money, travellers' cheques, press documents: nothing was missing. It was eight o'clock in the morning. Still time to make the boat to Crete. We stumbled down the four flights of stairs to the desk. "How did we get back here last night?" my husband asked the young clerk.

"I've no idea." He showed little interest.

"But weren't you on duty?"

"Only this morning. The night clerk leaves at seven."

We paid the very modest bill and clutching our suitcases raced to the dock and boarded the ship, the last passengers to cross the gangway.

We stood at the rail watching the rippling Aegean waters glide by. Islands appeared in the middle distance. How had we managed to return safely from the café, where we had undoubtedly been given knockout drops? Neither of us remembered anything after starting to drink the coffee. What Good Samaritan had led us, or carried us, back to the hotel and deposited us so neatly on our beds? It was not difficult to explain the drugging. In 1938 half of the people in Eastern Europe were trying to get away from the encroaching Nazi menace, and the most valuable thing just then was an American passport or, second choice, a British passport, into which a photograph of the new user could be inserted to replace the original. But if the motive could be guessed, who had rescued us? We did not recall anyone following us through the streets of Pireus or taking a particular interest in us at the café. The more we thought about it the more mysterious it all became.

Still a little shaky, we stayed on deck until we arrived in Crete. There we had breakfast in a sunlit outdoor café. With tea, not coffee.

The apparent intervention of a Guardian Angel occurred again some thirty years later in New Zealand.

One of the few places, perhaps the only place, where gannets can be seen nesting in their thousands, and at a certain time of the year setting off on their long migration, is at Cape Kidnapper on the east coast of the North Island. (All the other sites are on remote islands, usually inaccessible.) At low tide this gannet colony at the very tip of the cape can be reached via the sands, so I joined a small group of naturalists who planned to ride horses along the beach, a distance of about ten miles, where a track led up to the colony. We would return by a path that followed the top of a cliff.

It was a fine cool morning. The horses were fresh and spirited, and we let them run. Their hooves pounded the hard sand, the wind blew my hair and tugged at my orange Ecuadorean serape. Faster and faster. We were soon spread out and scattered right along the beach. Exhilaration began to give way to fear. I had a brief intimation that I was no longer in control.

Then nothing.

My husband, who was walking along the cliff path above, had seen a riderless horse gallop past on the beach far below, and then in the distance noticed a spot of orange against the grey sand. He climbed down the cliff and when I opened my eyes he was kneeling beside me. I was in great pain. The tide would soon be coming in, and above us loomed a precipitous cliff. No help was in sight.

At that moment a sort of large wooden sled on wheels, pulled by a tractor, appeared. On the sled were about a dozen children, and a woman who immediately scrambled down to us. "Can I help?" she asked. "I'm a trained nurse."

The tractor driver had a walkie-talkie and called a co-worker near the place where we'd started and told him to order an ambulance and then bring his own tractor-sled along the beach to rescue me. My Good Samaritan, named Enid Sutherland, said goodbye to the children, her Sunday School class, who were on their way to the gannet colony, and remained with us.

There was no time to lose. The tide was coming in. I was in no state to move, and in any case they could not possibly carry me up the two-hundred-foot cliff that rose above the beach.

I was too confused to be concerned, but I do remember hearing that in falling I had just missed a sharp jagged rock by inches. The sand was hard enough, and very cold. After what seemed ages but was not really a long time, the tractor-sled arrived and I was placed upon it. Every bump was agony, as there were no springs. At the Hastings end of the beach a St John's Ambulance was waiting. From the stretcher on which I was being carried to the ambulance I could look down to where the beach had been. The tide was swirling across it. We had made it just in time.

Except for being badly bruised I escaped lightly. I spent ten days in hospital at Hastings, during which period every possible test was made — no concussion, no broken bones, no internal injury. As at Pireus, I remember nothing of the blackout. I must have fainted and slid off the horse. I would have been more badly hurt if I had been thrown at full gallop.

But I will never know. Enid's two daughters have visited us in Spain. They say their mother believes it was divine intervention that brought her to the spot at the moment she was needed. She could be right.

Chapter 20

RUSSIA WITH LOVE

My husband had first been to the Soviet Union when he and nineteen other journalists covered the Foreign Ministers' Conference of 1947. General George Marshall was head of the U.S. delegation. The word "noble" is out-of-date now but it applies to him as to few others of his time — he was a gentleman, a patriot, and a statesman. The rescue operation, rightly named the Marshall Plan, undoubtedly saved Western Europe from disintegration and ruin.

The conference dragged on, of little interest to the readers of the *Chicago Times,* or for that matter to my husband. But what was of tremendous interest was Moscow and the Russian people: the way they lived, dressed, ate, thought (not easy to know, for this was the Stalin era), and so these matters were what he reported in articles carrying his by-line that were spread across the pages of his paper. Russia in the late 1940s was as remote and mysterious to Americans as China was when we visited it in the mid-'seventies.

Nearly twenty years after that conference, in the summer of 1968, we arrived in Leningrad with our seventeen-year-old son Tommy. We had come from Finland by plane. While we were waiting to have our luggage cleared in customs, Tom wandered away, keen to see everything, but soon returned and we took a taxi to our hotel, the Europa, which still showed traces of former grandeur in the size of its rooms, the enormous chandeliers and wide sweeping staircase.

We had a car and chauffeur, a guide, vouchers for meals, tickets for ballet and opera. We explored the city mostly on foot, the countryside by car. Our guide was always with us, a very pretty young woman with whom we conversed in Spanish. We learnt that her mother, a Spaniard, had been shipped from Spain to Russia during the Spanish Civil War as the Nationalist forces closed in on Bilbao. Our guide had been brought up by a mother whose greatest ambition was to return to her homeland. We were surprised to find that Tommy did not want go anywhere with us. He would appear every morning and ask for the vouchers he needed for meals. When we tried to find out why, he was evasive and would mutter something about "other plans". Before long we discovered that there was a *girl*. But little else. When we went to the Hermitage that houses some of the greatest paintings in the world, including a fine collection of the French Impressionists, we again urged him to come with us but he still refused. Then, a few days later he was limping slightly and gave out in explanation that he had spent five hours on a grand tour through the Hermitage, guided by a marvellous girl called Katerina. (So that was her name!) She had given him a complete history-of-art course during that time. But in what language? It seems she spoke only Russian and French, he Spanish and English. No matter; they understood each other.

Katerina, it turned out, was not permitted to enter the hotel. Only official guides could come even as far as the lobby. He used to meet her on a street corner and they would go to a café and drink tea. At night they went to cafés that had orchestras, or to hotel restaurants with dance bands, ones where Tom could use his coupons to obtain meals for them both. They had first met at the airport (when he'd disappeared), where she was working as a French interpreter during her college holidays. She was sixteen years old.

There were difficulties. One evening a man in uniform came up and spoke severely to "Kat", apparently reprimanding her for associating with a foreign capitalist. Katerina invited Tommy to her home, an apartment where she lived with an aunt, uncle, brother, and a cousin, the latter two being university students. He said afterwards, "I feel quite ashamed. They can recite poetry in English, and I don't even know any!"

On our last day in Leningrad we had planned to visit a monastery at some distance from the city. Just as we were leaving, Tom surprised us by announcing that he was coming with us. He was obviously upset by something but I could see he did not want to talk in the presence of our guide and the chauffeur. Later, as he and I walked in the monastery garden, he told me that Katerina had not met him at the usual place, though he had waited over an hour. "She was always there on time," he said. "It isn't that I'm worried about being stood up, I'm afraid something has happened to her. Perhaps she is in trouble for going out with me."

The train for Moscow was to leave about ten-thirty that evening. Tom was packed early, left his suitcases with us, and went out to look for Katerina. He came back more distressed than ever. "Not a sign of her," he reported.

We were in our compartment on the train, my husband reading a newspaper, Tommy deep in thought. I was standing at the window in the corridor, watching the crowds in the station, the farewells and leave-takings. Then I saw a girl running along the side of the train, blonde hair streaming behind her. "Tommy! Tommy!" she called. I turned back to the compartment. "I think there's someone looking for you," I told Tom. He was out of the train and on to the platform so quickly that I had hardly finished speaking. Katerina and he embraced fondly but only for a moment before he had to jump back on to the train as it began to move; she followed for a few steps then stopped and waved, the tears running down her pretty face. Her brother stood nearby, impassive, stolid. I thought of Anna Karenina and felt like weeping too.

Katerina had given Tom the address of a students' chess club to which he could write. He wrote cautiously worded postcards from Moscow, and later from Tokyo, Singapore, Kuala Lumpur, Manilla, Taiwan and Seoul, where we travelled that summer, giving as his return address Tabor Academy in Massachusetts where he would be the following autumn. He never received a reply.

Our hotel in Moscow was another in the once-elegant, now-dilapidated category. When my husband opened the window the whole frame came out in his hands. Everywhere we went, Tommy was beseiged by young men, offering to buy anything he had — camera, wristwatch, transistor? Did he have any Beatles records? His clothes were greatly admired, his shoes, anything "American".

But not by our guide, Galina, the daughter of Spanish refugees who had fled after the defeat of the Spanish Republic in the Civil War. For her, Spain and everything Spanish was the best. She had been born in the Soviet Union and her brother had done his military service in the Soviet Army. Her parents' nostalgia for Spain had manifested itself in what they had told their children — Spanish food, Spanish art, Spanish literature were unequalled. As exiles they had little hope of ever returning to Franco's Spain to live, but Galina hoped that some day she might visit. She knew nothing about Spanish politics. With some pride she showed us a copy (in English) of *Doctor Zhivago* on which the cover of a Russian grammar had been pasted.

We had friends in Moscow among the members of the press corps, particularly the United Press correspondent, Richard Longworth. The foreign correspondents lived in an apartment complex where the guards at the entrance asked your name and why you were visiting; they kept careful notes on who went to see whom, and for how long. Russians were turned away. It was a sort of ghetto, but the apartments were more commodious than those of most Russians, except officials.

To the Longworths — Richard, his wife Barbara and their small son Peter — it was all very frustrating after the freedom of working in London, their previous posting. Life was almost intolerably restricted: they were spied upon; their telephone was tapped; they were sure their apartment was wired (so, it was found later, was the American Embassy). But for the Russian-born wife of another colleague, Henry Shapiro, life was much better than it had been under Stalin. "No one expects to hear a knock on the door in the early hours, the way we used to — any night, it could happen. Now arrests are made in the daytime and at least your family knows where you are being taken: you don't simply disappear. There is a sort of trial. Bad, of course. But not *so* bad."

Chapter 21

PLAGUE IN PRAGUE

AFTER the Munich Agreement of 1938 that was to bring "Peace in Our Time", it was not long before Nazi Germany swallowed up the Sudetenland; Poland took what had been Czech Teschen, and Hungary completed the dismembering process by grabbing the long-coveted territories of Komaron, Kassa and Ungvar. My husband was sent to cover these "takeovers". We boarded a train filled to the brim with somewhat apprehensive Czech soldiers (we were the only civilians) on their way, so they thought, to the Front. But except for some random shooting across the Olza River by bored border patrols, the Polish occupation of Czech lands was unopposed and we entered Teschen with the "victorious" troops to the sounds of military music and a stage-managed welcome from crowds of onlookers.

That evening, after listening to a propaganda officer from Poland extolling the German-Polish entente, a French journalist interrupted. "Don't you *know*?" he asked.

"Know what?"

The Frenchman sighed. "That they hate you even more than they hate us!"

The same performance of soldiers marching, bands playing and flags waving, to the cheers of the dutiful population, was repeated when the Hungarians occupied their "Lost Provinces", maps of which had decorated ashtrays and bookends ever since the end of the First World War and the dissolution of the Austro-Hungarian Empire.

In Budapest, behind the public demonstrations of joy at the recovery of these lands, there was a secret and more sinister side. Journalists whose families were even part-Jewish had to prove

154

that the family had lived in Hungary for at least a hundred years in order to have their work permits renewed. Since many place-names had changed time and again in the past, this was not easy. It was also expensive, for obtaining necessary documents usually meant paying off local officials. The lucky ones were those who decided to leave. Those who remained, if they did not end up in Auschwitz, had to endure with other Hungarians first German and then Russian occupation.

My husband knew the Czech leaders Jan Masarek and Eduard Benes. The Czechoslovakian nation was born in Chicago at the Hotel Windermere, when Thomas Masarek, Jan's father, convinced Woodrow Wilson of its right to independent existence in the brave new world that was to follow World War I. After World War II when the Communists took over Czechoslovakia, a friend of ours received a letter from the widow of President Benes, describing the murder of Jan Masarek in 1948 — he was pushed out of a window — and denying official reports that his death was suicide. My husband published her account in his daily column in the *Chicago Times*. As a result, when we applied later for visas to visit Czechoslovakia we were told that he was *persona non grata*.

But on a holiday in Warsaw we found the Czech Embassy most cordial; the Consul-General offered us cigarettes, issued press visas, and even waïved the fee. We were surprised and delighted. Weeks later we were told he had defected to the West!

From our visit to Czechoslovakia came the following article that I wrote for the December 1950 issue of the magazine *Independent Women*. Peter and I were among the very last American newspaper correspondents admitted to the country before Russia's iron curtain came down.

In the ruins of the capital cities of countries that have been taken over by the U.S.S.R., you live amidst rubble; the rubble dust is omnipresent. It enters your throat and your eyes when you walk down the street; you taste it in your food; it finds its way into your scalp and under your fingernails.

In Prague, physically unscarred capital city of Czechoslovakia, there is another kind of dust. It is invisible, yet it permeates everything. That invisible yet pervasive dust is fear.

Why should I, a free American citizen, have been so gripped by fear in Prague? Because fear is a communicable disease and I caught it from everyone I met.

Perhaps I caught it at the ambassador's garden party that I attended the first afternoon of my visit to Prague. In the formal well-manicured garden of the embassy, the few remaining newspaper and wire-service men, the United States Information Service representatives and a couple of visiting professors of political science chatted with the nervous insouciance of French aristocrats awaiting the tumbrils which would carry them to the guillotine.

Over their glasses they swapped the latest stories. A former banker, a Czech, had imprudently bought a new Buick. The banker had disappeared, but the Buick was now being driven by the chauffeur of a high ranking member of the security police. That afternoon, a British and a Swiss correspondent had found microphones in their rooms; both were leaving the country with protests to the Czech Foreign Office. And for the umptieth time, the information service librarian had been ordered to remove from the shelves and to destroy the current issue of *Time* magazine and the *New York Herald Tribune*.

This sort of thing happens in all totalitarian countries. I'd been in Hitler's Germany, Tito's Jugoslavia, Communist-run Poland and Franco's Spain. Previously, I'd been worried about other people, but not about myself or my husband. I'd been in air bombardments, places that were being shelled and cities under attack, but I'd never felt the kind of creeping terror that seems to be endemic to Prague.

This fact can be described only in psychological, not in physical terms. In fact, the physical intactness of Prague — a few buildings were nicked during the fight for liberation and some of the bridges partly destroyed — only underlines the spiritual and moral destruction. The baroque solid beauty of the Czech capital remains untouched.

On Hradcany hill, President Gottwald resides in the ancient fortified palace of the Kings of Bohemia; headquarters of the security police seemed to be in a building in the courtyard of the tenth century cathedral of St. Vitus. The Brueghel-like medieval Street of the Alchemists winds down the hill, unchanged. And back in the heart of the city, the wonderful clock from which the twelve apostles, life-size, appear to mark the hours, still draws a crowd of admiring tourists.

But within the unchanged exterior, everything is different. Perhaps that is why Prague is more shocking than Warsaw, where it is comprehensible that violent social change should have followed physical destruction. But that is only one reason; there are other, more cogent ones.

Elsewhere in Eastern Europe, in Poland, Hungary and Rumania, the governments had been reactionary and corrupt before the war. In these countries the Communists could promise social reform, land distribution and better working conditions. But Czechoslovakia, with all its faults, was a progressive democracy; all the social reforms that the Communists could promise to the other countries were already in force there.

When I visited Eastern Europe in 1939, I was impressed by the bitter hatred of the landed nobility and upper classes of Eastern Europe for the Czech Republic. All this social welfare was giving their peasants and workers "ideas". Now, a weird sequence of this sentiment is apparent in the dispossessed and impoverished survivors of the upper classes. "You see, it didn't do them any good!" they say. Having liberal social institutions and being on friendly terms with the Soviet Union was no guaranty of survival. In retrospect, they point this out to justify the regimes of Smigley-Ridz, Antonescu and Horthy because it would have been all the same anyway!

The Czechs themselves are still puzzled by the motivation for the Communist coup. Czechoslovakia was already within the Russian orbit. In fact, she seemed like a beautiful example of how a nation could do business with the Soviet Union and remain independent. And because she did business with the West, too, she acted as a useful clearing house for East-West traffic of mutually needed commodities.

As it is, Czechoslovakia is much worse off than Poland. Whereas in Poland food is plentiful and good, food in Czechoslovakia is scarce and of poor quality. Bread, butter, meat and sugar are still rationed. Pilsen beer is still excellent, but the best grades are for export.

Nowadays a well-dressed person in Prague is noticeable. The Czechs were never chic — most of them are too solidly built for style — but the people in Prague used to appear comfortably dressed in good woollen overcoats, durable and neat suits, sound leather shoes. Now everyone is shabby; clothes are worn and threadbare. Soap is severely rationed and its lack is apparent. A housewife gets a single bar of laundry soap per month.

Most of the small shops have not yet been nationalized, but since they must buy their products from government-owned manufacturers, they are being forced out of business by fixed price levels and punitive taxation. Although we were there in the season when tomatoes and salad greens normally appear in the marketplace, these foods were unobtainable except in the most expensive restaurants. The official selling price was fixed so low that the farmers preferred to let them rot on the ground rather than pay the transportation costs to bring them into town.

We were staying at the Majestic Palace, an elegant hotel near the famous Wenceslaus Square. Bedspreads and draperies were of honey-coloured satin. The furniture in the formal sitting-room was covered with damask of the same tone and design; the service was as impeccable as before the war. But on the heavy silver serving dishes, the food was a pathetic parody of the once fine meals they served.

Our instinctive reaction to the fear-ridden atmosphere was excessive sociability. We accepted and proffered invitations to breakfast, luncheon, tea, dinner. We found ourselves feverishly eager to be continuously accompanied by someone — anyone.

Only much later did we admit to each other that, at the time, it seemed a good idea to have someone around who could advise the State Department just "in case". And when either of us had an appointment, we made a deadline for returning. "If I'm not home by five, call the embassy," was the unspoken agreement.

The S.N.B., security police, (dubbed "insecurity agents" by the Czechs) are everywhere, both in and out of uniform. Whenever we sat down — on a park bench, in a museum, at a café table or in the lobby of our hotel — ears bent in our direction. A thick-set, well-dressed man who was presumably assigned to us frequently turned up at a nearby table. When we lowered our voices, he tipped perilously backwards in his chair. We were tempted to whisper and see whether he would spill on his bullet-shaped head!

Everyone in Prague is afraid. Waiters glance over their shoulders. People look around in all directions before answering a simple question as to where a certain street or public building can be found. Even the officials themselves are scared. They are right to be, for almost all the officials who were in power when we were in Prague, including the Minister of Commerce and the Foreign Minister, have since been purged. As for the Army, the general staff has been replaced by Russians.

Marching squads of security forces are ubiquitous; their uniforms and bearing are reminiscent of the S.S. troops. A constant patrol by the police is maintained in front of the Archbishop's palace, the foreign embassies and the principal churches.

Remember Lidice? It is only twenty miles outside Prague. A friend took us there in his jeep. A tall stone shaft marks the spot where the entire male population of the town was massacred by the Germans and buried in a common grave. The stone shaft is inscribed in Russian, then lower down, in Czech. Although the new town of Lidice was built entirely with funds from the United States, there is no mention of U.S. help at all. And when the massacre happened, Russia was still an ally of Hitler's.

If you read the beautifully printed books on Czechoslovakia, you will learn that Clement Gottwald was elected President by an overwhelming majority of votes, and that the present government is representative of the people. Benes and Masaryk receive casual mention, but their names are being obliterated in the history books as well as on buildings and streets that once bore their names.

The Czechs were the most literate people in Eastern Europe. Now that both the British and American information services have been closed, there is nowhere they may read Western newspapers, magazines and books. These libraries and reading rooms were always crowded, despite the fact that the police kept careful watch on all visitors. In the bookstores "decadent" Western authors have disappeared — whether they have been sold out or whether the order was given to remove them from the shelves, no one knows. In their place, the latest Russian novels are featured. The same fact is true of the films; a few flickering old cowboy "westerns" are still showing in the neighbourhood theatres but the principal movie-houses show Russian and German films.

The only place where we saw people who looked happy was a workmen's restaurant in a Prague suburb. The masons and bricklayers laughed and joked as they sat down at the long wooden tables. Each brought his own bread with him in his jacket pocket. They ate the *prix-fixe* dinner, a sort of stew, mostly potatoes and gravy. They drank large steins of beer. As they started the meal a loud-speaker began to blast. "Turn that accursed thing off!" one of them shouted. The waiter shook his head and shrugged his shoulders to indicate that he couldn't. The music and patter from the loud-speaker filled the room with noise; the workmen finished their meal in resentful silence.

Despite the general shabbiness of the people of Prague, there still remains a class of people with money — people who once were well-to-do and who now are spending their capital, convinced that they might as well enjoy themselves while they can. You see them in the splendid restaurants on the Vltava River, where dance orchestras play far into the night.

This, too, was reminiscent of the last time we were in Prague, in 1939. Then during the Runciman Mission when the Czech Republic was being sold out, well-dressed and well-fed Czechs wept as they ate in-between-meal "snacks" of Thuringer sausage, dumplings and Pilsen beer. The restaurants are still there, but the food is skimpy and ersatz.

Now, as then, the United States is to blame for everything in the minds of many Czechs. At that time we were reminded that the Czech Republic was conceived in America and Woodrow Wilson's theory of national self-determination had brought her into being. Then why didn't we help in her crucial hour of need? Now they point out that if Patton's Third Army had not stopped in Pilsen but had continued on to Prague, and if the Americans, instead of the Russians, had marched into the Czech capital as its liberating force, everything would have been different.

The scrubbed, energetic, hard-working atmosphere of Prague has disappeared, and in its stead a slovenly Balkan-like indifference can be noted. And the paralysis and stagnation that are produced by a combination of fear and lack of incentive have clogged the wheels of Czech industry and commerce.

Individuals plan to escape into the Western Zone of Germany, and despite increasingly tight border control a surprising number manage to do so. But most Czechs live in a nightmare world of terror and intimidation from which there seems to be no escape. There is talk of sabotage, but none of revolt. The students at the famous St. Charles University demonstrate occasionally; the ring-leaders are arrested and sent out to work on the roads with forced labour battalions.

The sense of being trapped in Prague extends to foreigners as well as the citizens. Newspapermen hate living there, but they fear that if they get permission to leave the country for a holiday they will be unable to get back.

The feeling of insecurity remained until the last moment of our stay in Czechoslovakia. Our friend with the jeep brought us to the airport, but he had to say goodbye in an outer waiting-room. We proceeded into an inner room where our baggage and passports were examined. The customs officer pounced upon a small leather address-book suspiciously, and I was thankful there were no Czech names in it. Then he motioned to a uniformed police officer and together they examined the book, looking at me out of the corners of their eyes. Next the two of them called a third officer, who asked to see my passport again.

The customs official and the two security police disappeared with the address-book and my passport. Oh, why had I brought that silly book anyway? Our friend and his jeep were gone. If we were picked up no one would know what had become of us.

Outside, the plane for Vienna was ready to take-off.

The moments passed. Finally the customs official returned with my address-book and gave it back to me. "Your passports will be returned to you on the plane," he said. We were cleared.

A few minutes later, we were flying high over the peaceful rolling Czech countryside. My husband and I grinned at each other; for the first time since we'd entered the country we felt unafraid.

PART IV

A REVOLUTION
IN BEING

Chapter 22

IN CASTRO'S CUBA

On New Year's Eve, 1959, Fulgencio Batista and a few of his associates quietly left Havana in an airplane, making way for the triumphal entry of Fidel Castro. And our busy lives in Chicago ended suddenly when my husband received an offer he could not refuse.

The offer came from the American Universities Field Staff, an organization supported by fourteen U.S. universities and the Ford Foundation which sends men with both academic and journalistic backgrounds and the appropriate languages to places not covered regularly by news services. The idea behind it is that the work of historians takes too long before publication to be currently useful, and dispatches from reporters who dip in and out are often superficial and sensational. So the organization sends its own people to places undergoing transition, to stay in the country assigned to them and write their "reports in depth". After a year's stay they return to the U.S. and lecture to classes of undergraduate and graduate students, foreign affairs groups, and faculty clubs in the sponsoring universities.

My husband was assigned to Cuba to cover a "revolution in being". He obtained leave of absence from the *Chicago Sun-Times* and from Northwestern University, dropped his radio programme and scheduled TV discussion show appearances, expecting to return two years later. As it turned out, we never went back (except to visit).

In our fairly new Chevolet we drove to Key West to board the ferry to Havana, my husband, our nine-year-old son Thomas, and I. We settled into a luxurious apartment hotel, the Rosita de Hornedo, replete with restaurant and café and two enormous

swimming-pools; our terrace faced the Caribbean Sea and spectacular sunsets. Armed with introductions both official and personal we made a call on Fidel Castro, the first of several.

He did not keep us waiting; we were ushered into his office
(the locale of which kept changing, as did his residence). An
impressive figure, dressed in fatigues, he rose and shook our
hands cordially. The luminous eyes, the voice, his whole manner radiated friendly warmth and sincerity. He announced that
since Cuba was now a free country we could go anywhere we
wanted, see anything, speak to anyone. Facilities would be given
us to visit the new co-operative farms, the housing developments,
the schools, any and every government department.

It was still an era of enthusiasm and euphoria. After years of
guerrilla warfare and living in the sierra, the young militiamen
were to be seen everywhere, all heavily armed; their long hair,
sometimes below their shoulders, caught in a beret or pony-tail,
indicated their length of service, since many of them were too
young to have beards like their leader. There were daily rallies,
meetings, "concentrations", to which Fidel spoke — and spoke
and spoke: four- and five-hour-long speeches in which he repeated the same slogans, using dramatic illustrations. And
(almost) everyone listened, fascinated, almost hypnotized. When
he looked directly at you as he spoke, you felt convinced he
must be right, even though you knew better.

Our apartment in Havana was our base. From it we set off
in our Chevrolet to explore Cuba. We must have visited almost
every city, town, village, co-operative farm, school, and small
community in the whole country, as we drove sixty thousand
miles in less than a year. We met provincial administrators, sugar
refinery managers, ranchers, Jesuits, Protestant missionaries, editors, doctors. I had brought some U.S. schoolbooks for Tom, so
that he would not fall too far behind his class in Evanston, but
somehow they remained in a suitcase; instead, he learned Spanish, the geography of Cuba, and, in an oblique way, Revolution.

Because strange things were happening. We were interested
in the new system of education introduced by the Castro government (all the textbooks had pictures of Fidel as a frontispiece),
so one of Fidel's assistants, a slightly built, efficient, young man,
gave us a letter of introduction to his aunt who was superintend-

ent of schools for a large district in Pinar del Rio. The super-
intendent, her husband and her daughter were warm and
friendly. We visited schools, talked to teachers, attended classes,
stayed to dinner in their comfortable home, met their neighbours,
and sat talking till late at night. When we left they loaded our
car with fresh fruit and homemade cakes, some for us and some
for their nephew in Havana, to whom they sent loving good
wishes.

When we went back to the young man's office to deliver the
gifts and thank him for his introduction to his family, he was not
there and the people who were there didn't seem to know who
he was. It was as if we'd made up the whole thing. Much later
we heard that he was in Cabañas prison and had not "yet" been
executed.

They were strange times. Fidel Castro wore a Holy Medal on
a chain round his neck, and so did many of his lieutenants. He
had said: "Arms? For what?"; now he was saying, "Votes?
For what?" Private estates, property and businesses were being
seized (and their owners given what proved to be worthless documents), and a massive housing project outside Havana was
being launched to replace the slums. Almost every day there was
a mass meeting somewhere in Cuba at which Castro raised the
revolutionary spirit by four-hour-long perorations, martial music
and singing.

Simultaneously *la vita dolce* — the night-life, the cabarets, the
restaurants — continued to function. At a meeting of tourist
agencies "Visit Our Revolution" was the slogan that season.
Much of the former life of Havana continued, but according to
new rules. Long after all the country clubs and golf clubs had
been seized to be turned over to revolutionary committees, we
were invited by some well-to-do Cubans to have Sunday
luncheon at the Yacht Club. We were amazed to find that nothing had changed — the same perfect service, *haute cuisine*,
beautiful girls in bikinis disporting themselves near the limpid
pool. How could this be? Our hosts explained: the other clubs
had been seized as belonging to Batistianos — since Batista
was a member; but Batista had never been admitted to the
Yacht Club (it was considered that he was not white!).

But gradually at first, then with increasing momentum and finally at dizzying speed, havens like the Yacht Club of Havana and the private estates of rich people who had helped Fidel while he was still leading a band of insurgents in the sierra fell into the hands of the committees. We were invited to house-parties in the vast country homes of Cuban friends, who were entertaining, they knew, for the last time before the militia moved in.

A large section of the educated and well-off Cubans had helped Castro. They had smuggled in arms from the United States, provided money, sheltered militants; their sons had fought and some had died fighting for his cause. But everything was changing; Castro's middle-class supporters were being denounced, and the Communists who had passively assisted Batista were moving into positions of power.

Rufo Lopez-Fresquet, an economist and lawyer, who through banking connections within and outside Cuba had been largely responsible for financing the Revolution (a much more dangerous activity in Havana under Batista than fighting in the hills), was Finance Minister in Castro's first cabinet. By promising to forgive and forget all previously unpaid taxes if the taxpayers paid in full and promptly that year, he enabled income tax to be collected for the first (and last) time in Cuban history. But as the months went by the cabinet did not meet, and Fidel said openly that he did not want to hear advice that no longer suited his objectives. One day Rufo was walking home from his impressive government office when a passer-by, without stopping, said, "Don't go home. They're waiting for you." *They*, of course, were the secret police. Rufo walked on, not daring to call on anyone he knew for fear of involving them. Then he met an old friend who greeted him warmly.

"Rufo! I was just looking for you. I thought you might like to come fishing, since it's such a fine day."

Wearing only bathing trunks and carrying their fishing tackle, they went to where a small motor-boat was docked. The revolutionary guards wished them good luck with their fishing. They stayed just within sight until it was dark, then started the motor and headed for Florida.

*　　　*　　　*

Among the places we visited were church-related colleges and schools, ranches where the famed Gertrudis cattle were bred, sugar and banana plantations, tobacco farms, vegetable-growing projects, fisheries, rum distilleries, missions and newspapers. We often stayed with these teachers, farmers, managers and others and heard their views about Castro and the Revolution. They talked openly but it would not be long before these same people, if they were still around, would tell only what they thought it was safe to say.

Many Catholic priests, and even the Archbishop of Santiago Province, who had saved Castro's life after his hare-brained attack on the Montana barracks, defended his cause. And Protestant teachers and missionaries, and social workers, sickened by the brutality and corruption of the Batista régime, were willing to accept certain unlawful activities — such as the seizure of property and inexplicable arrests — in the hope that the new government, once firmly established, would become more moderate.

All the time surveillance was increasing. We wondered why one editor we talked to took us on something like a "pub-crawl", moving on from one café to another, until we noticed that a person nearby kept turning up at each place. A week later that editor's paper was shut down, and soon afterwards two Havana dailies were closed.

At his rallies Castro had railed against American Imperialists and Capitalists; now he was beginning to rail against Americans. At the U.S. base in Guantanamo we sat in the officers' club while the Cuban bartender turned up the radio for us to hear a savage attack on President Eisenhower by Castro's propaganda minister.

Next, Cuban employees of the U.S. Embassy were arrested. Lines of Cubans began to form in front of the modern steel and glass building (how vulnerable!), seeking U.S. visas, while photographers snapped pictures of them for the files of the security police. The mass meetings continued but people went now for reasons of expedience. Besides, for farm workers, being taken in trucks to a rally and provided with food and beer was a good day's outing, far better than working.

Newspapermen were being picked up, questioned, kept over-night and then released, a technique intended to insure their compliance with unofficial censorship. One of the few not molested was Ruby Hart Phillips, *New York Times* correspond-ent, for it was her predecessor Herbert Mathews whose famous interviews with Castro in the sierra first gave him prominence and a sort of tacit recognition as the future leader of Cuba in the minds of many U.S. people. Our own telephone was being tapped, and as a former wartime censorship official I could easily tell that our letters had been steamed open, read and resealed.

During this same period journalists from all over the world were being given the royal treatment and "shown" the wonders of revolutionary Cuba. Figures of international importance, like Jean Paul Sartre and Simone Beauvoir, came and went, and wrote panegyrics about the changes wrought. A government interpreter was always present at interviews to help maintain the correct level of enthusiasm. But there was still an enormous reservoir of genuine goodwill and wide expectation of a better life on the part of many sections of the population.

The day came when Russians moved into the Rosita de Hornedo apartment building where we lived. They were quite unlike the transient Hungarian, Rumanian and East German writers, artists and propagandists whom we often saw in the restaurants and theatres. The Russians kept to themselves and they moved in to stay. (Some were probably technicians sent to set up the missiles which caused the confrontation with Jack Kennedy a few years later.)

Our sources of information were beginning to dry up. No one wanted to be seen talking to an American, much less a journalist, and we did not want to implicate friends whose positions were already uncertain. Despite severe limitations on baggage and currency that could be taken out of the country, many of them were leaving for the U.S. One friend, who had entertained us at her beautiful country estate and on her yacht when we had first arrived — shortly before both estate and yacht were seized —called to say goodbye. Emilia recognized that the kind of life wealthy Cubans had led was over and done with, and rightly so. She waved a Pan Am flight-bag. "This is all I'm taking with me," she announced. She was wearing a tailored suit and white silk blouse with large glass buttons and cuff-links. Much later, in Chicago, she told me that the glass buttons were *diamonds*!

Emilia, the daughter of multi-millionaire landowners, had studied law in the same class as Fidel Castro, and knew him and his friends, though she was not part of the group. She met and married a U.S. naval officer who was later killed in the Korean War. Then began a strange dual life. For ten months of the year she worked as a legal aid in the juvenile courts of the Chicago area, helping young people, mostly Puerto Ricans and Mexicans. She lived in two austere rooms in Hull House, dressed simply, knew a few journalists, including us, but rarely went out. She received a dollar a year from the city government. For the other two months she returned to the extravagant life of the Cuban rich. She gave lavish dinners, luncheons, weekend house-parties, took guests on Caribbean cruises on her yacht which resembled a small ocean liner. Dressmakers, glove-makers, hat-makers, bootmakers came to her house to measure and to fit and to make-to-order masses of things that she wore only during her yearly holiday. At the same time she was providing sanctuary for Castro's guerrillas and money for their cause.

Now she was leaving Cuba forever. "In the future," she said cheerfully, quite undefeated, "I'll be paid for doing what I've been doing before. Every year the Mayor of Chicago has offered me a salary and I've turned it down. This year I'll accept."

In Havana we began to notice that our Chevrolet was being followed by cars whose number-plates started with sixty-six — which everyone knew belonged to the secret police. We used to let them tail us to the U.S. Embassy, wait nearby and then follow us back to the Rosita de Hornedo. They must have found it very monotonous for that is about the only outing we gave them; as a rule if we were going anywhere else we took a bus!

Like all revolutions, the Cuban Revolution was beginning to devour its children. Some of the most important leaders, men who had come with Fidel in the *Gramma* from Mexico, were in prison, at Cabaña fortress or the Isle of Pines; others had disappeared. The purges had begun. We had seen it all before in Spain: the early days of euphoria, exhilaration and high hopes become times of frustration, suspicion and fear.

Castro was taking no chances. He rarely slept two successive nights in the same place. He arrived at the mass rallies hours after the scheduled start. His favourite means of travel was by helicopter; he would, literally, drop in from the sky (this became so matter-of-course that whenever a helicopter appeared our son Tommy would say, "Fidel Castro?"). The fact that Fidel named his brother Raul as his successor was also thought to be a form of insurance: Fidel was known as implacable in his attitude towards his enemies, but Raul was considered downright bloodthirsty.

One day we had been swimming at a beach near Havana and returned to have lunch; it was late, even for Havana: about four o'clock. We were the only customers in a popular restaurant and had just been served when there was a great commotion outside and then Castro and an aide appeared. He came straight over to us, shook hands, and patted Tommy affectionately on the head. "Everything all right?" he asked, and we nodded and smiled. He strode — Castro never walked, he moved with long strides — to a nearby table where the owner hastened to serve him. Through the window we could see the street was full of jeeps and militia with machine-guns. Castro ate quickly. We ate slowly. Only after he had left did we finish our meal and depart.

Like normal tourists we visited the many scenic places mentioned in the guide-books. Most of the larger hotels had been taken over by the government and were being run by workers' committees, sometimes very well. Some of the small guest-houses were still operated by their owners, who were trying desperately to keep going, despite shortages and bureaucratic impediments.

In one such place, in Pinar del Rio, we stayed at a motel run by a French-Canadian. Canadians were popular in Cuba at the time because products from the United States, like tyres, automobile parts and agricultural machinery that could not be imported directly because of a U.S. embargo, now came via Canada. We were invited to dinner by the manager of the neighbouring sugar refinery. He and his wife had a large, comfortable house where they had raised their two sons, now grownup and living in the United States. After a fine dinner with French wines, they spoke of the uncertainty of their position. "We've lived here for thirty years," our host explained. "We are at home in the community. The company wants us to stay because it knows the moment we leave the refinery will be taken over by the government."

Two young women visitors (who were employed in the French Embassy in Havana) invited me to join them in a swim of about half a mile to a small island offshore where, I was told, a French woman, a recluse, lived. Off we went, enjoying the swim, and at the island we climbed up a small beach to a wooden shack but it appeared to be deserted; we plunged back into the almost warm Caribbean waters and swam slowly home. We were met by an excited motel proprietor and my husband and son, who seemed more than usually happy to see me. The French-Canadian had discovered us with his spyglass on our return trip. "Those crazy people!" he cried. Apparently the refinery wastes were dumped in the bay and it was one of the most shark-infested waters in the Caribbean. My husband and son rushed down to the beach to get the rowboat, discovered it was locked, ran up the hill to get the key, discovered that the oars were missing, found the key to the boathouse, found the oars, ran back to the rowboat, and were about to push off when they saw us happily approaching the beach. During the whole time we were in the water we had not seen a fin, or if there was one we had not noticed!

Shortly after this we spent a week on the Isle of Pines (possibly the site of R. L. Stevenson's *Treasure Island*), where there had been a large colony of U.S. expatriates and where there was now a large prison. Our fellow passengers on the little ferry-boat were mostly the wives and mothers of prisoners, all carrying parcels of food — it was the Thursday once a month when they could visit. We were all searched when we landed.

While we were at the Isle of Pines we met an American who had done what he called "the Columbus caper" — which meant travelling to Spain and back in a twenty-foot sailboat without a motor or two-way radio (he could receive but not send messages). He and his wife were anxious to sell their small ranch and fine horses, and the boat, so that they could start life again elsewhere, but of course there were no buyers.

We were staying at an elaborate resort complex — swimming-pool, golf course, tennis courts, shooting range included. When

Tommy announced, "Here comes Fidel Castro!" we smiled indulgently; how like a child to think every helicopter would be carrying the Maximum Leader. But he was right. Soon Castro and an aide strode past our table on the poolside terrace. He nodded to us but it was hardly a sign of recognition. Had he forgotten us, or did he now dislike all Americans? That was the last time we saw him.

More and more Russians were moving into the Rosita de Hornedo. Foreign journalists were being arrested; plots were being uncovered daily. Independent newspapers were being closed, either by official edict or by failure to obtain newsprint. A New Zealand journalist named Scott was arrested, held for days unable to communicate with anyone outside while he was questioned about supposed spying activities. When through the efforts of Ruby Hart Philipps, and the *New York Times* he was freed, told to leave at once by air, we brought some clothes to him from his rooms and wished him a safe trip. The plane taxied to the end of the field, waited a few minutes before take-off, and then circled above our heads before setting course. But Scott was not on it; he had been taken from the plane when it was at the end of the runway. It was a long time before he finally left Cuba.

The situation felt familiar. Madrid in 1936, Havana in 1960. The seizing of private property, the ubiquitous militia — sloppy, ill-kempt; an atmosphere of excitement interlaced with fear. But with a difference. Madrid had been surrounded by real enemies, a well-equipped army with the latest German and Italian weapons, long-range canon, planes that could bomb and strafe, and a Fifth Column within the city willing and waiting to stab in the back. And Havana? At that moment the only enemy was the bourgeosie, the middle-class that had helped Castro to power. It was as hard to find a Batistiano in Cuba as it was, after World War II, to find a Nazi.

Later on there were real enough enemies, real dangers — stupid "dirty tricks" plots, and finally the disastrous, tragi-comic invasion attempt. Just before that ill-fated and ill-conceived operation my husband and I were in Guatemala, where he had been interviewing the President. We were driving across country and as we approached the west coast we stopped for dinner at a restaurant. "You folks going to Retalaleu?" the affable waiter inquired. "Where them Cubans are training people to invade Cuba?" Such were the top secret preparations for the Bay of Pigs!

*   *   *

What turned out to be our last weekend in Cuba we decided to spend at Verdadera beach, once the exclusive resort of the rich whose hotels and chalets cut off access to the sea, now open to the public. Small apartment complexes had been built where a family could stay for two weeks holiday at a nominal rent. We booked in at a baroque guest-house, formerly run by an elderly Englishwoman. The place was filled with Victorian memorabilia, antimacassars, portraits of military ancestors, swords crossed on the walls. The owner had returned to England but the cook and the major-domo (waiter, manager, night clerk, chauffeur and gardener all in one) remained and nothing much had changed. This was our third visit. We went swimming, walked for miles along the magnificent beach, no longer divided into segments by walls or wire fences. Tommy was learning to water-ski. We were invited by a city official to take a trip along the coast in one of the many "liberated" launches and yachts moored at the marina. We tried to decline but he insisted. About ten miles from shore the motor stopped, and after a while the skipper announced that in the efforts to fix it a "pin" had been dropped and could not be found. He alerted the coast-guard and our imposing craft was towed ignominiously into port. It occurred to us that the skipper had deliberately sabotaged the engine to discourage such excursions.

We had left our elegant apartment in the Rosita de Hornedo on Friday morning, taking with us only our weekend bags, containing little except bathing-suits, change of clothes, and my typewriter; everything else remained there. My husband's notes for his reports on Cuba were always carried in the car (under the spare tyre). We had not mentioned the idea to each other before but on the road back to Havana my husband and I had the same thought: "Try the ferry?" he asked suddenly, and I nodded. Instead of turning into the street leading home, he drove to the dock where the ferry-boat to Key West was berthed. As casually as I could (at least in appearance), I bought tickets for the three of us and we drove up the ramp leading to the parking level.

The ferry was scheduled to leave at ten a.m. but instead of sailing she remained tied fast to the wharf. While the passengers gathered on the upper deck, an official with a list in one hand and a megaphone in the other called out names in alphabetical order: "Señor Alvarez, Señor Betancourt . . .", and these individuals reluctantly left the ship and were made to stand in a group on shore. We waited, afraid to look at one another, while the names of more and more people were called, sometimes couples, sometimes whole families. Inexorably, after Lopez, Martinez, Nolan, Ortega, he reached "P" as in Pflaum. But no "P" was called, and he moved on to Quiñones. At long last the list was ended, the man with the megaphone waved to the captain in sign of dismissal; with a loud blast on the ship's siren we moved slowly away from the dock.

Not until we were out at sea did we compare notes with other passengers. Each of us had reached the conclusion that his time in Cuba was up. We ourselves were certain that the police were waiting for us when we returned to that apartment in Havana. And, with a nine-year-old child, we felt it was too much of a chance to take. In the crowded bar, people spoke in whispers until the ten-mile limit had been passed and we were outside Cuban jurisdiction. Then it was pandemonium, with everyone ordering champagne and unknown fellow-passengers insisting on buying us drinks, proposing noisy toasts — "To Freedom!"; "To the United States!" — raising their glasses to us as that country's representatives. A comely blonde reached into her bulging blouse and from a seemingly generous bosom produced handfuls of Cuban banknotes. (She would discover all too soon that they were practically worthless.)

We will never know whether in fact Castro's secret police were waiting for us at the Rosita de Hornedo. We had left everything there, fully expecting to return, yet something during that weekend convinced us that it was time to get out. It was probably the culmination of many misgivings, the steadily growing feeling that events were closing in on us.

Anyway, we had caught the last ferry to Key West.

Chapter 23

INTERLUDE

AT Key West we drove straight to the Casa Marina, a handsome old hotel with miles of verandahs and endless gardens. It was almost empty. We took a suite (eight dollars a day, with breakfast!) and my husband settled down to write his reports, which later were published as a book: *Tragic Island: How Communism Came to Cuba.*

While he worked, Tommy and I swam in the net-enclosed seapool, and Tommy became a dedicated fisherman. He had made friends with two brothers, sons of the owners of a sports shop, and from morn till night they could always be found near the end of the long pier, three boys, silent, obsessed, enchanted. It was so difficult to get them back for lunch that the mother of the other two and I took turns in bringing them sandwiches and milkshakes at noon. Their catches were paltry, but their hopes remained undimmed.

During this time at Casa Marina I came to know Tennessee Williams, whom we had met years before. Every afternoon he brought a few friends to the pool and afterwards we gathered in the patio bar. (My husband, poor man, was working.) There Williams held court. We listened, rarely interrupting even to ask a question. Physically unattractive, Williams captivated you with his voice, his humour, his ability to catch the nuances of speech so that when he imitated someone you could almost see that person. His wit could be cruel, biting, waspish. And yet there was also compassion for human weaknesses. Unlike Ernest Hemingway, who believed you could "talk away" your novels so they'd never be written, Williams often seemed to be trying out episodes and dialogue on us, listening to the sound of the words as he spoke them.

A REVOLUTION IN BEING

Over the years I have met many writers — poets, playwrights and novelists — some internationally renowned; the ones we knew best were Hemingway, Williams, Steinbeck, Sandburg, and Elliott Paul (if you could include him in this rather elevated category). Many were close personal friends, including Carl Sandburg, Keith Wheeler, James Wellard, Pat Frank. Is there a common denominator? Something they all have that most other people do not? If there is, it is too elusive to define. Somerset Maughan and Eudora Welty both wrote superb short stories, but could any two people be less alike? And neither of them was at all like Katherine Anne Porter. Carl Sandburg with his guitar would sing all night — as long as the beer held out — and sleep on the couch at dawn; the poet of the disenfranchised and the unemployed, he was a populist, a romantic for whom Abraham Lincoln was the ultimate hero. How different he was from Nelson Algren with his drug- and crime-related Chicagoans, his jazz musicians! And they in turn from Steinbeck's Okies, victims of the Depression and the Dust Bowl, and the engaging petty criminals of Tortilla Flat! But then, perhaps this shows not the difference between the writers but between the times in which they lived: the hobo culture of the early 'twenties, the exodus west by drought-stricken farmers in the 'thirties; then the drug culture, no longer individualistic but organized, without a gleam of hope.

I was on a radio programme in 1957 with Nelson Algren whose book, *The Man with the Golden Arm*, and mine, *Bolero*, had just been published. At that time advertising billboards everywhere proclaimed, "There's a Ford in your Future". We were being interviewed by Studs Terkel and Algren remarked that for the characters in his novel there was no Ford in their futures!

True indeed. Yet my sons today cannot imagine a time in the United States of America when people actually starved to death in the big cities. Aside from private charity, political-boss handouts, or begging in the streets, there was really nowhere for a jobless man or woman to turn. No social security, no medical care. No old-age pensions. Inefficient and bureaucratic as the present social and medical services may be, they are vastly better than the humiliation, desperation and hopelessness they have replaced.

INTERLUDE

My father-in-law, after working in a bank for thirty-five years, the latter part as vice-president, received a gold watch and at the age of fifty found himself unemployed and unemployable among millions of younger men looking for work. He survived, thanks in some measure to a small insurance policy, but many of his contemporaries were not so fortunate.

During the depth of 1930s Depression we were living and working in Spain. But before we left Chicago, on my way home from the American Medical Association on North Dearborn Avenue, I used to pass a line of men wearing good overcoats, shoes and hats — everything from brokers to bankers — waiting for the old county jail (no longer in use) to open so they could get a bunk for the night. Failing that they slept under the Michigan Avenue bridge, wrapped in newspapers. In weather that was below zero.

Now, in 1985, under the Administration of Ronald Reagan, middle-class people who are unable to fill out the requisite bureaucratic papers are once again sleeping in doorways in New York. Soup kitchens are being opened again by the churches, and family farms are being auctioned off.

PART V

HERE AND THERE

Chapter 24

CHANGES IN SCENE

THE walk-on part I have played now for over fifty years has
been performed with an enormous and ever-changing cast of
characters in almost every country on the globe. Backdrops
include the Nile, the Amazon, the Congo, the Danube, the Ira-
waddy, the Yangse, the Moldau, the Volga, the Mississippi; the
Victoria Falls, Iguazu (where Brazil, Paraguay and Argentina
meet), and Angel Falls (in Venezuela), all more beautiful than
the renowned Niagara; the Himalayas (seen but not scaled from
Kashmir and Nepal), the Andes at Machu Pichu, Mount Kenya
and Mount Kilimajaro (partly climbed), the active volcanoes
of Hawaii, the Philippines, the North Island of New Zealand,
and Mount Fujiyama of Japan.

Islands have always enchanted my husband and me. Ever
since our first peasant house perched on the hills of Mallorca
we have tried, and usually managed, to visit the islands in the
region where assignments took us. And so to Sicily, Crete, Tahiti,
Moorea (which seemed to me as Tahiti must have been a century earlier), the two Samoas, Fiji, the New Hebrides, Mauritius,
New Caledonia, even the small isle at the southernmost tip of
New Zealand, Stewart Island. While we were teaching at a university in Puerto Rico, we visited all the islands of the Caribbean: St Lucia, Antigua, St Vincent, St Kitts and Nevis, Martinique, Haiti, and the Dominican Republic, and we spent a year
in Cuba observing Castro's revolution.

The difference between places you know and places you visit
is the difference between friends and acquaintances. We know
the Pyrenees through skiing, walking, and driving — we used to
ski at Font Romeu in France and L'Escalles in Andorra, and
drive from the Mediterranean to the Atlantic coast at San Jean

de Luz — in a way we will never know the Andes or the Himalayas, or for that matter the Swiss Alps. And we know the islands where we have lived — Puerto Rico, Mallorca, Cuba, Maui, the South Island of New Zealand — as we will never know those we have loved to visit, such as the Seychelles, the Ionian islands, Sicily, or Taiwan.

Although over the years we have stayed in hundreds of hotels, *pensions*, furnished flats, ranging from the most simple and economical to the most elaborate and expensive, we have had very few homes, a home being defined as a place where you have your possessions around you and to which you return after your travels. Thus defined our homes have been: the peasant house at Genova, in Mallorca; the *"atico"* in Madrid on the Plaza Atocha (bombed early in the Spanish Civil War while my husband was flying to Barcelona to see his newborn son, at an hour when otherwise he might well have been there); the big house at Evanston, Illinois (for almost thirty years); and, in a certain way, the little New Zealand house at Sumner, near Christchurch, to which we returned for many years. And now our house high in the hills above the Spanish town of Javea.

There are intermediate homes — somewhere between friends and acquaintances: the house on the Philippine island of Dumaguete, forty yards from the beach, when we taught at Silliman University; the flat in Doshisha University at Kyoto; the house up in the hills of San German, Puerto Rico, when we taught at Interamericana University.

I used to think I "knew" certain cities — Paris, Rome, Madrid, Chicago, for instance — but except for certain central areas that remain familiar, like Saint Germaine de Près, the Plaza Mayor, or Michigan Avenue Bridge, I feel like a stranger when I return on a visit.

Two houses that qualify only partially as homes were those at Collioure in France and at Arlington, Virginia, in the United States, because my husband, in both cases caught up in a war, could only visit me and the children there. Les Balettes in Collioure, a huge studio jutting out over the rocks so that you looked at the sea as though you were on a ship, was occupied in the earlier part of this century by Derain, Matisse, and Cézanne at various times, and the small hotel there was where the poet

Antonio Machado, a refugee, ill and almost penniless, was cared for by Madame Quintana, the proprietor, until his death. So the greatest Spanish poet of the Twentieth Century is buried at Collioure on French soil.

When we lived at Les Balettes, which was close to the Spanish border, my husband would visit us when he came out to buy supplies for the Madrid bureau and make uncensored telephone calls to the London office. As I had the necessary credentials as a journalist, I could occasionally return to Spain with him, leaving our two sons with my mother, and with Jeanette, our housekeeper-cook, who called the baby, Peter, "ma prune en sucre" (my sugar-plum).

We moved to Virginia before America's entry into the Second World War, when Colonel "Wild Bill" Donovan asked my husband to be his deputy as Co-ordinator of Information, an innocuous-sounding title for what was to become the O.S.S. which in turn fathered the C.I.A. My husband was sent to England as liaison with the P.W.E. (Political Warfare Executive) stationed in the Duke of Bedford's estate at Woburn Abbey. We didn't see him again until the tide had turned and the Allied forces were pushing into Germany. Although I knew about many of the colourful aspects of his life at Woburn, where strange animals (like white deer from China and long-necked geese brought by British gunboats from the Dowager Empress's park during the 1910 revolution, and rare species from the Czar's hunting-grounds brought over during the Russian revolution) wandered freely, I was never told of the official activities there. Only now, after more than thirty years' silence under Official Secrets restrictions, is much of this information coming out in now-it-can-be-told books. The Bedford estate has since become a "Stately Home" tourist attraction, complete with zoo and toy railway. Not far distant was the famous decoding centre where cryptographers broke the German code known as "Ultra".

During the years my husband was overseas I lived with my two sons (our third son was born much later) and the ever-faithful Martine, our housekeeper, in a white "Dutch Colonial" cottage in Arlington, Virginia, a small house with a large garden surrounded by a seven-foot box hedge which had formed part of the hedge of an estate long since subdivided. I worked in Washington, D.C., as the Chief of the Iberian Division of the Board of Economic Warfare, an agency devoted to buying strategic minerals and other materials needed by the Allies (and to keep them out of the hands of the Germans). Among the diverse items purchased by our agents from neutral Spain and Portugal were tin, tungsten, cork, amblygonite, iron, sardines, and wool.

The boys attended a nearby school and began to speak with a slightly Southern accent, influenced by their many playmates in the neighbourhood. In the adjoining woodland they built a fort and a tree-house. Having grown up a pacifist, I shuddered at the belligerent tones of their games but I realized that in an atmosphere of war and war-talk among adults it was to be expected. One day I returned home from my office and when I opened the door was almost overcome by the overpoweringly scented air. The reason soon became clear. The children had been given a talk on civil defence and first-aid and had decided to practise what they had learnt. They had improvised a stretcher with brooms and a sheet, and for medicines had used — yes, all the French perfumes which my husband had brought me from Martinique!

Chapter 25

OUT IN THE WILD

SEEING an animal in a zoo is like visiting a person in prison. Even modern, landscaped zoos, where there are moats instead of bars, are like prison-farms where "trusties" are allowed more freedom of movement but are still prisoners. Animals in large "safari parks" may be better fed than those in the wild, and safer from predators (though not always from the worst kind, human poachers), but they are not free.

The best places to see free-ranging animals are Kenya, Tanzania, Southwest Africa, and Zaire, followed by South Africa and Zimbawe. In Nepal, in Sri Lanka, and in India we have gone out "hunting" on elephants, or horses, and in Tunisia on camels, to photograph wild animals. Actually, I never carry a camera because I find the experience of looking at and being looked at by, for example, a lion or a rhino is much more exciting than trying to fit him into a viewfinder before he moves away. You are always aware that you are in his territory, that you are an intruder. Pictures I carry in my memory are far more vivid than those in a photograph album. As we approached the alkaline lake in the hollow of the great Ngorongoro crater, thousands of flamingos rose into the sky like a pink cloud. At a waterhole in Namibia, two elephant youngsters entwined their trunks and swayed together like teen-age lovers. A family of lions under a thorn tree leisurely dined on their prey — a young antelope — father first, then mother, then children, without taking any notice of us until the great sire lifted his magnificent head and stared directly at me, a momentary contact that sent a thrill down my spine.

At a waterhole in Savo National Park under a full moon we watched a dramatic performance of a precise hierarchical nature. First of all came a family of elephants, showering one another with their trunks, an hilarious opening. Then they retired, but the huge male elephant remained behind until a rhinoceros emerged from the bushes, whereupon he made his exit with quiet dignity, as though to say, "I was going anyway". This was the cue for the rhino's wife and son to appear on the scene. After them came antelopes and gazelles, followed as a finale by a chorus of birds, first big ones like the secretary bird, then the smaller birds. Before the moon set, we had seen most of the animals in the area — and witnessed not a single dispute; it was as though they had all been given their parts and came on "in order of appearance", as they say in theatre programmes.

After many days of driving about the dusty plains in a Land-Rover (which our Masai driver called a "Rand Lover"), we finally saw a leopard. He was crouched on the branch of a tree, stalking something below in the tall grass. He crept silently along the branch, his eyes intent on a prey we could not see. Then he sprang, and in that split-second a springbok jumped up and bounded away. The leopard saw us. With easy nonchalance he strolled back to the tree and climbed again to the limb, clearly indicating that he didn't really care about that springbok, the veldt was full of them.

The common giraffe, the reticulated giraffe, the hartebeeste, the wildebeeste, the topi, the duiker, the klipspringer, the oribi, Grant's gazelle, Thompson's gazelle, Hunter's antelope, the golden jackal, the marsh mongoose, the bat-eared fox — such a wealth in number and variety of creatures, sometimes a few, but in the case of the antelopes seen in their thousands. Their world is increasingly dependent on human beings for survival, and on our laws concerning ecology, poaching and hunting. Hundreds of species have disappeared already. If, inadvertently or deliberately, mankind starts a nuclear war, our own species, as well as all the others, may follow them to extinction.

To observe free animals in Africa requires time and patience. We walked twelve miles through jungle in Zaire to see a female gorilla for about twenty seconds (a view of *us* apparently quite long enough for her!). We have driven for hours over bumpy grasslands, trying to avoid termite hills, hard as rock, on which the jeep can be overturned, without seeing anything more than a few baboons and many vultures. And in the jungles of Nepal, we spent days riding elephants in grass so tall it almost covered them, to find one tiger and one rhino (but riding the elephants was fun in itself. When we saw the rhino I leaned over and my head-scarf fell off. I told the mahout, who whispered something to the elephant, who daintily picked up the small scarf with his trunk and handed it back to me over his shoulder.) It is often feast or famine on these expeditions: almost nothing one time, then perhaps on an early morning, lions, giraffes, elephants antelopes of all kinds. At dawn and sunset the odds are always better.

On one occasion I was quite happy that there were no wild animals (or snakes). That was the night we were "lost" in the hills above Pelorus Sound, in New Zealand. We arrived at the small settlement of Havelock rather late in the afternoon and, as we had been driving all day, decided to go for a walk. The owner of the motel suggested a track which led up to the reservoir; it was about an hour's walk, he said, and easy to follow. He neglected to mention that at the bend of the river we should cross on stepping-stones and continue on the other side. We followed the riverbank, up and up; the going became harder and harder, then the path disappeared and we climbed up slippery stones. A waterfall. Lovely. But where was the reservoir? Must be farther up. The sun was setting and only the top ridges of the gorse- and scrub-covered hills were still light. We were not dressed for this sort of hiking. My stockings were torn, my legs and hands scratched and bleeding. We made our way to the top, thinking we might meet a road. Nothing. It was getting dark. We could not climb down again — there were sudden drops of twelve feet or so hidden by the tall bushes.

Peter had a lighter for his pipe so we made a small fire and watched the smoke going straight up into the evening sky. "Someone's bound to see it," we assured each other.

It was cold. I wore a light tweed suit. We kept the fire going with twigs and small branches, but were careful not to make it too big in case we started a brush fire. The moon came out. We were not really "lost". We knew exactly where we were: we could see the lights of Havelock and even hear the buzz of motorboats on the Sound. We kept busy feeding the little fire; we talked to keep from falling asleep. About midnight we heard

"*Halloo*"s from below, and we shouted back. But nothing happened. The moon went down and the night was colder than ever. When dawn came, we carefully put out the fire and started on our way down. About halfway we met our "rescuers". They had tried to find us during the night but since they were standing *below* the waterfall, our replies were inaudible! Meanwhile, the local police constable had checked our motel room, seen our passports and given out our names, so that "U.S. PROFESSOR AND WIFE MISSING IN PELORUS HILLS" appeared in the New Zealand papers.

After a bath and a few hours' sleep we were refreshed and ready for the fine breakfast the motel-owner's wife had prepared for us. And except for the scratches were none the worse for our adventure.

Chapter 26

OF NOBLE SAVAGES

WHAT should we call them, the Igorotes of Luzon, the Negritos of Malaya, the Pygmies of Zaire, the Australian aborigines? Terms like "natives", "savages", "primitives", "Stone Age" are derogatory or banal, and in any case to lump such peoples together is absurd for they have far greater differences than similarities. But we in our complicated modern society are fascinated by these simpler cultures, because we feel that they suggest how our own prehistoric ancestors lived.

One of the most spectacular views in the world is at Bantoc, high up in the mountains on the island of Luzon in the Philippines. For miles and miles in all directions you can see alpine slopes covered by carefully maintained terraces. The ricefields here have been in continuous cultivation since before the birth of Christ, and they still supply large quantities of rice (and, more recently, potatoes and onions) to the city of Manilla.

The Igorotes of Luzon are short and stocky, with the large chests typical of mountain people. The men wear no clothes except a G-string, and the women only a brief skirt. No shoes. They live in stone huts, without furniture, sleep on straw mats. It is bitterly cold thousands of feet up in the mountains. We wore our thickest clothes and heavy ski-jackets, with lined boots and gloves, and still found it hard to keep warm.

The Igorotes have never been conquered — not by the Spaniards who held the Philippines for centuries, nor by the Americans early in the present century, nor by the Japanese who took the islands in the Second World War, nor even by the present government of Manilla. They have their own laws, and unless an outsider is involved they carry out their own judgments.

191

HERE AND THERE

From dawn to sunset they toil unceasingly. The terraces must be shored up by rocks to prevent erosion; the rice must be planted, cultivated and harvested. In the thin cold air, the rain and fog, they work for a subsistence living. They carry huge gunnysacks on their heads down the mountain slopes to places on the road where trucks can collect their produce.

My husband was allowed to attend a meeting of elders at night. Sitting on the cold stone round a small fire of twigs, they debated an important issue: whether or not they should have a holiday the following Tuesday, which was a national holiday throughout the Philippines, the birthday of Riscal the national hero of Independence. A decision was made after much thoughtful discussion. They would declare a holiday. They all bowed to one another and to my husband and trudged out into the darkness to their unheated stone huts.

A granddaughter of one of the elders, educated by French nuns in a convent below Bantoc, asked if she could accompany us back to Manilla. A handsome girl with red cheeks and big black eyes, she was studying medicine; when she was a doctor, she said, she would go back to serve her people. I wonder if she will.

While the Igorotes must be the hardest-working people in the world, the Pygmies of Zaire never work at all. They have no possessions, no clothes, no homes, no obligations, no debts, few responsibilities and fewer problems. They hunt with poisoned arrows and trade their kill with settled tribesmen for bananas, pineapples, manioca and vegetables. They wander freely through an enormous national park the size of Belgium, where they are the only people permitted to hunt and fish.

With the consent of their headsman, we spent a day with them on a hunt. It was difficult to keep up with them, as they darted along streams, slipped through bamboo thickets, vine-tangled jungle and cathedral-like forests where the branches met high overhead. We would tread silently, then suddenly be startled by amazing sounds — shrieks, roars, or shrill piping. A gazelle would dart ahead of us, and with a resounding *ping* an arrow aimed by an invisible hunter high up in a tree would drop the animal in its tracks. With the bigger animals, the first arrow paralyzed, then the other hunters completed the kill.

OF NOBLE SAVAGES

The largest Pygmy was the size of a six-year-old boy, the women smaller than the men. They all looked wizened, scrawny, underfed, and dirty, even the young mothers whose doll-like babies were carried in a sling of reeds on their backs. The families construct tunnel-shaped, temporary huts (for they are always on the move) of leaves and branches, less substantial than the tree nests of the neighbouring gorillas.

We watched the hunters make a fire of twigs, then heat the poison roots and catch the drops of poison in a plantain leaf into which they dipped their arrows. Now they were fully prepared for the next hunt. It was time for the ceremonial dances. With the old men and women who held the babies, a drummer who also rattled gourds, a flute player, and an ancient man who banged a stick on a hollow log, we sat in the outer circle.

The equatorial sun was high overhead, and although the day was cool when we started off that morning (at three thousand metres above sea-level), we now felt uncomfortably hot. There were four dances: the hunting dance, when the Pygmies mimed the hunt we had just seen; an elephant dance, at the end of which the dancer, miming an elephant, first attacks, then, wounded, slowly succumbs to his captors; a monkey dance, in which the Pygmies scurried up tree-trunks, swung from limbs, and made all the gestures of chimpanzees, then roared and threw sticks about just like the gorillas that lived nearby; as a finale came the wedding dance, in which the young men alternately chased and were chased by the young women, all this accompanied by a shuffling, stamping and kicking step encircling the small fire. The performance went on hour after hour and the Pygmies showed no sign of fatigue. Their only "props" were the stick that the elephant dancer used as a trunk and, for the wedding dance, garlands of leaves and flowers worn by the young women. Some of the babies were crying by now and could not be pacified by their grandmothers and grandfathers, who were unable to suckle them. One infant, just able to walk, staggered out towards the dancers and was snatched back, screaming hysterically, by an older child.

I was beginning to feel dizzy with the heat, the pounding and screeching noise, and increasingly aware of the many miles we had to cover on foot to regain our base. We were offered palm oil "wine", an extremely potent concoction, which after a few sips left us hotter and thirstier than ever. That song from *My Fair Lady* kept going round and round in my head: "I Could Have Danced All Night"; the Pygmies could and very well might dance all day and all night as well. The sun was setting by the time we returned to the lodge at the end of the long sinuous path through the tropical jungle.

In recent years, we were told, the Pygmies have been trading the meat and skins from their hunting expeditions for marijuana and palm wine, and substituting them for food, so they are now suffering from diet deficiencies. Whereas tribes of Pygmies once extended throughout central and southern Africa, their numbers have dwindled from thousands to hundreds. Since they are nomadic, they have no schools or hospitals, no churches, no police, no taxes, no social security. Their religion is animistic, a belief in spirits. When a man dies, his son leans over his body in order to catch his last breath, which will then enter the son's body and endow it with the father's strength and wisdom.

I suppose in time the Pygmies will become merely a "tourist attraction", selling their bows and poisoned arrows and flimsy musical instruments on the steps of the government-run lodge, performing their dances to entertain visitors, just as has happened in other parts of the world. Ugly (to our eyes), but unwarlike and (as yet) unacquisitive, they seemed to me to deserve something better from what we like to call civilization.

Zaire is one of the largest and richest countries in Africa, magnificent in a scenic sense, with the great Congo River (source of the White Nile), active volcanoes, forests and jungles, elephants, gorillas, every kind of gazelle, hippos, birds — and, in the south, valuable minerals like uranium, gold, bauxite, as well as diamonds, silver, tin, tungsten — and oil. Yet when we visited it in 1980, it was a country that had utterly collapsed. What infrastructure the Belgians left had virtually disappeared. In some respects this was worse than none at all. Except in Kinshasa (formerly Leopoldville) and Goma, there was no running water, no electric light, no telephone or post; the roads were a network of potholes, usually flooded. In the Volkswagen minibus in which we travelled, we took besides the driver a mechanic with a selection of spare parts and an enormous drum of petrol.

OF NOBLE SAVAGES

Arriving at a handsome lodge by a lake, we were assured by the Belgian housekeeper that although the normal water-supply was not working, her "boys" would bring hot water in buckets for our baths. After a long dusty day it sounded wonderful. Half an hour later two sturdy lads rushed into the bathroom and poured steaming water into the bathtub — without putting in the plug!

Because of a lack of petrol, air travel was chancy, to say the least. Intending passengers were taken to the airport when it was rumoured there would be a plane, then left there, sometimes for six or seven hours before departure. It was not unusual for an Air Zaire plane to arrive at a place quite different from its scheduled destination.

Three of the most remarkable women I have ever known were three nuns who were running a clinic school in the most remote and inaccessible mountain region. We visited them several times, and on the last occasion found they had just completed the almost unbelievable ordeal of innoculating all the local children, over two thousand, against poliomyelitis, during a period of sixteen hours. The youngest sister had brought the serum by jeep from a town fifty miles away via a hazardous mountain road, and since there was no refrigeration it had to be used at once. Members of a nursing order, they came from Navarra in Spain. Hardworking, cheerful, devout but not sanctimonious, these three women had, over some twenty years, created a centre to which the entire region looked for help and advice. We were shocked to learn that the government made them pay "import duty" for the milk-powder provided by U.N. agencies. When we left we took their letters to post on our return to Spain. A Dutch friend, on hearing our story of the nuns, brought it to the attention of "Caritas", a Catholic charity in Holland. Today, the nuns have a completely furnished clinic with its own electric generator.

Our driver, "Coeur de Lion" (Lion-Hearted), was well named. A short, sturdy, black man, a former prize-fighter, he converted frustrations and problems into challenges. Confronted by a six-foot-deep puddle, he drove the minibus along the steep embankment at an angle of forty-five degrees, without slackening speed, while we held our breath and closed our eyes. Once some villagers, hoping for a small toll charge, put up a barrier of sticks.

"Illegal!" he shouted, and simply drove straight through it. He had friends everywhere. He carried letters for some, photographs of weddings and baptisms for others (taken many months earlier and developed in town), or packages of cakes which he had picked up in one village and would hand to relatives in another distant one.

We stopped at tea and coffee plantations where he had friends who supplied us with drinking water, a most precious commodity, in very short supply, and usually bananas and pineapples, all amidst much laughter and camaraderie. The owners and managers of these estates were mostly Lebanese or Greeks; each estate was as far as possible self-sufficient, like a medieval village.

Chapter 27

LEADING A DOUBLE LIFE

SPRING. Summer, Early autumn, Spring. Summer. Early autumn. That was our year. During most of the 1970s we had two homes. One in Spain. One in New Zealand. When we were asked where we lived we would have to pause before replying. Where *did* we live?

For over a decade before that we had lived and worked in the subtropical Caribbean where we completely forgot about anything called winter. There were no hot and cold seasons, just wet and dry; no blooming and burgeoning, no autumn leaves, no sense of renewal.

We had visited New Zealand and Australia during an academic leave, and when an exchange professorship in New Zealand at the University of Canterbury, in Christchurch, was offered to my husband, we accepted it happily. And when retirement loomed on the horizon, as it must to all of us, we considered returning. There were difficulties, of course. Did we really want to jettison our past, our family and all our old friends, to live, literally, at the far end of the world, practically at the South Pole? (The U.S. polar operation, code-named Deep Freeze, is indeed supplied and manned from Christchurch.)

And there was an earlier, deeper love. Spain. Where we had lived for many years, the all-important young years, and where our two older sons were born. And where everyone could visit us — not only could but did. One summer we had, all told, forty-one visitors to stay between May and October; not, I may add, at one time.

So we bought a house on the Mediterranean coast in Spain, rented a house above the Pacific Ocean in New Zealand, and thus began a double life, combining the best of both worlds. No winter. We both grew up in the Middle West and if we never endured another season of cold, sleet, slush and bitter winds, it would be fine with us. This new way of life was not as extravagant as it sounds. With the exorbitant rise in prices all over the Caribbean, the cost of living in New Zealand, even including air fares, was no more than living in, say, Puerto Rico or Jamaica. We missed the warm Caribbean waters, snorkling among the coral and the tropical fish; no use pretending we didn't.

Physically there was a striking resemblance between our two homes. Both were high, high up, looking down on a sea, a town, and to one side a range of mountains. From our two sun-decks at Sumner, a coastal suburb of Christchurch, we could see the estuary of the Avon and Heathcote rivers, the sandspit of New Brighton, and the vast reaches of the Pacific. Away to the west rose the snow-covered Southern Alps, and below, closer at hand, the city. In Javea, where we still live, we have orange groves and vineyards, the tiled roofs of villas, and beyond, the blue Mediterranean; to the west the town of Javea, the Montgo, a solitary peak where Greek and Carthaginian ruins have been found, and and then range after range of grey and mauve mountains, not formidable except to motorists. Both houses had gardens; both had breath-taking views, and both sites could be very windy at times: an unimpeded vista means you are not sheltered from wind — you pays your money and takes your chance.

To the casual observer, the resemblance between the two places ends here. But we are no longer casual observers. True, no two countries could be more unlike socially and politically than New Zealand and Spain. New Zealand is possibly the most egalitarian, democratic and free nation in the world. Spain was in those days still a dictatorship. In New Zealand there is great social mobility; in Spain, even today, tradition is still powerful, the class structure apparently impregnable.

Nevertheless, there are similarities. Most New Zealanders and most Spaniards like Americans; in fact, there are times when I think they are the only people who do. Certainly not the Australians. In the 'fifties they were still thankful because we had saved them from the Japanese, but the Vietnam war changed all that. I remember the daughter of an American newspaperman who had grown up in Sydney and graduated from the university telling me she hated to go to parties because she seemed to be held personally responsible for whatever the Pentagon had been doing recently. Many New Zealand students opposed the war too but we found they didn't hold it against the few American students and professors in their midst. And in Spain, though young intellectuals generally feel that the U.S. upheld the Franco régime and they resent the military bases, our military profile is so low (our servicemen wear mufti in Madrid) that individual Americans are accepted as they have always been — as individuals. They are certainly inoffensive as tourists, compared with the more blatant Europeans.

There are other things that Spain and New Zealand have in common. The family survives in both places. The generation gap exists but only as a shallow ditch. I felt that there was less of a gap between our friends and their offspring than there was between our friends and *their* parents, in both countries! Some of the differences — the matter of class, for example –- are more apparent than real. A well-educated New Zealand woman, after meeting a friend of mine, a distinguished novelist, in a public library where they were both doing research, told me approvingly that the writer was "of good working-class stock", oblivious of her inverted snobbery. On the other hand, the "First Four Ships" that brought pioneer settlers to Christchurch little more than a hundred years ago long constituted a *Mayflower*-type of society, and families of the early "runholders" (whose sheep-runs were measured by the square mile) have shown a talent for survival. But if New Zealand is not the classless society it has sometimes been represented, it is probably still the fairest and most decent one on earth.

Indeed, years before we had seen New Zealand, my parents visited it and my father came back with glowing accounts of the natural beauty of the countryside, convinced that it was "the only place in the world where you don't have to feel sorry for anyone", as there was neither great wealth nor poverty. Things have changed somewhat since then, and New Zealand which was once the most advanced nation in terms of social security has fallen behind in recent years.

And what of the Arts? *Culture*? During the 'seventies the Madrid theatre revived and blossomed, with brilliant and original productions of new and old plays, many of them obliquely critical of authority or quietly satirical. The Prado Museum may well be the greatest art museum in the world. Madrid gets all the great musicians, the symphony is good, and even in Alicante you can hear the best string quartets and occasionally a soloist. When we yearn for theatre in English a couple of hours' flight takes us to London. In Christchurch at that time we found concerts, choirs and choruses, plays directed by the late Shakespearean director and mystery-novelist Ngaio Marsh. Except for visiting artists, most of the theatrical and musical activity was of a voluntary/amateur nature; almost everyone we knew seemed to be involved in something. Amateur standing was the thing in rugby football, in music and in theatre. So most of the young people who wished to work professionally would go away to England, Europe or North America. They still do, but there have been changes. Professional theatre is now established in a modest way, the national symphony orchestra and ballet are excellent, and many of the world's best performers include New Zealand in their touring circuits.

Friends and neighbours: On our hill in Sumner we had nearby a music critic and his English wife (who received all the latest records as soon as they were released, so in that respect we were very avant garde and "with it"), a world-renowned paleontologist and his China-born American wife, the advertising manager of one of the newspapers and her rowing-champion husband, a travelling salesman (or, as they put it simply, "a traveller"), and an American city-restorer (Old Town in Chicago, Old San Juan) and her seventeen-year-old son. On our hill in Javea we could muster an Uruguayan diplomat, a young American writer and his wife, and many summer residents from Madrid, Paris and Brussels. And among our frequent visitors, our old, old friends from Madrid, Barcelona and Palma de Mallorca, all Spaniards whom we have known for over forty years.

In one other important respect the two places were alike. The so-called quality of life. Pure air, water, an undefiled atmosphere. Little or no crime, juvenile delinquency, or drug-abuse. This did not last much longer in either place, but it was a joy as long as it did. And in comparison with so many other parts of the world, basic living costs were low, food plentiful and relatively untainted by chemicals. Butter in New Zealand, olive oil in Spain, we thought them both cheap and good. Beef and lamb, vegetables, fruits in season, bread and milk were all cheap in New Zealand, as I remembered them; even in Spain they seemed dear to us. On the other hand, where but in Spain could you get good red wine for about seventy cents a bottle? New Zealand's now flourishing wine industry was still in its infancy when we lived there.

If you poke a stick through the globe from one hemisphere to the other, Christchurch and Madrid are just about opposite. Auckland and Seville have almost the same climate, so have the Southern Alps and the Guadarrama mountains. Like the *rias* of Gallicia, the sounds of Marlborough have endless inlets. And in both Spain and New Zealand there are vast areas in the interior where you can drive and drive (the roads are good) and see no one, except flocks of sheep and a shepherd with his dogs. The reasons are different but the impression is much the same. New Zealand has about three million people (and sixty-five million sheep) and is underpopulated. In the 'seventies, of which I write, parts of Spain were depopulated, the former inhabitants of deserted villages working in the factories of Germany and the hotels of London. Reforestation has taken place in both countries on a considerable scale. Like the early pioneers in the United States, the first European settlers in New Zealand exploited the land; after all, there was plenty more.

Until recently, and for over a decade, one of Spain's principal exports has been people, unskilled for the most part, to work in the industries of Europe. We encountered Spanish porters and bellhops in Helsinki, Stockholm and Oslo. During the same period New Zealand imported people, from Pacific Islanders to man the factories to academics from Britain (all but one of the professors in my husband's department at the University of Canterbury were graduates of British universities). But this is changing. Because of the general unemployment in Europe and the increasing mechanization of industries, many Spaniards have returned to Spain. It is not unusual to find at least one French-speaking waiter or barman in the most isolated village in the most remote mountain regions of Andalucia and Granada and that their children had attended French schools. For better or worse, the men who returned were no longer the almost illiterate peasants who had left; they had jumped into the Twentieth Century and taken their families with them.

New Zealand's ties with "the Mother Country" (even now, older people who have never set foot in England still sometimes refer to it as "Home") were sharply broken by Britain's decision to join the European Common Market. New Zealanders no longer have special status, working privileges, and the right of residence but are treated almost (but not quite) like foreigners. Worse was the economic blow to the wool, lamb and butter trade, which relied on the traditional export market to Britain. New Zealand used to think of herself primarily as part of the British Empire. A little remote, true, but the contacts were kept up through sport, the BBC, travel, and family visits and correspondence. There was a time during World War II when the Japanese were getting uncomfortably close, most of the New Zealand forces were away fighting in North Africa, and the Pacific Ocean was no longer a barrier but a highway. So the main harbours were mined and concrete bunkers that would not have stopped a determined boy scout troop appeared along the coast. The British Pacific Fleet lay at the bottom of the sea. Most New Zealanders remain convinced that only the U.S. saved them. For a brief time, then, New Zealand was made aware that it was a group of Pacific islands, close to Asia. But everyone soon forgot and went on with the same trade patterns they had always had, supplying food to the homeland. Hence Britain's entry into the E.E.C. meant rejection and a rude shock. For a time there was indignation. Understandable, for New Zealanders, including Maoris, had fought beside Britain with exceptional bravery and distinction in three wars — against the Boers, against the Kaiser, and against Hitler — as monuments in practically every town record. The New Zealand attitude to the "Pommies", as the British are called, has long been a love-hate relationship, still strong in New Zealand hearts, but to the British a matter of indifference.

In Spain, too, many are taking a second look at the country's relationship with the rest of Europe. Being accepted into the Economic Community is all very well, some economists warn, but take care or you'll find yourself the supplier of unskilled labour in place of the Algerians and Senegalese, while Spanish manufacturers will be unable to compete with German or French products. Signs of the times are newspaper advertisements for physics and chemistry professors wanted by universities in Venezuela, Peru and Ecuador. The salaries offered are better than those of Spanish universities, but the cost of living is higher in South America.

Tourism remains Spain's greatest industry, and greatest headache. There are about thirty-seven million tourists each year. Statistics are not wholly reliable as the figures include people who live near the French border and cross over briefly to buy gasoline (it is cheaper in Spain). Foreigners have taken over the beaches, the hotels, the high-rise apartments along the coast, often in national colonies of Germans, Hungarians (Benidorm), British (Marbella), French (everywhere), Dutch and Danes. Middle-class Spanish families who used to spend a month at the seaside can no longer afford it, as they cannot compete with the foreigners. So the invasion is fine for maids, workers in the building trades (the rate of building is astonishing), shopkeepers, and waiters, but hard on everyone else (like schoolteachers and civil servants). The infrastructure (a word Americans love to use) isn't quite up to the strain sometimes and things break down. But the miracle is that the breakdowns are temporary and short-lived. Water fails, electricity stops; then after a while everything works again. In some ways we were more secure five decades ago when we lived in a peasant house in Mallorca with our well, lamps, fireplace, charcoal stove, none of which ever failed. But by the end of each September the foreign invasion is over, and both Spaniards and permanent residents sigh a deep sigh of relief. The discothéques and bars close down, along with most of the restaurants, and life becomes normal again.

Although New Zealand is now having her own tourist boom, particularly from Japan and the U.S., when we lived there people seemed scarcely aware of the seventy thousand or so who then came each year from overseas. Most of them arrived in group tours to visit the thermal areas of Rotorua in the North Island and Mount Cook and the lakes and fiords of the South Island, spending little more than a week to do it. We used to see large numbers of Australians driving rental cars on the scenic routes (the current fashion is campervans). When a New Zealander sees a beer-can-littered picnic place he is apt to blame it on "those bloody Aussies"; I found New Zealanders (except perhaps the West Coasters, hard-drinking descendants of the goldminers) scrupulously tidy.

In Spain, as in New Zealand, the summer roads are dotted with hitch-hikers, pack on back, thumb pointing. They are of all nationalities. Guitars used to be standard equipment, but are no longer. Few of the youths have beards; as a rule their hair is trimmed and clean-looking. The girls wear shorts or minis, and seem unconscionably young. In New Zealand I remember these young people were mostly English, Scots, Welsh, Canadian, with an occasional Dane or German. I do not count the myriad students who hitch-hike to and from universities or are going camping during the holidays. (There are youth hostels all over, ranging from sloppy to spick-and-span, depending on the warden.) They had an effective grapevine — word was passed on that there was a job for a ski instructor at Coronet Peak, for treeplanters at Taupo, that someone needed a crew for a cruise yacht at Picton. They had been around, some of these youngsters: to Ceylon, Fiji, New Guinea, Samoa, New Caledonia, Afghanistan, Iran. Some were Jesus freaks, others Hari Krishma disciples, but most of them were just following the snow or the surf through the seasons.

In Spain the hitch-hikers are Europeans, with an occasional American. Their chances of getting temporary employment are dim and work-permits almost unobtainable, which seems hard until you remember that in the countries they come from foreigners have an even tougher time getting work, except for the most menial jobs. Besides, most of them are tourists, too, who are travelling in a way they find more entertaining than by scheduled buses and trains.

New Zealand has scenery. Spain has scenery and history. Sometimes together, as in the mountain villages of Andalucia — Ubeda, Baeza, Caravaca, where Greek, Roman, Carthaginian artifacts nestle amidst crumbling Moorish fortresses, or Cazorla where you can drive and then walk to the source of the Guadalquivir River and alone among rocky crags and crystal rivulets pretend you discovered it. You can live in courtly splendour in palaces now converted to *paradores,* where the timbered ceilings are twenty feet above your carved mahogany bed.

In New Zealand everyone enjoys the country. Everyone plays golf, surfs or skis, everyone who cares to. There seem to be mountains and beaches everywhere. As you fly over New Zealand, you see a golf course and a racecourse next to even the smallest towns. Every few miles along the highways there is a stopping place for picnickers, with a View, tables and benches, barbecue pit, sometimes a spring with drinking water. Camping grounds cater for tents and "caravans" (what Americans call trailers), have shower-rooms and toilets, and attractive sites, and cost a pittance. New Zealanders use and enjoy their outdoors; visitors are welcome to share it. Unfortunately this is not true of Spain. The facilities are for foreigners, not for Spaniards. They look upon *"los campings"* with amused disdain; why anyone should choose to be so uncomfortable, eat such unsatisfactory meals, dress in shorts when they are not young or well-built, passes all understanding. Only a few years ago the Spaniards regarded beaches as the places from which fishermen launched their boats. And if a Spaniard, of any class, cannot live in what he considers moderate comfort on his vacation he prefers to stay home. In our neighbourhood near Javea, the wealthy Spaniards with villas come with cars, maids, chauffeurs, open their places for a month, then close them for the rest of the year. A few families also spend Semana Santa (Holy Week) here. And gardeners and caretakers keep the villas and their gardens looking splendid all year round.

But for most Spaniards a visit for a couple of weeks to some relatives in a mountain village or seaside town is the closest they ever get to Nature. And when they return, they tell you that it is undoubtedly very healthful and that the children enjoy it, but how happy they are to get back to Madrid. Or Barcelona. Many prefer to stay in town and go to a football match and perhaps a bullfight if there is a *torero* they like. The cities of Spain have not been taken over by foreigners, although there are foreign enclaves in all of them, and some, like Toledo, have become museums through which armies of tourists march all summer. So, despite the coastal invasions, Spain remains Spanish; it has survived many other, less benign invasions.

HERE AND THERE

Not long ago my husband and I were invited to a party by some friends who live below us on the hill above Javea. Both from Ohio. The occasion was the visit of some old friends and former university colleagues; both of the visitors were Mississippians from the Delta, the husband an English professor who supplements his income by giving folk music concerts and lectures at weekends. The guests, about forty, came from all over the region, from Denia, from Jesus Pobre (yes, it does mean Poor Jesus), from Ifach, from the Port of Aduanas, and from next-door. At least one member of every couple was American; for instance, a Dane with an American wife, a Spanish girl with an American husband, all long-time residents of Javea. Most of us had never met before. People sipped their drinks of *sangria*; talk was desultory, snacks were passed around. Then Steve, our visitor, picked up his guitar and began to play and sing in such a low voice that everyone stopped talking to listen. Slowly the spell was cast. Steve sang almost as though he was alone, beginning with all the old favourites. "Barbara Allen" — "The Blue-Tail Fly" — "Where Have All the Flowers Gone?". People began to suggest songs: Sing "Eleanore Rigby". Sing "Black Is the Colour of My True Love's Hair". Sing "Greensleeves". Sing "John Henry". Steve knew them all. It went on and on. It was as if no one wanted the evening to end. Ever. Work songs. Spirituals. Peter-Paul-and-Mary songs. Everyone singing, listening, remembering. It was dawn when the party ended.

Later, thinking about it, my husband and I agreed on the nature of the spell — it was nostalgia. Most of us there were homesick. Not for a particular place nor even for particular people. It was something else. We were, for the time being, exiles far from the shores of our native land. But our homesickness was for a country that no longer existed, if it ever had. What we were really nostalgic about was our younger selves when Life was ahead of and not mostly behind us.

Chapter 28

WITH SPANISH FRIENDS
IN CHINA AND EGYPT

"Amigos Españoles" was the way we were greeted by Chinese guides, schoolteachers, factory-managers, commune directors, acrobats, dancers and schoolchildren, through their interpreters. We were the only Americans in our group of "Spanish friends", the first to visit China after the official visit of King Juan Carlos and Queen Sofia; but not, by any means, the first Spanish-speaking group, as countless Mexicans and Latin-Americans had preceded us. We were in China before Teng's historic visit to the United States, the exchange of ambassadors, the setting up of news agency offices, and the rush of salesmen of American products. (Coca-Cola, however, had preceded us.) And we were in Egypt during what looked like a breakdown in the negotiations between Sadat and Begin, before Carter's fresh initiative and the eventual peace agreement. In a sense, we visited both countries as Spaniards, though we carried U.S. passports. Certainly, in each country, we were told many things by our Spanish-speaking guides and interpreters they would not have said to Americans.

Besides my husband Peter and myself, our group consisted of four physicians and their wives, an industrial chemist and his wife, a commercial artist, a champagne manufacturer and his wife, a woman gynecologist, and two young girls who were laboratory technicians. We met for the first time in Barcelona and we'd come from all parts of Spain — Irun, Andalucia, Valencia, Madrid and Aragon. There, too, we met our tour director, a handsome and capable young woman who remained with us until our return. Renate Mau possessed excellent qualifications: she was tall and could be followed easily in a crowd; she was polite but firm with bureaucrats. Realizing the dangers that too-outspoken Spaniards courted in China then (possibly because of having to exercise care for so long at home under Franco, Spaniards had become overly critical abroad), she warned us before we left Hong Kong: "Be tactful. If there is something you don't like, tell me, not them." She retailed the unhappy fate of a West German group who had complained about the food and accommodation, and the delays, and who had simply been ordered to leave China within twenty-four hours. There was no appeal. Out they went.

Renate need not have worried about this group. We accepted everything — inconveniences, delays, changes in plans — with stoicism and tolerance, sometimes hilarity (which completely mystified the Chinese guides!). We were, or appeared to be, tireless, indefatigably good-humoured, determined to enjoy and appreciate every aspect of our Chinese adventure. We behaved as well-mannered guests, exemplary travellers. When we were told to arise at five-thirty, pack our baggage, have breakfast and be ready to be picked up by bus at six-thirty, we were all standing on the steps of the hotel on the dot. Often laughing. It was so un-Spanish it was comical — particularly for some of the women, who had never awakened before ten o'clock in their mature lives.

During our month in China, our accommodation rose from squalor to magnificence. In Canton we were housed in a hotel that had been an officers' barracks. Peter and I had a large, somewhat musty room with bath. The beds were frames with wooden slats covered by a two-inch-thick lumpy pad. Over this was a clean white sheet. No springs, no mattress, no top-sheet, no blanket, no bedspread. Fortunately, it was warm in Canton. We used the large, frayed bathtowels as covers, and slept. Since visitors do not drink the water, we all ordered bottled water; we were also supplied with huge vacuum flasks of tea, constantly replenished.

In Changsha the bed had a thin mattress, two sheets, a solitary blanket and a bedspread. The room was cleaner; you could see out of the windows. In Shanghai we were given an old-fashioned European type of hotel, where the father of one of our friends had stayed in the 1920s when he went to China in answer to a call from the League of Nations for doctors to help in a cholera epidemic. There our shabby-grand room looked out on the river, with its endless boat and barge traffic. The constantly changing scene was a delight until about three in the morning when the noise of the horns and the loudspeakers broke all decibel records. Whether the shouts were, "Get out of my way!" or "How is your mother-in-law's lumbago?", friendly, menacing or practical, we'll never know.

It was only in Shanghai that my resolve to be a docile and co-operative traveller almost broke down. A verbal confrontation was but narrowly averted. The Americans and the Russians were the villains in all the propaganda we endured in the course of sightseeing — the Americans were Imperialists and the Russians were their allies! But in Shanghai we were subjected to a doctrinal lecture. A local guide presented an hour-long history of Shanghai. He told about the Foreign Concessions, including the well-known notice on the bridge that says that no dogs or Chinese may cross (it was still there, as a reminder); he told us the whole story of Chinese humiliations and ill-treatment by the foreign devils. All true. Then he went on to give statistics of death by hunger and cold and to describe the misery of the people of Shanghai in the years before their liberation by Mao's Army. But what he did not mention was the Japanese Occupation under which these horrors had occurred. No mention of the Japanese invasion, of the bombings, or of Japanese atrocities. In fact, no mention of the war. You would have thought that everything before the Liberation was the fault of the Foreign Concessions. Damn it, I thought; if it weren't for us Imperialist Americans, Shanghai might still be under Japanese rule. I started to say something when I caught my husband's eye and noted the definite shake of his head.

Somehow Shanghai retained a certain European atmosphere. Whole sections of the city still had the villas and apartment houses typical of *fin de siècle* buildings in Vienna or Prague.

Our visit to Changsha was obligatory in those days — it was a Mao shrine. We visited Mao's house, saw the fading photographs of Mao's brother, his first wife, rather touching groups of young men, among them Mao, seated on hard wooden chairs in the simple room where we stood, presumably planning the

Revolution. In the large new museum the photographs had been culled and doctored to eliminate Russian colleagues.

But it was in Kweilin that the magic of China, the legendary beauty of scenes made familiar by vases, screens, paintings on silk and engravings came to miraculous life. It was all there: the river valley encircled by the strange round mountains that rose suddenly from the flat plain, the caves with statues and carvings thousands of years old, the monolithic shapes — an elephant, a tortoise — of rock formations seen from a distance. The fields were emerald, the skies mauve. The day we spent in a barge (pulled by a tug; the river was too low for the larger vessels) was an artist's delight, every turn of the river bringing another enchanting picture.

From our window in the well-appointed modern hotel we could see a little park, and a sort of belvedere in the middle of a lake. Through the dusk a few lights were reflected in the water. For once there was no opera, play or concert we were expected to attend. So we took a walk to the little pavilion on the lake. Students with books, young couples strolled past, trying not to stare too obviously. But there, as everywhere else in China, we and any other members of our group were of great interest. In particular, our clothes. When some of us visited the Friendship Shops, department stores especially set up for foreigners, crowds of several hundred curious Chinese gathered and waited for us to emerge (we felt like Hollywood movie-stars). An official-type woman kept telling them to move back, and they would retreat a few steps and then surge forward again. The same interest was evoked by our attendance at theatres or public monuments.

The dull anonymity of clothes in China at that time — blue or grey jackets and slacks for both men and women, all nine hundred million of them — no doubt explains the interest. At first we thought their clothes made them all look alike (as the Chinese in Hong Kong or Taiwan never did) then we began to see subtle differences within the sameness: whereas common soldiers had only two pockets in their jackets, officers and officials had four; our chief interpreter's jacket and trousers were tailored, made of good material, he wore a white shirt under his jacket, his socks were silk or nylon, his shoes of highly-polished black leather. Secretaries going to work on their bicycles looked cleaner and better groomed than the factory workers jammed into their buses. Sometimes you caught a glimpse of a freshly-starched blouse, and even, occasionally, a locket at the throat. I remember an episode in a secondary school we visited. We attended a mathematics class, a science class and then a class in music. Afterwards, while the teacher played the piano, two girls aged about thirteen or fourteen danced for us. They looked very graceful, even in uniform, and we all applauded loudly. One of them, I noticed, was wearing a gold chain round her neck. The girls bowed, clapped for us, and ducked into the corridor. When they returned for an encore, the chain had disappeared.

If, in accommodation, Canton was the nadir, then the new Hotel Peking was the zenith. An imposing structure facing a wide boulevard close to the central square where Mao's tomb was situated (and where a block-long line of people waited patiently to enter), this was where most of the official visitors (including President Nixon) were housed. It was up-to-date, well-furnished, comfortable, splendid in the bureaucratic style characteristic of Communist régimes everywhere. Some of the "modern" gadgets were unexpected. When you wanted to open the curtains you pressed a button and an electric motor purred while the curtains slowly chugged open. In a country where everything was done by hand, such mechanization was mystifying.

Unlike other hotels where we had stayed and where we were given a dining-room for ourselves (other rooms were for Party visitors from the provinces, Japanese delegations, German tourists and so on), foreigners, diplomats and government bigwigs all ate in one enormous room. And, at least for breakfast, each table seemed to provide a different cuisine. Our Spanish friends, who customarily have only coffee and rolls, were intrigued by the three eggs (cooked any way requested), the assortment of breads, rolls and cakes, the yogurt in china pots, the coffee, tea, mineral-water, and beer!

Although more lavish, the food at the Hotel Peking continued the uniformly high level found throughout China. The question that our Spanish friends always asked us before tasting a dish was, "Pica?" They would not eat anything highly spiced (as much of it was). The two culinary highlights were, of course,

Cantonese roast pig and Peking duck, each served by traditional restaurants in the respective cities; both lived up to their reputations as gourmet food *par excellence*. In both places our parties were given private dining-rooms — the buildings were rabbit warrens full of separate rooms — and the service was flawless, in the best "decadent capitalist" manner.

Even if patrons eschewed the highly spiced dishes, they were in no danger of malnutrition. At every meal we were given a dozen varied dishes: chicken and fish soups, shrimps, mushrooms, leeks, all sorts of seaweed-type vegetables, rice, spring rolls, combinations of pork with vegetables and noodles, cabbage, apples and pears, infinite cups of hot tea, bottles of beer and mineral-water. In each town there were regional dishes, usually varieties of seafood, vegetables and cakes. The service was invariably efficient, pleasant, and helpful (in contrast to that in the Soviet Union where — at least in Moscow and Leningrad — the staff seemed to delight in keeping diners waiting). We had long before learnt to use chopsticks and our Spanish friends picked up the custom quickly; one of the doctors (a surgeon, needless to say) became an expert and could handle even slippery noodles and tiny shrimps with ease.

When we returned home people asked: Were you free to see things? Could you go anywhere you wanted by yourselves? The only answer is: yes and no. No one ever stopped us from doing anything or going anywhere in the region where we were staying. But our days were scheduled from six in the morning until almost midnight. And all the items on the programme were things we wanted to see and didn't want to miss. So there was neither time nor opportunity to depart far from the planned itinerary.

One place we visited was a silk factory where the whole process from cocoons to finished silk and painted screens was carried out. The building, its machinery, heavy wooden looms, great iron cauldrons, and huge, dusty, ill-lit rooms looked like those old engravings of textile mills during the Industrial Revolution. Many of the young women were housed in dormitories not unlike those of New England's paternalistic factories in the 1880s. Everyone worked a six-day, forty-eight-hour week. To us it seemed a hard life, with little diversion or freedom, and we were surprised at the apparent cheerfulness of the workers and their air of well-being.

That was before we saw the farm labourers. Then we understood why, in comparison, the girls in the silk factory led lives of comfort and ease. "I really thought I would never survive," a teacher of English from the University of Shanghai, whom we met in a tea-house, told us. "After graduating from university I was sent to live with peasants in a rice-growing province. I developed malaria and dysentery from working waist-deep in the cold water. We only had kerosene lamps, but I was so exhausted at night I couldn't have read anything even if there had been enough light. The first year, I even *hoped* that I would die." Her thin, intellectual face softened. "But the peasants treated me like a daughter, saved delicacies for me, sent good reports to the village leaders about my work and my behaviour, so that, although I abhorred the primitiveness of the place — no sanitation, no privacy — I wept when I left them after almost three years."

She smiled. "Things are better now. The government realizes it needs the skills and knowledge of trained people. Today I am teaching in a high-school; I share a small apartment with three other women teachers; we can afford to travel sometimes to other parts of China. Perhaps. . ." she paused, "one day we will go to visit Hong Kong."

We saw primary schools and secondary schools, watched gymnastics, attended operas, plays, concerts, and — most exciting of all — displays of acrobatics. These displays simply defied belief; you held your breath and kept thinking: it's impossible! The acrobats seemed to disregard gravity. Instead of the usual roll of drums finale to the various acts, the climax of these feats was accompanied by soft music, the performers behaving as if there was "nothing to it", leaving us gasping.

Two things we wanted to see and didn't were a university and a hospital. In Shanghai we were taken to a special school for talented children — they included painters, musicians, dancers, even young (six-year-old) would-be architects and engineers building model bridges, aircraft and housing units. At every factory or school, park or historical monument, we were always welcomed by the director or manager and served hot tea (sometimes with cakes and nuts) while he explained the operations or the history of the place.

During the long bus trips covering hundreds of miles, we had ample opportunity to see agricultural China. Sometimes, as far as the eye could see, the landscape looked like a Bruegel painting, with peasants in heavy wooden yokes pouring water (or night-soil) from wooden buckets into the furrows. Everything was being done by hand much as it had been done for a thousand years. We were shown a tractor plant in Shanghai but we never saw one in use. On the rivers, men pulled barges by ropes from the bank, only occasionally did we see a horse used. Men and women hauled heavy wagons and carts, walking between the shafts like draft animals — often with someone else pushing from behind.

City transport was by crowded bus and by bicycle: seemingly millions and millions of bicycles. Except in Peking where the diplomats and high government officials resided there were almost no automobiles, and when a rare one passed the occupants usually had the inner curtains drawn and could not be seen.

If transport, housing and agriculture were antiquated, there was one compensation: food. Everyone looked well-fed. In the cities, minute stalls sold hot soups, rice and noodles combined with fish or chicken and served in bowls; people ate standing or crouched on the pavement. Peasants sold vegetables, fruit and sweets. Walking through the crowded streets of any city one found the most prevalent smell was that of cooked cabbage. The children in particular, seen in groups being led to kindergarten or primary school by their teachers, looked well nourished, warmly dressed, and happy.

We wanted to see a commune and, finally, we were told we would visit one. It was more than a hundred miles outside the city, which meant a long, dusty, bumpy trip in a fairly new Volkswagen bus. The driver kept stopping to ask directions. He followed little side-roads and when we kept seeing the same square several times it was clear that he and we were lost. Eventually, a young man joined the bus and there was a long argument about how to get to our destination. Again we went in circles. At last the young man pointed to a very small hand-painted sign and an unpaved lane took us to the commune.

The director and his two assistants had been waiting for us for hours and seemed relieved that we had arrived. We were welcomed into a meeting-room, served tea, and lectured on the commune. A large-scale map showed the location of the various facilities: the school, the community centre, the clinic, the units for ducks, pigs and poultry. We were taken to the clinic — I walked in the door and turned back; the smell was overpowering. Later the doctors in our party told me they were shocked at the dirt and lack of sanitation. They had seen some acupuncture performed, which they found very interesting as it is becoming popular in Spain. The commune had one young doctor, the others were paramedics.

We were escorted through the buildings where the pigs were kept, shown the chickens and their large feed mixer, the pond for the thousands of ducks, but we were hurried back to the bus without seeing the housing for the commune members or anything that would give us an idea of their lifestyle.

Physical fitness was given great emphasis everywhere. If you looked down to the courtyard of any hotel in China at around six in the morning you would see hundreds of people doing calisthenics, sometimes in unison with a leader calling out the movements, sometimes each person apparently doing his or her own thing. At one secondary school we watched the mid-morning exercises of the entire school, including the teachers. Many of the exercises were the sort I remember we used to have in gym classes in the United States, but some were quite different. At the order of the instructor, all closed their eyes, pressed the bridge of the nose with forefinger and middle finger; they then pressed the back of the neck, and finally their temples. "It is good for relieving eyestrain," our guide explained. I hope it worked, as the light in many of the classrooms and in the factories where fine embroidery and delicate painting were done, seemed to me quite inadequate.

The China of fable, Marco Polo's Cathay, still pervades Peking. The vast Forbidden City with its reminders of many dynasties, the Summer Palace where you ride in a boat on the artificial lake surrounded by painted pavilions, the Ming tombs approached by an avenue flanked by enormous stone animals, but, above all, the Great Wall and its apparently endless encircling defence of the Chinese Empire, all these wonders give the visitor a *déjà vu* feeling. We've all read the books and seen the movies; we remember the scrolls, the paintings, the bronzes, the ceramics, with their wealth of detail. Yes, this is how it must have been.

Most of our fellow-visitors comprised large groups of Chinese from other provinces: schoolchildren, students (often art students), delegations of Party leaders. Next most numerous were Japanese businessmen, salesmen and tourists. After the ubiquitous Japanese came French, Mexicans, and small numbers of Germans, Scandinavians, Canadians, each with an appropriate guide.

No matter how much time one spent in China it would still be insufficient to allow one to absorb the vastness, the unique combination of grandeur and delicacy in the architecture, the sensitive use of colour and the intricate motifs on ceilings, walls and archways on such an enormous scale.

We were given booklets describing exhaustively the ancient history of palaces and monuments. But only in one of the museums outside Peking did we find a photograph of Sun Yat-sen, the founder of modern China, and his handsome wife, the elder sister of Madame Chiang Kai-shek. (It reminded us of Czechoslovakia where we found Benes and Mazaryk had disappeared completely from the history books, and the Museum of the Revolution in Moscow where Trotsky had been painted out of photographs and group portraits.) The great National Museum has gigantic collections of everything from ceramics, scrolls and tapestries to weapons, but some individual works of art in the Taipei Museum in Taiwan are probably superior. At least they are better presented, and more securely guarded; we were in Taiwan when the Cultural Revolution was raging on the Chinese mainland and youthful fanatics were smashing priceless Ming vases.

Despite their drab dress, it was not hard to imagine some of the Chinese clad in the magnificently embroidered robes of the old courtiers, moving about the manicured gardens or standing in the rich anterooms of the throne, whereas in Egypt none of the Egyptians in their heavy robes looked anything like the beautiful, smooth-skinned, graceful figures pictured in the ancient tombs. Perhaps there were a few. The bellhops in the Hotel Mena at Cairo, dressed or rather undressed differently, could well have modelled for the archers and attendants of Tutan-khamen shown in the frescoes. There is a vast time difference, of course; the great works in Egypt are several thousand years earlier than the high peaks of Chinese culture.

The Pharoahs were intent on immortality and they achieved it, although not as they envisaged. No ancient palace or municipal edifice survives — not even ruins of the sort that exist in Iran. Yet we know the most minute details of their lives because they are pictured in the tombs, carved and painted, wrought into gold ornaments. We know how they dressed: was the climate hotter then or is the current surfeit of robes and wraps a Moslem introduction? The camel-drivers wore what looked like far too many layers of clothing in the broiling heat, though I have been told they keep you cool. Surely the ancient Egyptians with only short miniskirts on the men and diaphanous gowns on the women must have been cold when the breeze swept in from the Nile at night.

As for the Moslem religion, our Spanish friends (a smaller and younger group than those in China) were equivocal in their feelings about it. The Moslems conquered almost all of Spain and remained in some areas for seven hundred years, mixing with the Iberian-Roman-Celtic-Greek-Carthaginians already there. But this fact is never acknowledged, except by scholars. After the expulsion of "the Moors" and of the Jews, many Moslems and Jews, converted to Christianity, remained, and the Holy Inquisition set about the task of eradicating any who secretly practised the proscribed faiths.

All Spaniards today take great pride in the magnificent architectural works left by the Moslem conquerors, such as the Alhambra and the Generalife in Granada, the mosque in Cordoba. In practically every city there are evidences of their occupation, particularly Toledo and Seville, everywhere except in the north of the country. The Spanish language is filled with Arabic-derived words, and most of the towns along the Mediterranean coast beginning with "Al" or "Beni" (meaning "the" and "son of") are named after Moorish chieftains. Many of the vegetables, fruits and creature-comforts were brought to Spain from Persia. Yet, apart from the two young men from Seville in our group, all the Spaniards referred to "them', not "us", when speaking of Spain's Moslem past. These young men, one a high-school teacher and the other a librarian, did speak of "our ancestors" in comparing the mosques and fortifications, the palaces and gardens of Egypt with those of Spain, which they extolled as far superior. Both men were good Catholics.

Our Egyptian guides, all Moslems, talked about the wonders of Arab workmanship and architecture in a way that blurred the distinctions between Egyptian and Arabian. Cairo is a city where many religions are practised. We visited the Coptic church and the beautiful Coptic museum, an ancient synagogue, several magnificent mosques, a Roman Catholic church and a Baptist chapel. The widely credited myth that "everyone speaks English" was dissipated for us one morning when a whole series of taxi-drivers shook their heads to indicate ignorance of where we wanted to go; until, eventually, someone pointed to a cab across the square where the driver, black and Sudanese, understood us.

There are some places in the world that cannot be appreciated from photographs or even the best documentary film. Nothing had prepared us for the sense of grandeur, in scale and in time, that we experienced at the Pyramids and the Sphinx, or on seeing the temples and statues at Karnak and Luxor, the Valley of the Kings, the mountain-high figures removed to safety when the Aswan dam was built, and where the frescoes could have been painted yesterday.

At night, at the Pyramids, as the narrator related their history, one after another of the vast monuments was gradually flooded with light and then faded away into the darkness. There were thousands of people sitting around us, yet the sonorous voice and the subtle, changing illumination gave the sensation of witnessing in solitude the passing of milleniums under the stars of the desert. The same atmosphere was true of Karnak: by day, awe-inspiring; by night, magical. And sailing on the Nile in the dhows, once away from the city, one felt the whole scene belonged to antiquity.

Although the Tutankhamen exhibit was away in the United States when we visited Egypt, the enormous National Museum in Cairo contains more than enough art and artifacts from the tombs to mount dozens of equally dazzling displays. Dusty and rather unsystematically organized, it is filled with marvels of ancient craftsmanship — all the objects destined to accompany the Pharoahs to the hereafter. Every detail of their daily lives can be seen — their wars, hunts, worship; what utensils they used, the chariots they drove, the jewels they wore. In the tomb of Rameses II there is a painting that reminds one of the Sistine Chapel: on one hand are shown all the ruler's good works, on the other his bad ones — portrayed vividly for the Final Judgement much as Michelangelo showed the Blessed rising to Heaven and the Damned falling into Inferno.

As the great monuments of Egypt go back thousands of years, the Roman era seems quite recent. "Why, Cleopatra was *yesterday!*" one of our Spanish friends remarked. In Egyptian history she is a very minor figure.

At the time we were in Cairo (it was when Sadat was in Washington), security was tight, or at least it was meant to be. Police blocked the entrance to our hotel. Women were required to surrender their handbags for inspection. Mine was investigated with great thoroughness by a swarthy, heavily-built officer. But no one took any interest in the fact that over my arm I carried a bulky coat that could have concealed a machine-gun or at least a clutch of hand-grenades. On internal flights, from Cairo to Aswan for instance, our passports were collected first thing in the morning (we often rose before five and had to be at the airport by seven for a nine o'clock plane) and were studied minutely by a whole series of officials; they were returned to us with the boarding pass just before we went out to the tarmac. But no one ever seemed to compare the picture or description on the passport with the actual person. Any of our passports could have been used by anyone of the same sex.

I should have been prepared for the dramatic extremes of Egypt by books like Durrell's *Alexandria Quartet,* but I wasn't. The difference between the magnificence of the past and the squalor of the present was numbing. One walked out of the air-conditioned fantasy-world of a modern luxury hotel into the nightmare of Cairo poverty — the noise, the dust, the heat, the smell, the begging children, the sheer press of people, and the taxis that broke down in the middle of their journey. Yet old-hands told us that conditions were much better than they used to be.

Of course, the life of the lowly in ancient Egypt could not have been very pleasant. Nevertheless, our guides insisted that the Pyramids were not built by slaves but by tradesmen: masons and carvers whose wages were recorded on clay tablets according to their skills.

"But what about captives, prisoners-of-war, weren't they forced to work?"

Our guide shrugged. "Captives? Oh, that's different."

Chapter 29

THE CARE AND NURTURE
OF A NOVELIST

THE novelist is like the panda. Useless, nocturnal, inoffensive, almost extinct. Soft to the touch. But if held in the wrong position, capable of producing sharp claws. He (or she) has few natural enemies, and likes to be stroked gently and admired.

And, like the panda, though constantly threatened with extinction, the novelist survives. A precarious existence to be sure. The world could get along without pandas or novelists but if they were to disappear, people might miss them. According to some pundits, the novel and the novelist are already extinct. The documentary film, the fictionalized news-report, the non-novel, the anti-novel, and of course television are all that anyone really requires today. Yet here and there, in the icy wastes of the "Now" people, in the steamy tropics of middle-class suburbia, or the trackless saharas of urban lofts, a solitary figure can still be glimpsed. One of that almost vanished species, the novelist.

The work of the novelist is by its nature solitary. Yet people are indispensable; hundreds for a Tolstoy, a few dozen for a Jane Austen. As pandas know exactly the kind of bamboo shoots they must eat to live, so a novelist knows the kind of people, the kind of society, the sort of problems and situations he (in the Unisex sense; I can't keep on saying "he or she") can use as grist for his mill. Life has texture and taste, moments when one lives more fully. Intensity and aliveness are as seductive to the novelist as the freshest and juiciest shoots are to the panda. Some novelists resemble the weaver-bird that picks a piece of ribbon here, a bottle-top there, a length of twine from somewhere else to construct an effective nest. From seemingly disparate snatches of conversation, flashes of light and colour, changing atmospheres, they weave a pattern of startling clarity.

Novelists are plagued by two questions often put by friends and colleagues. First: what is the novel *about?* (With the underlying implication that if it's *about* something the questioner isn't interested in he won't read it.) Unfortunately, if you could tell him what it's *about*, you wouldn't need to write it, or he to read it.

The eminent critic V. S. Pritchett said of my first novel, *Bolero*, that the theme was that of Balzac's *Comédie Humaine*: an excess of virtue becomes a vice; the generosity and understanding of my hero encouraged the selfishness and irresponsibility of others. With which I must agree. But I hadn't thought of it until it was pointed out to me.

The second quesion is: who are the characters in Real Life? My novel, *Windfall*, has a university setting and I was worried about this until three different professors from three different universities "positively" identified themselves and the circumstances. Unless a novelist is writing about Martians, his characters will inevitably resemble people the writer and the reader know. But recognition of this by the reader is quite a different matter, far removed from the facile "Of course, So-and-So in the book is actually Such-and-Such; it's quite obvious!".

Once when we were visiting Ngaio Marsh in her lovely cottage in the suburb of Cashmere, high above Christchurch, I asked her if she'd ever had problems with people identifying themselves with characters in her books. "My dear," Dame Ngaio replied. "They are perfectly *furious* at first." She smiled. "But then, later, they rather like it."

Identification in the sense that the reader identifies with the character — "Yes, that's just how I felt when. . ." — draws the reader into a feeling of complicity with the writer. The reader becomes concerned with the fate of the characters, shares their moments of trial and exaltation. And yet — and this is the great mystery — the reader stands apart, remains the observer, noting the irony, the humour, the elements of tragedy, the interplay of motives and emotions which offer an extra dimension of understanding and insight into the human condition.

THE CARE & NURTURE OF A NOVELIST

Who exactly is this reader? Once there used to be what was called "the reading public". No more. Today there are dozens of publics, all different. Even the term "best-seller", an encomium to many, repels many others. Our culture is fragmented. So the novelist must seek through the fog that enclave of readers with whom he can communicate. It may be his language, his viewpoint, or his ability as a story-teller that appeals; when it does, then a symbiosis occurs. Perhaps this is the strangest part of all: the reader brings to the novel all of his own experience of life, his remembered sensations, his prejudices, his judgments. Thus in the most profound sense, a novel remains unwritten until it is read. Without readers, a novel is a message in a bottle bobbing about in the ocean, far from shore.

Life, however, is a reflection of literature. We may not have read *Lord Jim* or *Moby Dick*, but our view of the sea has been fashioned by the works of Conrad and Melville. We look at Nature through the eyes of the poets. Our understanding of personal and social themes is conditioned by the novels we've read, the plays we've seen. Often our words and even our behaviour are determined in part by the nature of our reading.

Have all the novels been written? Is it time to call a halt? I do not think so. Today's problems require deeper analysis than that offered by television commentaries or newspaper editorials. The novelist considers, notes, points, describes; he can act as a scout in unknown territory, he can show patterns, create some sort of order from seeming chaos. For novelists are like monkeys as well as pandas; they watch, they listen, they imitate. They spy on life, catching a phrase or a gesture, capturing the way language is used to express and to conceal meaning. In their literary habits, they are neat and economical. Nothing that happens to them goes to waste. The delights and heartbreaks are all stashed away for possible use later, when "recollected in tranquility".

Unlike the panda, novelists can be found in most latitudes, the young and hungry peering anxiously through their typewriter bars, feral specimens trying to sustain life in a shrinking environment; domesticated examples are sometimes seen stumbling about the thorny wasteland of government grants, or glimpsed in the groves of Academe, nibbling contentedly on succulent sabbatical leaves. Like other threatened species, the novelist should be treated with kindness and preserved from extinction. After all, his wants are few — lots of paper, a new typewriter ribbon now and then, and, far off — beyond the quicksands of publishers, editors and proof-readers, past the slings and arrows of outrageous critics — finally, on the distant horizon, that one indispensable requirement for survival: the understanding reader.

APPENDIX

SOME CLIPPINGS

SPRINGTIME IN SPAIN

(From the *New York Herald-Tribune,* May 1938)

A SECOND spring of war. Here in Barcelona the Rambla is filled with flowers; music blares from the open doors of the radio shops; the girls wear bright new clothes. Spring and death are in the air.

I am beginning to understand why death does not interfere with the springtime. The thought first came to me in London, when Philip Jordan, of the *News Chronicle*, said he wanted to go back to Madrid. It was in the Cafe Royale. I had just come from Madrid, and thinking of the cold, the shellings and the bad food, I wondered why anyone should want to go back to Madrid just then.

"It's an escape from the world, from obligations, from all problems except the most immediate ones," Jordan explained. I thought of Charles Morgan's book, and the man who liked being kept in a prison in Holland because he was free there. While we were in London we met many of the newspapermen who had spent last winter in Madrid. They all wanted to get back there as soon as possible. They spoke longingly of the Hotel Florida, the shellings, the censors.

They were homesick for Madrid. They longed for the freedom and inward peace that comes only when you live close to death. If you are in danger of being killed, all the little worries and annoyances of life mysteriously disappear. The thought relieves you of all obligations. You have nothing to worry about except death.

As for death itself — you avoid it by adroit mental processes. Henry Gorrell, of the United Press, did it by using statistics. "Look here," he would say when the shells started to fall around the bar where we were sitting: "Now, there are a thousand people killed here in Madrid out of a population of a million — figure out the percentage and you get the result that you have the same chance

227

of getting run over by an automobile in New York as you have of being hit by a shell in Madrid. Maybe it's a little safer in Madrid."

Ernest Hemingway has his own angle on it. Bullets and shrapnel are an old story to him. "The critics think I drink a quart of blood for breakfast," he said, and laughed. "Dying is the easiest thing to do — there's nothing to it."

One newspaperman carries a lucky dime. He has had it with him at all the fronts and in many tough moments. "If I lost that dime, I'd leave Spain in twenty-four hours," he confided to me. We were walking to his office. "I always go down the same streets," he explained, "so if something happens it won't be because just that one day I went down a different street."

Colonel Fuqua, the American military attache, doesn't worry about what he does or where he goes. He holds the other fellow responsible. "If the fellow had pulled the lever twenty seconds sooner, he would have hit the hotel," he explained after an air raid the other day.

The path of superstitition is the easiest. I have scoffed at it, but find myself making strange concessions. For instance, I hate to name the restaurant or cafe where I will meet friends. I would rather that they name the place and the hour; then if we are bombed it will be their own fault. I don't like to insist about going to a definite place. In the back of my mind I think that perhaps the other person is being guided by some instinct that warns him of danger.

All this came about gradually, after twenty months of war and after many "miraculous" escapes. Since everyone has had innumerable escapes of this nature, they cease to seem miraculous. Each person attributes it to his "system".

Somehow, at the front I have felt safer than in the cities. The presence of soldiers and guns gives me a feeling of protection. I felt more confident of safety in a dugout than I do on an unlighted boulevard at night in Barcelona.

Last Saturday night there was an alarm every hour, on the hour, for five hours. I'd bet some German on the other side thought that one up. Like the old medieval torture of letting water drip into a lonely cell. Actually, the bombings were not as severe as on other occasions. But when a new hour approached, lights went out and the anti-aircraft guns began booming away. People began to look at their watches and made jokes that weren't very funny but everyone laughed.

On Friday night the opera season opened with a French cast. It was *Samson and Delilah*. In the midst of the third act Delilah was all alone on the stage; the lights were dim anyway — then they went out altogether, and the anti-aircraft guns on the roof popped away. For a moment there was a fearful silence. Would there be a panic? No one moved. The orchestra leader started up on the Republican air, followed by the Catalan anthem and then the *Marseillaise*, in honour of the French opera singers.

In Madrid they said that the Catalans were cowards. I decided, there in the opera, that they were not. Their courage is not as theatrical as that of the Madrileños, and they have seen less of war.

After the people in a city have been subjected to bombardments and shellings for a time, they begin to feel that if nothing has happened to them so far, nothing is going to happen.

Here in Barcelona people are getting used to air raids. But the thought of a rebel boat near the coast that may shell the city fills them with alarm. It is all a matter of acclimatization. Madrid has a million war veterans; in Barcelona the people were rookies up to now.

At the Ritz the Sunday afternoon tea dances in the Crystal ballroom differ little from pre-war days, except in the number of uniforms. There are two large orchestras; the girls are well coiffured, well dressed. It seems impossible that a bomb could fall upon such an assembly; war seems far away. So long as they ignore danger, these people feel safe.

Up in the mountains that surround the city and in observation posts along the coasts are the gods who hold vigil over the city. Their instruments to detect the noise of approaching planes and their anti-aircraft guns are the fates which seal the destiny of the city and of us all. All our childish superstitions depend on them and their alertness.

We are free. There is nothing to worry about except death, and each of us has his own method of escape from that too. A second spring has come. I will go out and buy a gigantic bouquet of flowers on the Rambla to take the smell of death out of the air.

MIDAS IN MALLORCA

(From the *American Mercury*, November 1948)

THE most powerful private citizen on the continent of Europe — and the richest — is Juan Albert March, a man who literally rose from rags to incalculable riches. This metamorphosis occurred in Spain, a nation that has been undergoing the process in reverse since the seventeenth century.

Hawk-nosed, high domed, with small, piercing green eyes, Juan March, now in his seventies, holds the reins of his country's economy in his fleshy white hands. Like Paul Barras, the French millionaire who spun his devious political webs during the days of the Bourbon Louis, the Revolution, the Directory, the Napoleonic Empire and the Restoration — all without losing his head or his fortune — March has survived the Monarchy, the Dictatorship of Primo de Rivera, the Republic, the Revolution and the Dictatorship of Francisco Franco. He has had only temporary setbacks, and he has always managed to emerge with a bigger pile of chips at the end of the game. Kings, Dictators, Presidents, Prime Ministers and Revolutionary Juntas have come and gone — but March has remained.

March can get along well enough without the men who govern Spain politically, but they cannot get along without him. His backing is well-nigh indispensible for any régime. His opposition spells its doom. In a moment of prophetic foresight, Manuel Azana, a former President of Spain, once remarked that either the Republic must control March or March would control the Republic. History provides the answer as to which won that contest.

Today Juan March controls the economic life of Spain as completly as General Franco controls its political life. But although Franco depends on March for financial and economic backing, Juan March does not depend on Francisco Franco. He could do business with Don Juan — the Bourbon pretender of the monarchy, as he once did business with Don Juan's father, Alphonso XIII.

MIDAS IN MALLORCA

It was in March's chartered plane that General Franco flew from the Canary Islands to Spanish Morocco in 1936 to start the insurrection against the Spanish Republic. It was March who financed the Insurgents and, with German and Italian co-operation, secured their victory. Today the Franco régime might be overturned by a *coup d'état*, with relative ease, but the thick tentacles of March's control have wrapped themselves so tightly around Spanish shipping, finance and industry that nothing short of a social revolution would pry them loose.

A financial *condottiere*, like the early Goulds and Vanderbilts, March believes there is only one way to handle competition, and that is to eliminate it entirely. What he wants is monopoly. The tobacco monopoly, the petroleum monopoly and the Mediterranean traffic between the Balearic Islands and the mainland are his. Formerly, when you went to Palma de Mallorca you had to go on Mr March's boat. Now you have a choice: if you like, you may now go in Mr March's plane.

Today Juan March owns five hundred million tons of Catalonian potash, the largest natural source in the world of this indispensable industrial and agricultural chemical. He owns banks, railroads, olive and almond groves, wine-making companies, soap-manufacturing plants and the bulk of all Mediterranean shipping. His brokerage firms handle the sale of grains, oranges, lemons and almonds grown in Spain, and his ships carry these products to their destinations in Stockholm, Liverpool or Marseilles.

In Mallorca, he owns most of the fertile land and the business property, the hotels and the public utilities. What he does not own is mortgaged to him, *i.e.*, to one of the three March banks in Mallorca. There is another in Ibiza and still another in Valencia. He owns the drydocks and shipyards of Valencia and Cartagena. And the London branch of March Interests, Inc., is the broker for all trade and shipping between Spain and Great Britain. No man in modern times has ever held such absolute control over the economy of a nation as Juan March holds over the economy of Spain. He is a one-man cartel.

II

Juan March started as low down on the social scale as is possible in Mallorca — as the son of an impoverished fisherman. (The peasants are relatively prosperous on that fertile island.) He had no education. Until his late forties he could neither read nor write; now he can do both, though only with great effort. But he had a natural ability with figures, and has always been able to multiply large numbers mentally.

Being bright as well as ambitious, he realized at about the age of ten that there was no future to being a fisherman unless one had a sideline. The sideline he selected was smuggling tobacco.

On dark nights, he would row his dory out to where the large boats were anchored in the harbour. A member of the crew lowered a parcel containing cigarettes, pipe tobacco and snuff down by a rope. March rowed his small cargo to a cove, where he disposed of it to the *contrabandistas*. Thus the tobacco was sold, tax-free, and a nice profit was made by everybody except the Spanish govenment.

When he was fourteen, he became the errand boy and handyman for a wheat merchant in Palma, whom he managed to interest in the growing of tobacco in Morocco. With the money earned from his nocturnal activities, he speculated in wheat, and before long he owned a controlling share of the Moroccan tobacco business. March, the tobacco-grower sold his tobacco at a profit to the government tobacco processors, while March the smuggler continued to fleece the government of its tax revenues.

Juan March bought several small cargo ships and a sugar refinery. He now divided himself three ways. March cargo ships carried March-grown tobacco from the mainland to the island. On the way, part of the cargo would be lost to March, the *contrabandista*. All three businesses — tobacco growing, shipping and smuggling — made money.

When the first World War broke out, Spain found neutrality highly profitable. The country sold food, textiles, mules and information to both sides. March was in a position to capitalize on this trade, for he was now in the shipping business and owned a small fleet of old cargo ships.

He is supposed to have insured his vessels and their cargoes at high figures. They would be sunk. He collected the insurance money and bought more vessels. He sold olive oil and oranges to the French and British; then he would tip off German submarines to the routes of the vessels. The story is told of how one of March's captains, instead of following the straight course March had indicated to him, ran a zigzag route and arrived safely with his cargo in Marseilles. He was promptly fired.

March was altogether neutral. He sold oil to the German submarines, but it is said that only a few tanks were filled with petroleum; the rest was water. The German submarine crews never knew they had been cheated. As soon as they left harbour, March informed British naval units at Gibralter, who torpedoed the submarines. When the first World War ended, he was a rich man.

When Primo de Rivera came into power he accepted March's financial help in his campaign against the Riffs in Morocco. In return, March was granted the tobacco monopoly. Under de Rivera's Dictatorship, March again became twins. He now held the tobacco monopoly for Spanish Morocco, Ceuta, Melilla and the Protectorate. He sold French Moroccan tobacco, which was carried to Palma de Mallorca in March's own ships (while officials carefully looked the other way) and then transhipped to the mainland on other steamers. Thus March the contrabandist sold his tobacco to March the monopolist, and cornered the tobacco market "band and contraband".

It is said that when he was temporarily out of favour with Primo de Rivera, who was pledged to rid Spain of the *contrabandistas*, Juan March went to Paris. There he bought up a controlling interest in the tobacco monopoly — the *Compania Arrendataria de Tabaccos* — for all of Spain and Spanish possessions everywhere. Returning to Madrid, he walked into the meeting of the directors of that company as one of the directors was denouncing him. March took his seat and listened attentively as the wretched man attempted to weasel-word out of what he had just said.

March now controlled both the legal and the illegal tobacco trade. The legal sale of the commodity was in his hands and the smuggled tobacco brought him additional revenue. If a foolhardy smuggler failed to pay a percentage to March, he found the *carabiniere* waiting for him the next time he brought his boat into some obscure grotto.

III

March began to expand his interests. He bought Mallorquin real estate just before the tourist boom hit the island. He also invested in sugar refineries, olive and orange groves, and shipyards. After the fall of Primo de Rivera, he was sometimes seen in the company of Queen Ena and Alfonso XIII. He was said to have a private fortune of two hundred million pesetas. He was called *el yanqui* because of his ability to make money.

But although he was a welcome guest at the palace of the King and Queen of Spain, he was still unable to get into the aristocratic Club Balear — the equivalent of the Union League club in his home town of Palma de Mallorca. He still could not read or write, except to sign his name.

Further, besides being of lowly origin, he was a *chueta*, which means Jew in Mallorquin. This appellation has led American journalists to describe him as Jewish, and to express surprise that his constant crony was an old priest, with whom he played backgammon and chess. Actually, *chueta* refers only to the fact that in the sixteenth century, the ancestors of Juan March, who were Jewish, preferred conversion to exile. (The Inquisition gave them their choice.) So the March family has been Roman Catholic for four hundred years. But the memories of Mallorquins are long, and to them certain names common in Spain, are *chueta* names. March is one such surname. (Franco is another.)

I was living in Mallorca when one of March's sons was married to the daughter of a titled family, then in reduced circumstances. "The Archbishop of Palma will perform the ceremony in the Cathedral, of course," an acquaintance of mine said. "But then, after all, the Archbishop is a *chueta* too." Hitler and Goebbels were novices; their Nuremburg laws went back only to great-grandparents.

Spanish society was too rigid to accept even the richest parvenu. Juan March might own all the valuable property on the island; he might control the elections — Mallorca was his pocket borough — but he could not get into the Club Balear, nor would the aristocrats invite him to dinner in their cold stone palaces on the Borne Boulevard.

He helped Primo de Rivera finance his Moroccan campaign. He helped King Alfonso financially, too. Whether or not he was personally loyal to the King is not clear. But when Indalecio Prieto, a Socialist editor and one of the leaders of the group who wanted to overturn the Monarchy, asked March for money, March turned him down. Perhaps March felt that his investments in

Spain would be protected better under the Monarchy than under a Republic.

In the early 'thirties, several suits were brought against March. At one point he was accused of selling arms to the Riffs. But strange things happened to the witnesses; they became bored with life in Spain and migrated to America, where they were set up in business. Documents in the cases against him were inexplicably lost. Judges discovered that their health required an immediate change of climate. The cases dragged on, but nothing happened.

When the King decided to leave rather than risk civil war and bloodshed among his subjects, the new Republic sought to bring March to justice. On April 30, 1931, he was arrested on the charge of selling arms to the Moors during the Moroccan war. Enrique Iglesias, the Radical Republican leader, was expelled from the Cortes on the charge of attempting bribery as March's agent under Primo de Rivera.

In the November elections, Juan March was elected deputy from Mallorca. (The laws allowed men under arrest to run for office.) But on November 7 he was tried before the Cortes on the smuggling charge, and on the eleventh he was expelled from the Chamber for "moral incompatibility".

March was now imprisoned in the ancient fortress of Alcala de Henares. He remained there for eighteen months, awaiting a judicial trial. Then he became impatient: he left the prison, taking the jailor and the guard with him in his limousine. They went to Gibraltar, and attempts at extradition proved fruitless. Shortly afterwards, he arrived in Marseilles.

For once, Juan March was something of a popular hero in Spain. His nonchalant escape delighted people of all classes, even those who disapproved of him socially. His case had been reviewed by the Court of Constitutional Guarantees but he had never been accorded a legal trial. Everyone knew why: the government was afraid to try him because it had no proof. The Madrid press (which, except for the *Heraldo* and *Ahora,* was owned by March) crowed with victory.

The Republican government annulled March's tobacco monopoly. He travelled in France, making business contacts, building up his shipping interests and petroleum business. He bought into the great orange and olive companies of Spain. He was re-elected to the Cortes and in 1933, under the régime of Lerroux, he returned in quiet triumph to Spain. He was also elected to the Court of Constitutional Guarantees and granted immunity from arrest. In a test of strength with the Spanish Republic, he had emerged the winner.

March added petroleum refineries, municipal utilities in Madrid and Barcelona and Catalan textile plants to the many interests he already had. He began to acquire the bonds and stocks of railways, power plants and more newspapers. "I've so much money, I don't know how much I have," he is quoted as saying at this time.

When Maunel Azaña came into power as premier in 1936, March made a strategic retreat to Biarritz in France. Azaña was his bitterest personal enemy, and March had no desire to return to jail. The hatred between the two men was so great that on a previous occasion, when President Azaña had come on the Spanish flagship the *Jaime Primero* to the port of Palma for some special dedication service, he refused to land when he heard that he would be welcomed by Juan March as the Deputy from the Balearic Islands.

IV

It was Juan March who financed the military insurrection in July 1936. At first, the Generals who led the revolt allowed him to give them money but had little to do with him personally. General Emilio Mola, who headed the revolt, snubbed him and Quiepo de Llano sneered at him publicly.

Only General Franco, who succeeded Mola as leader of the Insurgents after the latter's death in an airplane accident, seemed to appreciate that March could be useful to the Movement.

As early as July 1936 March bought eighteen Italian transport planes and hired the pilots to ferry troops from Tetuan, Morocco, to the Spanish mainland. These troops came to the rescue of Quiepo de Llano, who had taken Seville with a handful of men and a brilliant bluff, but who could not hold it without a force of trained troops.

March knew that he had committed himself to the Insurgent cause. They *had* to win. He immediately placed at their disposal five million U.S. dollars, ten million pesetas and 500,000 British pounds — all his liquid assets. This was not a loan; it was an outright gift. But March judged shrewdly the nature of the men with whom he was dealing. He knew that if they won, he would get back his money — and more.

Juan March & Co. was organized in England. This company, headed by Senor Mayoraga, 19 Fenchurch St., London, was given control of all Spain's trade relations, imports, exports and credits, with the British Empire and the rest of the world. The March interests in Spain were used as security for the credits advanced. Across the street, at 20 Fenchurch St., the firm of J. M. Kleinwort did the bookkeeping on Spanish Civil War finances.

On April 9, 1937, March arrived in Naples. On the 11th, he arranged with Count Ciano in Rome for further aid to the rebels, for despite the guns, tanks, planes and pilots — not to mention men — that had been furnished them by Germany and Italy, they had not yet managed to win the Spanish Civil War.

Meanwhile, the Loyalist government had confiscated March's Mediterranean Steamship Company as a war measure. March's tobacco and petroleum monopolies were also confiscated. In France, Leftist members of the Chamber of Deputies insisted that March should be expelled from his palatial residence in Biarritz, from which they claimed he was directing the Civil War.

They were wrong. He was merely financing it.

It was March who arranged the barter agreements between Germany and Spain and Italy, by which Spain supplied these countries with agricultural commodities and minerals in exchange for bombers, fighting planes, ammunition, artillery, bombs and shells. For a while the going was tough. March spent some fifty million dollars of his own money. That hurt. But it put him in solidly with General Franco, and March was now so deeply committed that he had to make certain Franco won.

March went to Portugal and helped arrange the "friendly" neutrality of the dictator Salazar, by which mercenaries or volunteers on their way to join the Insurgent forces became invisible to the border guards. He was active, travelling back and forth from Rome, Berlin and Lisbon, and keeping the stream of money and supplies pouring in to Franco's armies. He dickered; he made deals; he purchased; he made promises to Mussolini and Hitler. He did this as a private citizen, without a title; he was merely financial advisor to the Burgos government.

But he did not return to Spain, for despite his activities on their behalf the Falangists did not like him. (Like the Nazis, the Falangists expressed a hostility to "bourgeois capitalism".) Neither did the Carlists, who would not admit to themselves that their "Holy Crusade" depended on the vulgar riches of an illiterate low-born *chueta*. And Spanish Army officers disliked everyone who was not a *militar*. In Loyalist Spain, hatred of March seemed at times to amount almost to an obsession. The beautiful actress, Tina de Jorque, was murdered in government territory, apparently for no other reason than that she was March's mistress.

In the spring of 1939 the war ended. March waited discreetly in France for a time before returning to Spain. After the "gifts" he had made to the Franco government, he had held a virtual mortgage on the entire economy of Spain.

He put this to use almost immediately. When the second World War broke out, March went back into the business of selling to both sides. He sold oranges, sardines, textiles, minerals and olive oil to both the allies and the axis. Both sides made a practice of buying not only what they required themselves, but also materials for which they would have no conceivable use, but which they wished to keep away from the enemy. British and German agents bid against one another for cork, tungsten, tin, mercury, lead, olives, wool, fruit and, particularly, olive oil. March, who had interests in all these commodities, made more fortunes.

Mallorca became a centre of espionage for both sides. And all the agents, with their unlimited funds, stayed at March's hotels. Business was good. Italian pilots, German submarine crews, Gestapo officers on vacation with their mistresses, British intelligence officers — the clientele was rather strange, but it paid well.

V

Today Juan March holds no public office, although he has made two visits to Portugal (in 1943 and 1945) and arranged for trade agreements with that country. He has no official government post. He still has no title or military rank.

But at long last, Juan Albert March has achieved his goal. He has made good, socially, in his home town of Palma de Mallorca. He is now a member of the Club Balear. Both of his sons married into aristocratic families who were in financial difficulties.

MIDAS IN MALLORCA

Today he is courted and fawned over by the same *Marquesas* and *Duquesas* who used to laugh at his diction and peasant manners. All the old Mallorquin mansions are open to him now. After all, there are sons' futures to think of. And business and financial opportunities lie in the hands of Juan March. Besides, his political influence is such that no one would dare offend him today. Times have changed.

In the summer of 1947 I returned to Mallorca for the first time in a decade. Between the soft pinkish stone of the Cathedral of Palma and the gray stone of the Governor's residence, an enormous structure was being completed. I watched landscape artists and plasterers putting the finishing touches to a white marble and stucco palace that extends for several city blocks. It is a Graeco-Roman, Italian Renaissance, Byzantine atrocity, like nothing else among the graceful ancient buildings around it.

This is the new home of Juan March, the visible symbol of his social success — a house on the Borne (now Avenida Jose Antonio Primo de Rivera).

Agents of Juan March have been buying up works of art in all the galleries of Europe. The new March palace will house paintings by Titian, Van Dyck, Rubens and Fra Lippo Lippi, bronze statues by Donatelo. Whether this art-purchasing campaign is inspired by a desire to live up to his newly acquired social position or whether March is shrewdly investing his pesetas in the one commodity that does not lose value, no one knows.

Over a decade ago, I first saw Juan March drinking coffee in the Hotel Mediterraneo in El Terreno, Mallorca. He was a portly man, with strong shoulders and a long neck. He has a hawklike nose and a receding chin; he looks like a bird of prey. It was a sweltering hot day, but March was dressed in a heavy black cloth suit and did not appear warm. Instead there was a cold, clammy look to his yellowing skin, his thin pale lips. His sharp eyes darted about the dining room suspiciously.

Few people have ever seen his wife. She was a large, dark-haired woman who kept herself carefully out of sight. This is frequently the case in Spain. Neither of the March sons has been in the limelight, either. Where they were and what they did during the Civil War is a matter of conjecture. But it is certain that they will inherit the largest financial empire in Europe.

239

SOME CLIPPINGS

Today, Juan March is the most powerful man in Spain. He owns everything worth owning. He has outlasted a Monarchy, a Directorship and a Republic; and he may well outlast the Dictatorship of General Franco. He has gained the social recognition for which he yearned. And no matter what happens, he continues to make money, to enlarge his network of commercial ventures.

He can now look back over his career and find it good. If you asked him the secret of his success, he would reply that it was due to hard work, perseverance and honesty. And he wouldn't even smile when he said it.

[Postscript. Today (1986) the March Foundation offers scholarships to young artists and musicians and sponsors expositions, concerts, scholarships in many fields in much the same way as the Ford, Rockefeller and other U.S. Foundations have done. The grandsons of robber barons have become philanthropists.]

3

THE ROAD TO TERUEL

(From *Revista/Review Interamericana*, Winter 1973)

IT was certainly *déjà*, but the *vu* was quite different.

"It was just about here," my husband said, and stopped the car. Ahead lay a straight road, then the high escarpment of the fortress city of Teruel. On either side of us in the bright autumn sunshine stretching endlessly across the Aragon plain were vineyards with fat clusters of purple grapes, orchards with pears and apples ripening, a picture of peace and tranquility.

It was here, however, when the great plateau was covered with a crust of white snow, the road slippery and icy and a piercing cold wind howled through these leafless trees that we were attacked. First a shell landed ahead of us, then one behind us, then one on the left side and one to the right. With each explosion our little Vauxhall seemed to jump with fright and the glass rattled but, miraculously, did not break.

Between the warm autumn day redolent of sun and ripening fruit and the freezing winter day on the same road lay more than a season. In fact, thirty-six years.

My husband and I looked at each other and smiled; here we are again, alive and well, on the road to Teruel. But were we, I wondered, really the same people as those two young, reckless war correspondents who set off from Valencia with our chauffeur Federico in our "liberated" Vauxhall, our little American flag flying bravely from the radiator (Couldn't they see we were neutrals?). Apparently not. Or, as we were the only moving object on the cold white endless plateau, the bored artillery officers far up in the fortress on the high escarpment were amusing themseves with a bit of target practice. In fact, we seemed just then — those artillery officers and ourselves — to be the sole survivors on a frozen empty planet.

Like Tobruk in a later war, Teruel was taken, defended itself, finally fell, was taken, defended itself, finally fell, time after time.

And each time its capture was headline news for each side; it had come to represent far more than its actual strategic importance, an almost legendary, talismanlike quality guaranteeing final victory in the civil war to the army that managed to keep it. For this reason, Teruel became a regular "milk run" for the correspondents then located in Valencia where the Republican government had moved from Madrid. Since the communiqués of both headquarters lied consistently, the only way to find out what was happening was to go there and see for ourselves.

Well, we could see all right. The Nationalists were clearly in control of the city of Teruel and its fortifications and of the road leading to it. The only question that now remained to be answered was whether we would survive to tell the story. It looked doubtful.

Federico turned around and said quietly, "Perhaps we should go back?" We nodded eagerly. But the road was narrow and slippery; could he manage it? Without consulting us he stopped the car, ran into the adjacent snow-covered field and jumped up and down. (Federico was about four feet tall and weighed 98lbs.)

Then, still without saying anything more, he hopped back into the car, turned into the snow-crusted field. The Vauxhall sank into the snow, slowly. We could see only a bit of light at the very top of the windows. The shelling had stopped. And there we were in a snowdrift near the Teruel road between two armies. "But I jumped on it," explained Federico, puzzled.

This was it. We broke into wildly hysterical laughter. We were perhaps slightly shell-shocked. We lit cigarettes and considered the situation, which was, we decided, desperate but not hopeless. Meanwhile, Federico had succeeded in snaking his way through the opened window on his side, which since he was the size of a small boy and more agile was a remarkable but not miraculous feat. "Something will turn up," he assured us, smiling.

That seemed unlikely. If he succeeded in digging enough snow away from the window for us to get out, we'd still have to walk thirty miles on the icy road which, since it was under shellfire, was not likely to be used by anyone. Our hilarity was giving way to dire forboding.

Then it was that what seemed like a miracle did happen. "Listen!" Federico shouted, and we heard a rumbling noise. Federico climbed up on to the road and waved at something he could see but we couldn't. Soon a tank came up, then another and another one. There was a lot of noise and shouting, and a tank stopped. Soon we were being hauled out of the snowdrift amidst raucous laughter and cheery obscenities exchanged between Federico and the tank crew. The officer who gave the order to pull us out was a fellow Anarchist taxi-driver from Madrid. Federico had friends everywhere.

But now we were moving against the current of an army division, threading our way between armoured cars, halftracks and trucks. And now the Nationalist planes moved in to bomb and strafe and all hell broke loose. I held my ears and closed my eyes, then opened them to see that Federico kept going. He was whistling now, in his element (perhaps even philosophically, moving against the current, going in the other direction from all the others). And his cheerfulness was infectious. Although we were now in more real danger than before, we didn't feel as frightened in this traffic jam as we had alone on the icy road. Men waved to us, greeted Federico whenever the planes swooped away and left time for the amenities.

At one point when we were stalled, an officious militia officer (probably a Communist, the Anarchists were very laissez-faire) came up and asked us for our credentials. My husband and I promptly produced ours. "I don't have any," Federico said lightly. My husband and I looked at each other; here we go again.

Now although Federico was about four feet tall and weighed 98 pounds, his head and shoulders were those of a normal, even good-sized man.

"Why not?" the officer demanded.

"Well, when my class was called up in Zamora, they told me I wouldn't need to serve." Then he went on with the story we'd heard a dozen times before. And by the time the officer was enraged at what sounded like a cock-and-bull story, Federico opened the door and got out. "Now here is my driver's licence, if you want that," he said. The militia officer looked down (about two feet) at Federico. He blushed. "Never mind," he said, and waved us on.

It was the same thing every time. Just as they were about to arrest him, he'd get out of the car and make fools of them. And

for an Anarchist, making fools of the representatives of any authority, of any government, makes his day.

*   *   *

We looked around once again, at the surrounding plateau. Where
was the snow, the tanks, Federico?
Où sont les neiges d'antan?
My husband started the car and we went on, this time, to Teruel.

THE HEALTHY LIFE
IS TOO DANGEROUS

(From *Vogue* Magazine, November 1947)

HEALTH is a fine thing. I am in favour of it. But whenever a friend of mine announces that he is going in for a "health programme", I think of Monsieur Cuvier and shudder.

My sister Barbara and I met Monsieur Cuvier on the beach at Collioure. Collioure is a fishing village in the French province of *Les Pyrénées Orientales* — next to Spain, on the Mediterranean. But even before we knew him, we were fascinated by his remarkable consistency. Every morning at ten o'clock, Monsieur Cuvier would arrive at the beach, resplendent in a coffee-and-gold striped beach robe and a bath towel tied like an ascot scarf at his throat. He was well over six feet tall, with pale blond hair. When he removed his robe, his bronzed chest and shoulders looked like the "after" part of the body-building advertisements.

Monsieur Cuvier's appearance would have attracted our attention in any case, since he was the only other person besides us who frequented the rocky, sea-urchin studded shore. (Collioure is not a place for tourists and is proud of it.) But it was his routine that really intrigued us.

For two weeks, he appeared not to notice us. He walked directly to a particular, small, flat rock. He removed the ascot-like towel, folded it with precision and placed it on the rock. Next he removed his beach robe, folded it, and placed it carefully on top of the towel. Now, clad in his bathing trunks, he walked forward ten paces and, standing with his feet about ten inches apart, proceeded to go through a series of bending, twisting, and breathing exercises, all the time counting, "*Un, deux, trois,*" quite audibly. After this he walked up to the sea and removed his sandals. Then he walked slowly into the water. He picked up a handful of seaweed, rolled it into neat pellets and inserted them in his ears. He slapped a bit of water on his chest. Then he took a deep breath. He was ready for his swim.

His swim was five lengths of the beach, up and down, turning when he came opposite to a certain rock near the edge at either end. It was as though he were swimming in an invisible pool, the limits of which were visible to him alone. Afterwards, he came out and went behind a high rock and changed into dry trunks, dried himself, and combed his hair. Then he spread his towel out and sat down on it, turning around every five minutes to keep his tan equal on all sides.

This routine never varied. We waited hopefully, thinking that some day he would omit some part of it. But he never did.

After two weeks, he smiled at us before he removed his towel. We smiled back. The next week, he said, *"Bon jour,"* to us and we replied. Then, a few days later, after he had finished his swim and had put on his dry bathing-suit, he walked over to us and bowed.

"May I present myself? I am Monsieur Cuvier. Monsieur Charles Cuvier, to be exact." His French was Parisian French. There was no trace of the Catalan accent which distinguishes the *Pyrénées Orientales* folk.

We presented ourselves.

"Yes. I know, *Les Américaines. La brune et la blonde."* (I was the brunette, Barbara the blonde, and we were known thus in the village.)

That was the beginning of our acquaintance with Monsieur Cuvier. Every day, after his swim, he took his sunbath on a nearby rock and talked to us. He had only one topic of conversation. That was health. It was his religion, his cause, his life.

When he had lived in Paris, he said, he and a group of his friends went swimming in the Seine every New Year's Day. From the way he spoke about it, it seemed that renouncing this yearly event was the worst thing about leaving Paris. He was also an enthusiastic *alpiniste*, or mountain-climber, and he had displayed his talents in the Alps and the Pyrenees.

He talked a great deal about his *"régime"*, which had nothing to do with politics. His *régime* was his health programme. He did not drink. He did not smoke. He ate only raw vegetables, fish, liver, and certain fruits (apparently those which were out of season and which had to be procured at great expense).

He owned a rowboat and he took us out on "excursions" in it. He rowed at an even distance from the shore for about a mile, and then back, at the same speed. He had a determined look as he never talked to us while he was rowing, and the consecrated look on his face made us feel that conversation on our part would be unseemly.

When he did ask us questions about America we were embarrassed. He was interested only in health and sports and he knew a lot more about the status of both in America than we did. He thought Americans were *formidable* because they did so many healthy things. Somewhere he had picked up the fact that American college men and women drank milk more frequently than wine. He congratulated us on this achievement, as though we were personally responsible for it. We were a nation with a magnificent future, he assured us.

We thanked him.

The only remark he ever made on international affairs (this was 1939) concerned the Germans. They went in for health and sport for *ulterior motives*, he confided in us. They just wanted to have strong soldiers. Monsieur Cuvier strongly disapproved of someone who had turned "professional".

For Monsieur Cuvier *believed* in the healthy life. "I shall live until I am one hundred — perhaps longer," he would say.

There were a couple of smallish mountains in the region. La Madelaine and Le Madeloc — he proposed that we climb the latter, which was the higher. He hired a guide, and when he called for us we were impressed by his get-up — heavy sweater, corduroy trousers, and climbing boots with spikes in them. He was obviously not pleased by our attire — shirts, shorts, and gym shoes. But he controlled himself — after all, *les Américaines* were different from other people. He and the guide had brought along what seemed to us like a lot of unnecessary equipment — ropes, a pick, flashlight, whistle, and first-aid kit. The guide carried a heavy rucksack, too.

It was a hot day and we felt fine. Monsieur Cuvier followed us with difficulty, laden down by his heavy clothes and boots. And way back in the rear came the guide, also heavily laden. We kept

247

going up and up and eventually reached the top, where we stopped. There was an old, crumbling, Moorish watchtower. Below lay the Mediterranean on one side and the higher Pyrenees stretched up endlessly on the other side. The guide had a hard time finding the place. Monsieur Cuvier blew his whistle and finally the guide showed up, carrying the rucksack and our lunch. It was a health lunch prepared by Monsieur Cuvier. There was warm salad; cold, greasy liver; some bruised and battered peaches; and some liquid soupy stuff which had been chocolate bars. We were polite. Besides, we were hungry. So we ate some of it. Monsieur Cuvier seemed to find it delicious. But the guide was obviously disheartened when he discovered what it was that he had lugged up the mountain. He refused to eat and went off and smoked his pipe in injured silence.

Later that night, Barbara and I were in the Café du Sport talking to René, the proprietor of Collioure's principal café. By this time, the whole village knew about our excursion to the top of the Madeloc with Monsieur Cuvier. It also knew how we had dressed for the occasion and how little time it had taken us to get there and back. Unwittingly, we had spoiled something almost sacred. rises and you never get back before the moon rises. You dress For, to climb the Madeloc, we learned, you start before the sun appropriately for the adventure and you prepare for the dangers of falling and being lost and the possibility of rainstorms. And you haul great quantities of food along to sustain your efforts. By leaving at ten in the morning and returning at four in the afternoon and by dressing the way we did, we had spoiled tradition. We had disparaged the *alpinistes* of Collioure.

We were saddened and chastened. But still curious about Monsieur Cuvier.

"Who is he and what does he do?" we asked René.

"Oh he is a most important man. The banker in Perpignan. Much money." He made an appropriate gesture with his thumb and forefinger. "He always spends his vacations here, although he could well afford a resort on the Riviera. Occasionally, when his friends come down from Perpignan, he comes here to the café. And you know what he drinks? Milk!" René waited for this piece of information to sink in.

SOME CLIPPINGS

Monsieur Cuvier's vacation lasted all summer. But he kept coming down to Collioure for weekends all through the fall. (It is a fifteen-mile drive from Perpignan.) He continued to go swimming. By this time, we knew that the reason he put seaweed into his ears was to keep the water out. In fact, he had explained the *rationals* of all his health rules. We knew just why he did what. He had theories on how to walk (like a savage — heel, arch, toe), how to breathe (so the diaphragm moved), and how to sleep (on a very hard bed with only one light, all-wool blanket). No matter how much he would enjoy going to theatre occasionally, he made himself go to bed *every night* at ten. He did not believe in indulging or spoiling himself.

Once he confided to us his private fantasy. It was being wrecked on a desert island, where his physique and his boy scout training (he was born a boy scout) would come in handy. We questioned him closely and discovered that what he really dreamed of was being rescued from a desert island. He relished the thought of the amazement he could produce in his rescuers when they came and found him getting along so well on his own.

The last time we saw him was at the end of October, just before we moved into Perpignan ourselves. He was still bronzed from the sun, still engaged actively in leading the healthy life.

Two months later, I was reading the *Dépêche de Toulouse*. A name caught my eye. It was the name of Monsieur Charles Cuvier. I called Barbara and we read the story together. It said he was a Perpignan banker, so we decided it was not just coincidence.

For what the story said was that Monsieur Charles Cuvier had been murdered. The well-known banker, it said, had been shot by his ex-wife. (We didn't know he'd ever had a wife.) She still had the key to his apartment, and she'd gone there and hidden in the closet until he went to bed (promptly at ten, of course). While he was sleeping (on his hard bed with only one light but all-wool cover), she had shot him right through his (sunburnt) temple.

She went to the police and gave herself up.

The day of her trial in Perpignan, crowds in front of the Palais de Justice waited for snatches of news on the progress of the case. We went to a café and ordered Pernods. We were sitting by the big glass window. Suddenly, all the rest of the patrons of the café were surrounding our table, looking at a woman passing on the street.

"There she is!"

We asked who. "Madame Cuvier, of course."

We stared, too. She was a small, youngish, smartly dressed woman. She walked slowly, as though she were rather proud of herself. We were mystified. Later we drove to Collioure and René's Café du Sport. René was delighted to see us. He knew about the verdict in the Cuvier case.

"But didn't she admit killing him in cold blood?" I demanded.

"One moment," said René, slowly as though speaking to a child. "In France, when a woman marries, her *dot* — dowry — goes to her husband. But when she is divorced she gets it back. Madame Cuvier got divorced. But does she get back her *dot*? No! Her husband, the fine honest banker — he has spent it all!"

We must have still looked puzzled. So René continued, "She explained it all to the jury. So they let her go. *Enfin* —" his tone implied that some unwritten law had been invoked. We nodded our heads, because he had quite obviously said all there was to say.

That is why I still regard the "healthy life" as rather dangerous.